D0672703

Doing God's Business

Doing God's Business

MEANING AND MOTIVATION
FOR THE MARKETPLACE

R. Paul Stevens

WILLIAM B. EERDMANS PUBLISHING COMPANY

GRAND RAPIDS, MICHIGAN / CAMBRIDGE, U.K.

© 2006 R. Paul Stevens

All rights reserved

Published 2006 by

Wm. B. Eerdmans Publishing Co.

2140 Oak Industrial Drive N.E., Grand Rapids, Michigan 49505 /

P.O. Box 163, Cambridge CB3 9PU U.K.

www.eerdmans.com

Printed in the United States of America

13 12 11 10 09 08   8 7 6 5 4 3 2

Library of Congress Cataloging-in-Publication Data

Stevens, R. Paul, 1937-

Doing God's business: meaning and motivation for the marketplace / R. Paul Stevens.

p.   cm.

Includes bibliographical references and index.

ISBN 978-0-8028-3398-3 (pbk.: alk. paper)

1. Work — Religious aspects — Christianity.

2. Business — Religious aspects — Christianity.   I. Title.

BT738.5.S74 2006

248.8'8 — dc22

2006014245

Unless otherwise noted, all scripture quotations are from the New Revised Standard Version Bible, copyright 1989, Division of Christian Education of the National Council of the Churches of Christ in the United States of America. Used by permission. All rights reserved.

To

Walter C. Wright

Director, DePree Leadership Center

Mentor

Contents

CONTENTS

1

◆ ◆ ◆

What Business Is God In?

The Christian Church has never found it easy to
come to terms with the marketplace.

Brian Griffiths, *The Creation of Wealth*

What if Christians could change their attitudes towards business, and what if Christians could begin to
change the attitudes of the world toward business?

Wayne Grudem,
"How Business in Itself Can Glorify God"

G od and business? God in business? Such thoughts have been, in
the Western world at least, almost unthinkable. "Leave your
soul at the workplace door" has been the unspoken and sometimes
overt message of business establishments. Nevertheless, the July 16,
2001, cover story of *Fortune* was entitled, "God and Business: The Surprising Quest for Spiritual Renewal in the American Workplace." In

this article Marc Gunther speaks of "breaking the old taboo." He describes a groundswell of executives who "want to bridge the traditional divide between spirituality and work."[1] It is a welcome and long overdue movement.

For too long the separation of God and business has resulted in a double life: God on Sunday, work on Monday. People of faith often have been enthusiastic theists on Sunday and practical atheists on Monday. One lawyer said, "I have never figured out how to wear my three piece suit and my faith simultaneously." What does faith have to do with making money, creating goods and services, and delivering value to customers, stakeholders, and stockholders? An executive observed, "I sense that what the church really values is my volunteer time — teaching Sunday School, being an elder, serving on church committees or leading a small group. I suppose if I'm really going to be committed as a Christian I need to go into full-time Christian service and become a pastor or missionary."

God and Business?

Feeding this unfortunate split between faith and work is a hierarchy of holiness in the mindset of most people of faith. Missionaries and pastors are at the top, and then people in the "helping professions" — medicine and law, followed by homemakers or the trades, the latter being physically dirty but morally clean. Then, farther down, there is business, which is physically clean but, in most people's minds, morally questionable. And somewhere near the bottom on the scale of holiness there are stock brokers and politicians. This heretical hierarchy is often reinforced by the real situations in which people find themselves in the business world.

Ivan develops design proposals for a ceiling tile manufacturer. He is working on a proposal for a new airport in an Asian country. But to get the contract his company will have to pay a user fee (read "bribe") to the government official. Should he do it?

1. Marc Gunther, "God and Business: The Surprising Quest for Spiritual Renewal in the American Workplace," *Fortune*, 16 July 2001, pp. 58-80.

Samuel is CEO of a large multinational oil company that has a division in an African country deep in a civil war. He knows that the duties and royalties his company pays to the government of that country for the extracted raw material are being used to purchase weapons to fight the rebels and not to enhance health care and education, which the country desperately needs. Can he make peace with himself, his God, and the demonstrators outside his office by saying that he is doing more good for that Third World country than harm? One thing he knows is that today business is irrevocably global. (Find out more about this in chapter 6.)

Bill had formed a business partnership with Robert in a high-tech assembly operation, New Age Electronics. They now employ twenty-five people. One day Robert dropped a bombshell on Bill: "At the mission conference I got the call — just as clear as my wife's voice. In fact, she heard the call too. We are both absolutely convinced that God is calling us to the mission field to do student work in Zambia. We are called to do the Lord's work!" This case, which we will take up later, underscores the dualism in people's minds about vocational calling, some called to "Christian service" and others not called at all.

Stephanie is a pastor of a large church in Toronto. She knows that most of her parishioners are professionals, university professors, and businesspeople. Just last week one of the executives said to her, "I don't believe the church really validates what I do in business — except as a means to another end. What I do is considered of Christian significance insofar as I evangelize or witness at work, earn a good income, and contribute generously to my church. All these validations are only instrumental. I've received no inherent validation from the church for what I do as a Christian in business." What can she do to help this executive see things differently? How can she serve the church she loves in equipping its people for their service Monday to Friday? We will return to Stephanie's situation.

Horacio Gutierrez is a skilled metallurgical worker. "When the company closed down, overburdened by debt and overwhelmed by competition from abroad, I thought I would find work quickly. How wrong I was. Those over forty in Peru are considered too old." He does the housework while his wife is a "micro-businessperson" — a euphemism behind which a precarious job lurks. "She is self-employed, selling trinkets one day and sewing clothes the next."

Halfway around the world, James, along with the eleven other vice presidents at the bank's branch in Hong Kong, finally made his way to the board room. James could feel the icy-cold tension in the room. He and his peers were being delivered an ultimatum by Paul, the international VP: focus on top-tier clients who generate incomes for the bank of more than 100,000 USD. Paul ended the meeting with these words: "Now, I want remedial actions to be taken immediately. If anyone of you cannot take the heat, he or she should get out of the kitchen. I will not hesitate to turn the color of the carpet in this board room *red* if I have to." James wondered whether he could take the heat.

Tom works for a large British firm of consulting engineers. The project group to which he is attached is working on the renovation of a number of factories in Uzbekistan, part of the former Soviet Union. The factories, all in various states of disrepair, have been bought by an Anglo-American tobacco multinational corporation which is planning to renovate them, put in its machine lines, and start producing cigarettes to sell to the local Uzbek population. Tom's grandfather died of smoke-related lung disease. He is not sure what to do.

All these case studies and the ones in the following chapters are based on real situations but the names, places, and content have been changed, often bringing together more than one situation. Beside sharing these cases, I have a personal connection with the subject of this book.

In My Father's Business

I grew up in a business home. My father was president of a steel fabrication company. I worked in the company for several summers — warehousing, operating punch-presses, making tools and dies, and doing payroll and clerical work in the office. My father had an open-door policy. He was always available to his employees. He was fair and deeply respected for his integrity. He loved *making* money though he did not love money. He had one deep anxiety, however, and it was this: While he was a Christian and active in the church, he did not feel his work had any lasting value apart from making money through which he was able to support generously various mission and humanitarian causes.

I know personally how deeply this dualism runs. When I left the pastorate of a large university church, apprenticed as a carpenter, and eventually bought into the construction business as a partner, people said, "You have left the ministry. You are wasting your talents. You are denying your call." In business I worked on the construction site, prepared invoices, hired staff, and kept on top of the accounts. I also had to deal with dissatisfied customers. Was this holy work? Good work? Lasting work? Soul-engaging work? God-pleasing work? These questions raise issues of significance and permanence. It is relatively easy to see we are loving our neighbor when we work as doctors, counselors, or pastors, but just how does providing personal banking services to very wealthy people or running a hair salon do that? And what will last?

God and Humankind in Business Together

When we open the Bible we find God at work, *separating* light and darkness, land and sea, and so on. We also find God *filling* — making the world and all living things flourish. The Bible ends with God at work — renewing everything, including material things: "I am making everything new" (Rev. 21:5). In between, God is working in incredible ways: shaping, molding, speaking, communicating, showing outcomes, destroying, embellishing, making things beautiful, fixing and mending, restoring, designing, keeping things running, and bringing things to conclusion.[2] That is God at work, God doing business. But what about humankind?

2. As I read through the Bible I also find God designing, beautifying, nurturing, imagining, embellishing, leading, crafting, teaching, guiding, forming, disciplining, directing, shaping, warning, unifying, sustaining, showing outcomes, saving, organizing, destroying, mediating, separating, helping, rescuing, speaking, healing, mending, communicating, feeding, listening, completing, overcoming, judging, instructing, bringing rest, and comforting.

Human beings made in God's image have the enormous privilege of entering into God's ongoing work in every kind of good and humane occupation. This includes everything from agriculture to genetic engineering, from designing software to manufacturing electronic circuits, from making toys to marketing jeans, from repairing automobile engines to counseling the depressed. The Genesis account of creation mentions two things about the dignity of being God-imaging creatures — relationality and regency. The first, relationality, means that we are called to be community-builders ("in the image of God he created them; male and female he created them," Gen. 1:27). But the second, regency, means that we have the wonderful role of representing the absent monarch's interests, for that is what a regent does. In this case the King is not absent. God says, "Fill the earth and subdue it. . . . Till [the earth] and keep it" (Gen. 1:28; 2:15). So in both community-building and regency we are included in the ongoing work of God.

God the Creator makes new things. God is as creative today as when he started to make this thirteen-billion-years-old universe. He invites us to co-create with him in the entire human enterprise: information technology, art, music, systems design, and so on. *God the Sustainer* keeps everything running. We couldn't breathe another breath without God holding everything together. The apostle Paul says in Colossians, "In [Christ] all things hold together" (Col. 1:17), making the universe a cosmos rather than a chaos. When God speaks to Job out of the whirlwind he advises his blustering and pestering saint that He is maintaining the universe quite well, thank you. He is sustaining patterns of time (Job 38:12, 19-20), weather and climate (38:22-30), the universe itself (38:31-33), and life systems (38:39–39:30). Most homemaking tasks and work in the service industry are forms of "maintaining" work: housecleaning, servicing road systems, office maintenance, keeping the urban infrastructure and government itself functioning. People doing these things are doing "the Lord's work."

God the Redeemer invites humankind to join him in fixing, mending, and transforming. We do this work, of course, in witnessing to the gospel of the kingdom of God, the irruption of hope and new life in Christ. But we also do this when technicians work on automobiles or broken-down appliances, when counselors heal the broken-hearted, when physicians bring physical and emotional health, and when lawyers bring justice. *God the Consummator* brings the whole human story to a wonderful conclusion. He had the "Marriage Supper of the Lamb," that great rendezvous, in mind from the beginning (Rev. 19:9). The work of authors and people in media points to the meaning of things. Educators, pastors, and parents are working to bring people to maturity and to their unfolding destiny. They are doing the Lord's work too. But let's look at a concrete case.

• IN THE BEAUTY BUSINESS •

Diane realized that the decision would be more difficult than she had first thought. The job offer was a lucrative one — a good salary and company car, plus benefits. Colleen, a former business associate, a woman with whom Diane had worked for several years, was opening a business of her own and wanted Diane to run the company. On the surface it sounded like a great opportunity. But Diane's conscience was not at ease.

Colleen was a successful hairdresser. She earned a six-figure income working independently. She was now preparing to open a full service salon of her own. Diane and Colleen had worked together as employees in another day spa that Diane had managed, but Colleen had always wanted her own business. She had leased an expensive space in one of the city's trendy neighborhoods, located near the homes of her clients. Tenant improvements were under way. The professionally designed interior had the tastes of the wealthy patrons in mind; no expenses were spared.

Diane understood as few people did what it meant to pander to personal vanity, whether male or female, young or old. Image and appearance were enormously important components of the identity and self-confidence of the elite she served. Beyond all reason, middle-aged women often expected to look beautiful, young, thin, and perfectly groomed, despite the limitations of their genetic endowments. The young wanted to look sophisticated and chic. Because these clients were impatient and demanding, it was a daily struggle simply to make satisfactory appointments. They rarely took "no" for an answer and were practiced in the art of manipulating staff members to get their way. The astronomical amounts they spent on services annually seemed completely unrealistic by any standard.

On the other side of the coin, Diane had to consider her long-term relationship with Colleen. They worked together very well, and Diane admired Colleen's determination to fulfill a life-long dream that would not only profit Colleen, but would provide a stable income for fifteen to twenty employees as well. Colleen's responsibility as a small business owner was an enormous weight to bear. Diane's years of experience in the industry and common-sense approach would be needed if Colleen expected to continue to work "behind the chair" full time after the business opened.

It was also obvious that the salon staff provided more than just "beauty treatments" for many of the clients. The caring, professional touch and sympathetic ear of the technicians created an opportunity for friendships to grow. Time and again, the staff had walked with clients through family crises, terminal illnesses, surgeries and deaths, as well as preparations for weddings, reunions, and gala events. The salon had its own role to play in the community.

As a Christian, Diane believed that consumerism and narcissism were empty pursuits with no redemptive value. Was it prudent to continue to pour her time and talent into an environment that seemed to embody Solomon's lament that "all is vanity"?

• •

So Whose Work Matters to God?

Let's analyze Diane's dilemma by first asking whether she would be doing work that has intrinsic value through administering a hair salon, overseeing employees, training, and dealing with customers. Work that only has *extrinsic* value is done for what it produces: pay, prestige, or possibly a platform for mission. Work that has *intrinsic* value is good in itself. Most people think that so-called secular work has only extrinsic value, while ministry and people-helping professions have both extrinsic and intrinsic value. In the Bible, work that is the "Lord's work" and has intrinsic value is not determined by its religious character or even the fact that God's name is being used openly.

First, such work must be *mandated by God.* It must be part of God's call in Genesis 1:28 and 2:15 to take care of and develop the potential of creation, and to take care of people as image-bearers. In so doing workers enter the "Lord's work" of creating, sustaining, redeeming, and consummating.

Second, it must be *synchronized with God's purpose.* God's purpose is not that human beings should become angels, or even religious, but that they should become fully human. We become fully human by relating to God, building both the human community and the faith community, and blessing the nations. My personal future is not to be a saved immortal soul in heaven "up there" — that is a Greek idea — but to be a fully resurrected person in a totally renewed creation in a new heaven and new earth.

Third, work must be *undertaken virtuously* — God's way. Faith, hope, and love are the main virtues, often repeated as a triad in scripture and mentioned singly dozens of times. We will develop this in a later chapter. But Karl Barth, the twentieth-century theologian, summarizes brilliantly the criteria for considering what makes work good, humane, or virtuous:

- The Criterion of Objectivity — One can be immersed heart and soul, really get into it.
- The Criterion of Worth — It must contribute to the advancement and adornment of human existence.
- The Criterion of Humanity — Work that uses people as mere instruments is excluded.
- The Criterion of Reflectivity — The internal work of reflection and contemplation must not be excluded.
- The Criterion of Limitation — It must be restricted by Sabbath.[3]

3. Karl Barth, *Church Dogmatics,* III/4, pp. 528-63, summarized in Gordon

Fourth, the work should have *lasting value*. Many people think that only soul work will last. I grew up on the poem, "Only one life, 'twill soon be past. Only what's done for Christ will last." Certainly, on the surface of things, a hair-do will soon be undone, and most of our products will end up on the garbage heap, or so it seems. But what lasts, as Paul makes clear in 1 Corinthians 3:10-15 and 13:13, is not faith, hope, and love as "pure" virtues unattached to our lives, but *what is done in faith, hope, and love*.[4] In the end, these works, purged of sin as fire burns out the dross and leaves the pure metal (2 Pet. 3:12-13), will find their place in the "new heaven and the new earth." We too easily drop the "new earth" from the "new heaven and new earth" (Rev. 21:1; Isa. 66:22). Even some of my own work will last and find its place there in some way beyond my imagination: cedar decks I have made; classes I have taught; a business plan, a couple of books, and a sermon or two I have written; a kayak I built for my grandchildren; and my special made-from-scratch pancakes.

Good work is good for us, good for our neighbor, good for creation, and good for God. If she joins Colleen's business, Diane's work will in some way enter into "the Lord's work" and that work will have both intrinsic and extrinsic value, though she still may have good reasons not to accept this offer. One thing is sure. Human fallenness pervades everything, and she will encounter sin in the workplace and in herself with both the elite she might serve in Colleen's salon and the more ordinary clients in the salon where she is presently working.

But I have said that good work is also *good for God*. Our work matters to God. I mean this in five ways. First, God *prizes* the work and the worker. God is not passive and unappreciative. In the Parable of the Talents God said, "well done" (Matt. 25:21). Second, God *energizes* the work. We are co-workers with God, not just workers for God (1 Cor. 3:9). Third, God *receives* our work. The enigmatic statement of the master in Matthew 25:40, 45 means just this: "You did it to me."

Preece, *Changing Work Values: A Christian Response* (Melbourne, Australia: Acorn Press, 1995), pp. 178-80.

4. John Haughey, *Converting Nine to Five: A Spirituality of Daily Work* (New York: Crossroad, 1989), p. 106.

The apostle Paul says something similar two times in Colossians 3:23-24: "You serve the Lord Christ."

Fourth, our work can *glorify God*. Of course God is glorified in worship and evangelism, in giving to others and in the exercise of faith. But, as Wayne Grudem shows in his essay, "How Business in Itself Can Glorify God," God is also gloried through imitating God in undertaking activities that are unique to human beings, God-imaging creatures.[5] This includes ownership (imitating God's sovereignty), productivity (imitating God's creativity), and employment of others ("Paying another person for his or her labor is an activity that is uniquely human"[6]). Further, buying and selling are fundamentally good activities and, again distinguishing us from the animal kingdom, they allow us to move beyond subsistence-level living. Grudem also explores the gifts of money, competition, and profit, which is the "ability to multiply our resources while helping other people. . . . Through it we can reflect God's attributes of love for others, wisdom, sovereignty, planning for the future, and so on."[7] And, a subject to which we will return, business is the best long-term strategy for helping the poor to overcome their poverty by enabling them not only to have the next meal but to create new wealth. In this way God is also glorified as he has commanded us to remember the poor and love them (Gal. 2:10; Matt. 25:39-40). These activities are all fundamentally good, designed to honor God through enterprise and exchange, though they all provide opportunities for sin and corruption.

But fifth and finally, God *enjoys* our work. The deepest spirituality of work and business in particular is simply the word given to the five-talent person who made five more: "enter into the joy of your master" (Matt. 25:21) — sharing both the joy and work of the Master. This book has that ultimate purpose.

---

5. Wayne Grudem, "How Business in Itself Can Glorify God," in Tetsunao Yamamori and Kennth A. Eldred, eds., *On Kingdom Business: Transforming Missions Through Entrepreneurial Strategies* (Wheaton: Crossway Books, 2003), pp. 127-51.

6. Grudem, "How Business in Itself Can Glorify God," pp. 134-35.

7. Grudem, "How Business in Itself Can Glorify God," p. 139.

Where We Are Going

What will you gain from reading this book? This is not a "how-to" book on leadership or management. But it does encourage some of the soft skills and spirituality that will, in the long run, increase the bottom line of a company or enterprise. Great companies have great leaders who know who they are and what they are about. Great leaders also bring their whole selves to work — body, soul, and spirit. They have integrity. They know that what they are doing is significant and they know why they are doing it. So this book is essentially a "how-*come?*" book; it is more about "why" than "how." We deal with meaning and motivation rather than method. If we have a "why," we can easily find a "how."

So there are two parts to this book. The first part, *Meaning,* develops a theology of marketplace activity. Don't be afraid of theology. Even the comic strip Peanuts once said that theology was good for the soul. Puritan preacher William Perkins said it better: "Theology is the science of living blessedly forever."[8] Good theology is like fresh rain on a weary land, or like a bracing wind on a hot sultry day. It is practical and wonderfully refreshing. In this section we will explore business as calling, ministry, community-building, mission, and globalization.

The second part, *Motivation,* explores a marketplace spirituality, that search for wholeness, inspiration, and integration that empowers us to give our best, to realize our potential, to be found by God in the whole of life, and to contribute to a better world. So the chapters in this section will investigate taking our soul to work, the spiritual sources of ethical decision-making, motivation for creativity and entrepreneurship, letting life speak through the experience of time, money and success, and finally, the possibility of vocational holiness. We look at what it takes "on the inside" to function with integrity. We consider some of the disciplines needed to live and work contempla-

---

8. "A Golden Chain" (1592), in *The Works of William Perkins,* ed. I. Breward, The Courtenay Library of Reformation Classics, 3 (Appleford, UK: The Sutton Courtenay Press, 1970), p. 177.

tively in a high-stress job. But, at the same time, we explore how the work itself is a spiritual discipline pointing us Godward and confronting us with ourselves, the double-knowledge of God and self that Calvin said was the mark of true religion. I know this to be personally true.

When I became academic dean at Regent College, the president at that time, Dr. Walter Wright Jr., told me several important things. First, he said that in this leadership role I would have to deal with myself; in other words, it would be a spiritual discipline and a means of sanctification. Second, he said that I did not need to worry about failing. He guaranteed my success. If I failed, it would be because he had failed as my supervisor. The annual review would contain only affirmation. There would be no surprises. "But," he said, "we will have breakfast every Thursday and deal with things as they come along." I learned more about leadership, about spirituality in enterprise, and about myself in those six years of being mentored by Walter than in any other period of my life. It is in gratitude to him that I have dedicated this book. I learned how leadership is really a ministry, a subject we will take up in chapter 3.

I am unashamedly approaching this subject from a Christian perspective, but I sincerely desire that this might be readable and helpful to anyone who is seeking a deeper and more reflective practice of business. So this book provides:

- a theological framework for marketplace activity,
- an understanding of corporate culture and the task in cultivating it,
- an explanation of how faith relates to vocation, work, and ministry in the workplace and gives it lasting and satisfying meaning,
- a perspective on how spirituality is not merely a means of cranking up motivation in weary workers but the very source of creativity and entrepreneurship,
- a motivational perspective on dealing with awkward ethical dilemmas,
- a plan for living contemplatively in the thick of a demanding career.

Most chapters include case studies and questions for discussion at the end, which can be used individually or in a study group. I have reserved some scholarly reflections for the footnotes.

A few months ago, I undertook a four-day pilgrimage to Mount Athos, the monastic center of the Orthodox Church where fourteen hundred monks live in over twenty monasteries. The peninsula is one of three fingers thrust into the Aegean Sea in northeast Greece. This monastic state, the only one in the world, is accessible only by water and footpath. In the early days, as many as ten centuries ago, monks came from all over seeking God. Some lived in trees (dendrites), some on pillars (stylites); some walled themselves in caves clinging to Mount Athos, which rises awesomely six thousand feet from the sea. Over the four days, besides walking and praying, I had the opportunity to talk with one of the guest masters in the monastic communities that have settled there. "What do you teach at Regent College?" asked Father Damian. "Marketplace theology and spirituality," I answered. "What's that?" he continued. I tried to explain a difficult phrase, "It is the integration of Christian faith with work in the world." He bluntly responded, *"It is not possible. And that's why I am a monk."*

I pondered that for a long time, particularly in light of the siren appeal of the religious life — detached, contemplative, prayerful, and peaceful. Hordes of people of faith have been driven into professional ministry, not-for-profit activities, and some into the monastery, looking for something worthwhile, holy, and of lasting value, many in mid-life. Monasticism has fed into this, claiming to offer the ideal Christian life. Orthodox theologian Tomáš Špidlik says, "The ideal model [of work] would be the work of monks. It is performed in an atmosphere conducive to prayer, accompanied by explicit prayers; it becomes in itself a prayer, because its motivation is charity."[9] As I hiked from monastery to monastery along the rough and stony donkey trails that link these communities, I pondered a saying from the Eastern monastic tradition: "Keep to your cell, and your cell will teach you everything! Only in his cell is a monk in his element, like a

9. Tomáš Špidlik, *The Spirituality of the Christian East: A Systematic Handbook* (Kalamazoo, Mich.: Cistercian Publications, 1986), p. 168.

14

fish in water."[10] I thought about the businessperson and professional in the world that I serve and I came to an ironic conclusion. Do not leave business and join a monastery or become a pastor. Keep to your office, your work station, your cell. Go deep where you are. Your business will teach you everything. Martin Luther, the Protestant Reformer, used to say that you have as many teachers as you have transactions and tools.[11] Today the tools are not only the wood plane and the beer barrel but the computer, the spreadsheet, the staff meeting, and the board room. But going deep requires that one become a contemplative worker, a reflective practitioner, the very matter we will take up in both parts of this book.

For Discussion

1. Make a list of jobs that you think should *not* be done by Christians.

2. Analyze why you think the jobs you listed for question 1 should not be done by Christians: Because they are specifically forbidden in scripture? Harmful to the worker? Harmful to one's neighbor? Harmful to creation?

3. Reconsider Diane's dilemma. In what ways would her proposed employment be good work? In what ways not? Since Diane is a Christian and Colleen is not, are there other things she should take into consideration? What are the issues in this case? Who will be affected one way or another? Are there biblical reasons to take one approach rather than the other? If both ways are "good"

10. Špidlík, *The Spirituality of the Christian East,* p. 213.

11. "If you are a manual labourer, you find that the Bible has been put into your workshop, into your hand, into your heart. It teaches and preaches how you should treat your neighbour . . . just look at your tools . . . at your needle and thimble, your beer barrel, your goods, your scales or yardstick or measure . . . and you will read this statement inscribed in them. Everywhere you look, it stares at you. . . . You have as many teachers as you have transactions, goods, tools and other equipment in your house and home" (Martin Luther, *Works,* vol. 21 [St. Louis: Concordia, 1956], p. 237, quoted in Paul Marshall, *Thine Is the Kingdom* [Grand Rapids: Eerdmans, 1986], p. 25).

(though mixed with the potential for sin) how should Diane decide?

For Further Reading

Ciulla, Joanne B. *The Working Life: The Promise and Betrayal of Modern Work.* New York: Three Rivers Press, 2000.

Graves, Stephen R., and Thomas G. Addington. *The Fourth Frontier: Exploring the New World of Work.* Nashville: Word, 2000.

Meilaender, Gilbert C., ed. *Working: Its Meaning and Its Limits.* Notre Dame, Ind.: University of Notre Dame Press, 2000.

Preece, Gordon. *Changing Work Values: A Christian Response.* Melbourne, Australia: Acorn Press, 1995.

Sherman, Doug, and William Hendricks. *Your Work Matters to God.* Colorado Springs, Colo.: NavPress, 1987.

Schumacher, Christian. *God in Work.* Oxford: Lion Publishing, 1998.

PART ONE

MEANING

Towards a Marketplace Theology

2

$\blacklozenge \quad \blacklozenge \quad \blacklozenge$

Is Business a Calling?

Can we *entirely* alter what we do, so that here and now we practice the occupations of heaven? Of course not. Can we *somewhat* alter what we do, so that our occupations come closer to becoming our God-issued vocation? Usually, yes.

Nicholas Wolterstorff,
quoted in Gordon Preece,
Changing Work Values: A Christian Response

Scholar Calvin Seerveld once described his father working in the family fish store more than fifty years ago. As a customer and Calvin's father were making a deal, his father held up a carp and extolled its features — fresh, the tail even and spare, the eyes bright, the gills of good color, and the flesh firm. "Beautiful, beautiful, shall I clean it up?" he asked the woman. She grudgingly assented, ruefully admiring the way the bargain had been struck and said, "My, you certainly haven't missed your calling."[1] I doubt that this would be said very often today to a tradesperson, a merchant, or a business leader. It might possibly be said to a professional. But why not? And what difference would it make if one sensed that she or he is called to a specific work in the world?

Our work in the world is not something we just "have" to do, or something we choose as a career for personal fulfillment. It is part of the delightful and liberating summons of God. But today we hardly ever use the word "calling," especially for careers in business.

The current situation in the Western world is not hard to read. The term "calling" is reserved for the work of those who are going into "full time ministry," while in fact, a "part time" option for discipleship is not available. The term "vocation" is now identified with career, a path normally chosen for personal fulfillment rather than the public good. Calling has been secularized in the world and clericalized in the church.[2]

Calling and Career

Without a sense of calling we become magicians, inventing the meaning of our lives through careerism and professionalism. We are susceptible to the siren calls of the media, which tells us that we find our identity in consuming or achieving. We are driven about like dust in a windstorm with no abiding sense of direction. In contrast, a sense of calling gives our lives direction and purpose because our Creator summons us into a personal relationship with God and into a wonderful purpose that will outlast the world. The English Puritans, who

1. Calvin Seerveld, "Christian Workers, Unite," in *In the Fields of the Lord: A Calvin Seerveld Reader*, ed. Craig Bartholomew (Toronto: Toronto Tuppence Press, 2000), p. 242. Quoted with permission.

2. Michael Novak, *Business as a Calling: Work and the Examined Life* (New York: The Free Press, 1996), pp. 37-39. Novak argues that calling can be secularized. People speak of knowing themselves, finding what they ought to do, doing what they sense inwardly they are here to do, and in so speaking, says Novak, they are witnessing to calling even though they may be uncomfortable with religious language.

history tells us had a clear sense of calling, have been described as people who had swallowed gyroscopes: They always knew where they were heading!

It is important to distinguish the question of whether a Christian might *work* in business from the question of whether she or he might be *called* into business. In chapter 1 we have concluded that the first is permitted. In this chapter we are now exploring not mere permission but persuasion. While much is written on the subject of calling or vocation, precious little relates to business and professional life.

The English word "vocation" comes from the Latin *vocare* — which means "to call." Unfortunately, in common usage "vocation" usually refers to an occupation and a self-chosen career. It would be helpful if we could eliminate the word "vocation" from everyday speech and substitute the word "calling," which invites the question, "Who is calling?" For there to be a call*ee* there must be a call*er,* and that caller is God. If one were called to business that person would not only be *allowed* to work in an enterprise as an acceptable human occupation but actually *summoned* by God to this work to fulfill God's will and purpose. But calling to any type of work is only part of a much larger calling.

First of all, we are called to follow Someone before we are called to do something. So calling starts with the invitation of Jesus to come to him just as we are and to be enlisted as his followers. Significantly Mark's gospel describes Jesus' calling of the twelve disciples, and through them of us, as a summons "to be with him and to be sent out" (Mark 3:14). And Paul, in his correspondence to the Corinthians, says that God has "called" us "into the fellowship of his Son, Jesus Christ our Lord" (1 Cor. 1:9).

Such a call into fellowship with God's son constitutes the most common sense in which Paul uses "call" language in his New Testament letters (1 Cor 1:9). The call primarily has to do with salvation. Paul refers to the members of the church as "called to be saints" (1 Cor. 1:2) — chosen ones and beloved (Col. 3:12). In his ground-breaking work *Toward a Theology of the Laity,* Hendrik Kraemer says, "All members of the *ekklesia* [church] have in principle the same calling."[3] We are also called into holiness (1 Thess. 4:7), to freedom (Gal. 5:13), to hope (Eph. 1:18; 4:4), to the ministry of reconciliation (2 Cor. 5:18-19), "according to his purpose" (Rom. 8:28) — that we would become conformed into the image of his son (8:29). Thus calling involves belonging to God (a relationship), being (a way of life), and doing (serving God and God's purposes). Having called us to himself to become his daughters and sons, God then enlists us in his work in the world. It is to this second part of calling that we now turn.

As we explore the subject of calling bear in mind these questions: Would it have made a difference if my father had sensed God's summons to the steel fabrication business? And what difference? Does the comment made to Calvin Seerveld's father ("You certainly haven't missed your calling") really sum up what calling is about — summoned to a specific occupation? Why do pastors and missionaries speak of being "called" but few in the world of enterprise or trade use such language? Does God call everyone or only believers? Does the sense of "oughtness" and "I was made for this," which many not-yet-Christians experience, indicate a summons or calling from God, whether or not you believe in a transcendent personal Being? And if you are a manager, can you help your employees discern their own callings?

While no specific biblical texts indicate that people are summoned into a societal occupation by an ecstatic call of God, strong biblical reasons support the idea that business is part of God's summons to some people.

Called to Develop the Potential of Creation

Kenneth Kantzer argues that "being in business is itself a divine call."[4] He insists that scripture speaks of the conduct of business not

3. Hendrik Kraemer, *A Theology of the Laity* (Philadelphia: Westminster Press, 1958), p. 160.

4. Kenneth C. Kantzer, "God Intends His Precepts to Transform Society," in *Biblical Principles and Business: The Foundations,* Christians in the Marketplace, vol. 1, ed. Richard C. Chewning (Colorado Springs: NavPress, 1989), p. 29.

in a direct textual way but as a corollary of the cultural mandate, which posits a good creation, once corrupted by sin and Satan, now partially redeemed, and into which God calls his people to serve.[5] This means that *business is a legitimate part of undertaking the stewardship of creation to make a human imprint on the earth.*

In a 1984 essay on "The Lay Task of Co-Creation," Michael Novak explores the "innate virtue of enterprise":

> The task of lay persons in the economic order, whether investors, workers, managers, or entrepreneurs, is to build cooperative associations respectful of each other's full humanity. Such enterprises should be so far as is feasible participative and creative, in order to bring out from creation the productive possibilities and the human resources that the Creator, in his

5. In *Minding God's Business* (Grand Rapids: Eerdmans, 1986), Fuller Theological Seminary theologian Ray S. Anderson outlines the doctrine of creation using four theses:

"*Thesis 1:* The existing cosmos is a world order originally designed by God as Creator and Lord; this order is determinative for the existence of human persons (social order) as well as of the world order. . . . The present order of human society, as God created and intended it to exist as part of the world order, is 'good.' There is no intrinsic evil embedded in the created order, nor is the created order to be despised as unworthy of our attention. Christians sometimes forget this, and make the mistake of thinking that the 'business' of the world is basically evil and therefore cannot be 'of God.' The created cosmos is intended to serve as an environment of space and time for the preparation of human society to be the people of God.

"*Thesis 2:* The existing cosmos has suffered a radical disorder that cannot be renewed through the natural world itself; this disorder alienates both social and cosmic structures of creation from their created order and destiny. We know how bad it really is only when we know how good it is meant to be.

"*Thesis 3:* Through God's intervention by the giving of his Word, first of all to Israel as his new order of humanity, and finally through Jesus Christ as the new humanity, both human society and the cosmos are brought back under the creation mandate.

"*Thesis 4:* This present world and social order, though under the power of the new and creative order established through Jesus Christ, continues to suffer a tension between the new and old order. This present and continuing ministry of Jesus Christ takes place through the provisional forms of the church and its organizations as a sign of the kingdom of God" (pp. 22-34).

bounty, has hidden within it. Economic activity is a direct participation in the work of the Creator Himself.[6]

Some will shrink from using the word "co-creativity" for our engagement with God in the work of creation, preferring to speak of "sub-creativity." But we are called to work with God, though not of course as equal partners, in the continuing work of creation. God is as creative today as he was when he was first making the universe. And in a continuing act of divine condescension God invites us to join with him in his own work, business being a small part of that. We are to do so in an environmentally responsible way because this is what stewardship means — a matter with which business has a tarnished record. But business also is a partial expression of God's call to participate in the work of redemption.

Called to Improve and Embellish Human Life

The calling to improve human life seems apparent from the list of occupations of the descendents of Cain:

Jabal — "the ancestor of those who live in tents and have livestock" — implying commerce

Jubal — "the ancestor of all who play the lyre and pipe" — implying culture

Tubal-Cain — "who made all kinds of bronze and iron tools" — implying crafts (Gen. 4:20-22)

Adam and Eve and their descendents were called to be world-makers: image-makers, food-makers, home-makers, health-makers,

---

6. Michael Novak, "The Lay Task of Co-Creation," in *Toward the Future: Catholic Social Thought and the U.S. Economy, A Lay Letter* (North Tarrytown, N.Y.: Lay Commission on Catholic Social Teaching and the U.S. Economy, 1984), pp. 25-45, quoted in Max L. Stackhouse, Dennis P. McCann, Shirley J. Roels, and Preston N. Williams, eds., *On Moral Business: Classical and Contemporary Resources for Ethics in Economic Life* (Grand Rapids: Eerdmans, 1995), pp. 905-6.

garden-makers, account-makers, research-makers, tool-makers, beauty-makers, music-makers, comfort-makers, communication-makers, transportation-makers, toy-makers. Significantly, the Chinese word for "business" is composed of two pictograms that mean, separately, "to create" and "meaning." Business is a way of creating meaning for human beings. To say that business will *always* be good work is saying more than we can in this fallen and partially redeemed world.

The Bible's teachings about salvation and transformation point in the direction of a this-worldly and whole-person mission. Philip J. Wogaman says, "Attending to business matters practically and creatively, seeking to solve problems of economic life and thereby to serve humanity can surely be a worthy ministry for many Christians to undertake."[7] God is interested in saving not only souls but also bodies, systems, and even the entire creation. It started with God's work under the Covenant with Israel, sometimes called the Old Testament. God's redemptive purpose through Israel, which includes the stewardship of the land, economic laws, and the development of creation, sought "to restore a measure of conformity to the original economic purposes of God in creation."[8] Failure to see the unity of the Hebrew and Christian scriptures has contributed to the erroneous view that "the New Testament is more 'spiritual' than the Old, and is, because of this, superior to it."[9] They belong together.

Turning to the New Testament we discover Jesus working, healing, confronting, forgiving, and releasing. The Greek word in scripture for "save" *(sozo)* means "to make whole." It is close to the Hebrew word *shalom,* which connotes wholeness, integration, and rest. Jesus announced his ministry in terms of the Jubilee, that wonderful every-fifty-year release from bondage that was ordained in the Hebrew scriptures. And thus Jesus declared the full extent of his kingdom

7. Philip J. Wogaman, "Christian Faith and Personal Holiness," in Chewning, ed. *Biblical Principles and Business: The Foundations,* p. 50.

8. Christopher J. H. Wright, *Living as the People of God: The Relevance of Old Testament Ethics* (Leicester, England: Inter-Varsity Press, 1998), p. 89.

9. David J. Bosch, *Transforming Mission: Paradigm Shifts in Theology of Mission* (Maryknoll, N.Y.: Orbis Books, 1991), p. 405.

ministry — to make people fully human and to humanize the earth. He came to "bring good news to the poor . . . to proclaim release to the captives and recovery of sight to the blind, to let the oppressed go free" (Luke 4:18). He was quoting Isaiah 61:1-2 but in doing so he declared that his mission was the actual fulfillment of the Hebrew scriptures' Jubilee. The Jubilee, as described in Leviticus 25, involves even economic *shalom* — release of people from hopeless debt, rest for the land and people, return of assets to families so they may provide a living, and economic and social salvation. Colossians 1:15-20 and Romans 8:29-30 show us that God's plan for redemption extends to all things. The kingdom of God is not just a spiritual rule but is the dynamic saving rule of God in all of life and all of creation.

Business itself is an opportunity for the businessperson to function in a redemptive manner. In his fine study of business theology Richard Higginson suggests that we enter into the Lord's redemptive work in a quasi-redemptive manner through humble service, through the creation of new beginnings, through bearing the cost, and through taking the blame.[10] In the same vein Lesslie Newbigin asserts, "It is in the ordinary secular business of the world that the sacrifices of love and obedience are offered to God. It is in the context of secular affairs that the mighty power released into the world through the work of Christ is to be manifested."[11]

In the light of this, Bill Droel, editor of *Initiatives,* says that according to Catholic social thought, work has several purposes:

- To put money in the pockets of workers and in the portfolios of investors (some of whom might also be workers), thus providing for families and individuals now and in the future.
- To manufacture goods and deliver services that are needed in the community, thus helping society to thrive.
- To contribute to God's on-going creation and redemption.
- To contribute to personal development, and through self-

10. Richard Higginson, *Called to Account: Adding Value in God's World — Integrating Christianity and Business Effectively* (Guildford, Surrey: Eagle, 1993), pp. 139-41.

11. Lesslie Newbigin, *The Gospel in a Pluralistic Society* (Grand Rapids: Eerdmans, 1989), p. 230.

discovery to help people learn more about God. Because God is a relational Trinity, Catholic social thought says personal development involves solidarity with one's co-workers.[12]

This last purpose needs to be explained.

Called to Build Community on Earth

Kenneth Kantzer says, "By creation, human beings are social beings, never intended to live alone. Because of our social nature, we are specialized (each person is in one sense unique), interdependent and, therefore, necessarily dependent on exchange. Exchange is built into our very nature. And this *is* business."[13]

This starts in the first chapter of Genesis. There God places the woman and man in a sanctuary garden and gives them three full-time jobs. The first is to live in *communion* with God. Their eating, working, and relating are all to be expressions of their love and worship of God. The garden is actually a sanctuary, and they are placed in it as the image of God, just as images are placed in all temples. In this case the image of God is not an idol but humankind, male and female (Gen. 1:27). Communion is not to be merely on the Sabbath or for twenty minutes in the morning but 24/7. The second full-time job is *community-building.* They are created in God's image as male and female. Males are not the image of God and neither are females. We are designed for community, to experience it, to build it, and to extend it by being fruitful, multiplying, and filling the earth. The third full-time job to which they are called is to be *co-creators:* to unpack the potential of creation, to "have dominion" over everything except themselves (Gen. 1:28), to "till [the earth] and keep it" (2:15). Since this is undertaken in the presence of God and as an expression of God's purpose, Adam and Eve are priests of creation.

12. Bill Droel, *Initiatives,* 123 (May 2002), 1. See also "worker solidarity" in Pope John Paul II's *Laborem Exercens: On Human Work* (Washington, D.C.: Office of Publishing and Promotion Services, United States Catholic Conference, 1981), pp. 17-19.

13. Kantzer, "God Intends His Precepts," p. 24.

A company is also a community. In business we experience community, whether in a village marketplace, e-commerce, trade fairs, or the small mom-and-pop store in the neighborhood. But there is a larger neighborhood to be served as well.

Called to Global Enrichment and Unity

God's call to humankind is a global call: "Fill the earth" (Gen. 1:28). Business can be an agent of the kingdom of God by bringing a measure of *shalom* to people and to nations. Engaging in business is one way in which we are called, with Abraham and his descendants, to bless the nations and to build intercultural and international unity. Michael Novak addresses this eloquently:

> Commerce, as several of the Eastern fathers of the Catholic church wrote, notably St. John Chrysostom, is the material bond among peoples that exhibits, as if symbolically, the unity of the human race — or, as he dared to put it in mystical language, shows forth as a material sign the "mystical body of Christ." The human race is one. The international commerce that shows forth the interdependence of all parts of the human body knits the peoples of the world together by the silken threads of a seamless garment.[14]

Novak argues that the founder of Western monasticism, St. Benedict (480-547), learned from early Christian hermitages the value of frequently changing leadership in monasteries and staking out unsettled and remote lands. These monasteries swept north into Europe and became, as many historians note, the West's first transnational corporation. "They introduced scientific agriculture thus enabling entire regions to advance beyond subsistence living."[15] Through the surplus generated by monasteries, arts and sciences such as botany,

---

14. Novak, *Business as a Calling*, pp. 46-47.
15. Michael Novak, *The Fire of Invention: Civil Society and the Future of the Corporation* (Lanham, Md.: Rowman & Littlefield Publishers, 1997), p. 28.

metallurgy, and architecture were nourished, and schools, music halls, and other aspects of civilization developed.

While it is true that we eat breakfasts, wear clothing, and use electronic instruments that are manufactured all around the world, all too often, the "seamless garment" is a Western one. And globalization has been more the homogenization of culture than a rich unity through diversity — unitarian rather than trinitarian.[16] We will develop this idea in chapter 6.

Called to Create Wealth and Alleviate Poverty

Business can have a redemptive purpose in alleviating poverty, creating new wealth, and enhancing human existence. The Bible clearly teaches that we are called to do all we can to help the poor overcome their poverty. "How does God's love abide in anyone who has the world's goods and sees a brother or sister in need and yet refuses to help?" (1 John 3:17). What the poor need is not merely hand-outs, though this is part of our ministry to them, but hand-ups, equipping the poor to become producers of wealth. Novak has probably overstated the case: "Business is, bar none, the best hope of the poor. And that is one of the noblest callings inherent in business activities: to raise up the poor."[17] This point is particularly difficult to make in the context of a world where the rich are getting richer and the poor, poorer.[18]

16. Gilbert Meilaender notes, in critique of Novak's assertion that commerce binds people together and is what people do when they are at peace, that "the very same business that testifies to and encourages human solidarity becomes — or can become — a means by which we acquire the wealth that gives us a considerable measure of independence from others." Gilbert Meilaender, "Professing Business: John Paul meets John Wesley," *The Christian Century,* 4 December 1996, p. 1201.

17. Novak, *Business as a Calling,* p. 37.

18. In his review of Novak's book, Prabo Mihindukulasuriya notes that while earlier migrations to North America in the late 1800s and early 1900s show the superiority of the capitalist system, the current economic migration from developing countries is composed of predominantly skilled workers and elites, thus actually hindering the development of healthy economies in those countries. "And so it will

Generally people are better off today than they were in previous centuries because of enterprise, even though huge discrepancies still exist.[19] Globalization of business holds both promise and peril.[20] But Novak is right: "To rise out of poverty, the poor need jobs; prospective employees need to find employers; and inventors and originators need to create new industries."[21] The work of the Mennonite Economic Development Associates (MEDA), Integra in Central Europe, and Opportunities International are stunning illustrations of the redemptive value of work in business and poverty alleviation on a global scale. Wealth creation is not evil, as some preachers have asserted. Wealth creation is the process by which needs and wants are satisfied. It is not a zero-sum game that makes one person's gain another's loss, although that might have been the case before the Industrial Revolution, when supply was limited and one person's meal was at another's expense. Wealth creation is part of bringing *shalom* to people and the world, as Brian Griffiths ably shows in his classic book, *The Creation of Wealth*. In a more recent work Clive Wright opines:

> The Malthusian prediction that the Earth could not support its growing population proved unfounded. That there are finite natural resources on the planet remains true. But human creativity has demonstrated over more than two centuries an ability to provide for a much larger world population.[22]

But business activity is not only for this life and this world.

---

not be capitalism *per se* that will offer the solution to Two-Thirds world development." Prabo Mihindukulasuriya, "Business as a Calling: Work and the Examined Life" (review), *Crux* 34, no. 2 (June 1998): 46.

19. Steven Rundle and Tom Steffan cite supporting statistics from the World Bank 2003 in *Great Commission Companies: The Emerging Role of Business in Missions* (Downers Grove, Ill.: InterVarsity Press, 2003), p. 47.

20. See my student's study, John A. C. Morrow, "The Global Economy and Global Free Market Capitalism: Towards a Christian Perspective" (Regent College, November 2000).

21. Novak, *Business as a Calling*, p. 60.

22. Clive Wright, *The Business of Virtue* (London: SPCK, 2004), p. 79. See especially Wright's chapters on "Wealth" and "A Theology of Wealth Creation."

Called to Invest in Heaven

I have often reflected on the fact that the whole culture of ancient Egypt was directed to the sunset of life and the known end of the world, for all the pyramids and tombs were built on the west side of the Nile. In contrast, biblical faith looks towards the dawning of a new day. A similar contrast has been made between the perspective of African traditional religion and the Christian faith. The comparison is made between a person standing on a bridge over a river and looking one way or another, downstream or upstream. In African traditional religion the person is looking back, at the influence of the spirits of the ancestors coming towards her or him, while the biblical perspective looks forward to where we are being led by God. The biblical view of the end times (the technical term is *eschatology*) is not looking back to the garden of Eden, an idyllic past, but forward to a totally transfigured creation and the wedding supper of the Lamb.

Theologian Jürgen Moltmann refers to this biblical view of the end as the "doctrine of the return to the pristine beginning" through which God will achieve his purpose for creation in "'the new creation of all things' and [in] the universal indwelling of God in that creation."[23]

Even business activity may last and find its place, purged of sin, in the new heaven and the new earth. The question of what work lasts is a vital one. Typically the church has taught that only "soul work" lasts. The resurrection of the body as the Christian's future means that "in the Lord your labor is not in vain" (1 Cor. 15:58).[24] As scholar Miroslav Volf notes, "The continuity or discontinuity between the present and future orders is one of the key issues in developing a the-

23. Jürgen Moltmann, *The Coming of God: Christian Eschatology,* trans. Margaret Kohl (Minneapolis: Fortress Press, 1996), p. 57.

24. "The resurrection of Christ redeems from meaninglessness the whole of our life and work. It is in the resurrection of Christ that we find the final vindication of all the work we do in this life, our assurance that all our toil and struggle and sufferings possess abiding worth." Alan Richardson, *The Biblical Doctrine of Work* (London: SCM Press, 1952), p. 58.

ology of work."[25] This has led some theologians to consider that there might be marketing in heaven![26]

The Bible offers ten evidences of why we can expect that some of our work in non-evangelistic activity may last and contribute to the new heaven and the new earth:

- There is continuity between this life and the next — the new Jerusalem is related to this world — a city, the land (Rev. 21–22);
- The kings of the earth bring their glories into the new heaven and new earth (Rev. 21:24);
- The glory and honor of the nations is found in God's holy city (Rev. 21:26);
- The Old Testament predicts that during the reign of the Messiah we will not cease to work: "My chosen shall long enjoy the work of their hands" (Isa. 65:21-22);
- The resurrected body of Jesus bore scars from this life — but these scars were transfigured (John 20:27);
- Jesus declares that, in the final judgment, he will personally receive even humble acts of service done in our everyday lives (Matt. 25:31-46);
- The fire of judgment (2 Peter 3:7) does not mean annihilation but transformation, for "in accordance with his promise, we wait for new heavens and a new earth" (2 Peter 3:13);
- 1 Corinthians 3:10-15 indicates that our work will be tested by fire and may even survive!
- Romans 8:19-22 proclaims that the earth groans and waits for liberation from bondage, this being associated with the revelation of the children of God;

25. Miroslav Volf, "Human Work, Divine Spirit, and the New Creation: Toward a Pneumatological Understanding of Work," *Pneuma: The Journal of the Society for Pentecostal Studies* 175 (Fall 1987): 173-93. Volf contrasts the view of work as cooperation with God in *creatio continua* (which has dominated Reformational theology) with work as cooperation with God in *transformatio mundi*.

26. Todd Steen and Steve VanderVeen, "Will There Be Marketing in Heaven?" *Perspectives*, November 2003, pp. 6-11.

- Revelation 14:13 indicates that the deeds of the Christians will follow them, "the indelible imprint" of their work on their lives.[27]

Miroslav Volf wisely cautions that while God will somehow include our efforts in the new creation, we must not imagine that the "results of human work should or could create and replace 'heaven.'"[28] Along the same lines and with consummate wisdom Lesslie Newbigin says:

> We can commit ourselves without reserve to all the secular work our shared humanity requires of us, knowing that nothing we do in itself is good enough to form part of that city's building, knowing that everything — from our most secret prayers to our most public political acts — is part of that sin-stained human nature that must go down into the valley of death and judgment, and yet knowing that as we offer it up to the Father in the name of Christ and in the power of the Spirit, it is safe with him and — purged in fire — it will find its place in the holy city at the end.[29]

A Specific Calling?

1 Corinthians 7:17-24 is a critical passage in the question of whether God calls people to a specific occupation including, of course, business. The New International Version offers a nuanced difference between verse 17 ("Each one should retain the place in life that God assigned to him and *to which* God has called him") and verse 20 ("remain in the situation which he was in *when* God called him"), suggesting that the call is both to a place of service and life (v. 17) and that the place is the location for receiving a more all-embracing call

27. Volf, "Human Work," pp. 175-79.
28. Miroslav Volf, *Work in the Spirit: Toward a Theology of Work* (New York: Oxford University Press, 1991), p. 92.
29. Lesslie Newbigin, *Foolishness to the Greeks: The Gospel and Western Culture* (Grand Rapids: Eerdmans, 1986), p. 136.

(v. 20). This apparent distinction does not seem to be supported by the original language.[30] Verse 20, however, is a critical verse for the Reformation doctrine that each person is called, some to be magistrates and some to be scholars. "Every one should remain in the state [*klesei*] in which he was called [*eklethe*]."[31] Commenting on the crucial implications of this for the Reformation, theologian Donald Heiges says, "For all practical purposes Luther uses vocation *(Beruf)* to cover both calling into the church and calling into a station."[32]

Both Luther and Calvin leaned heavily on this verse to argue for a worldly calling, as did the Puritans later. But the point Paul is making is that change, which the Corinthians wanted, whether in marriage, ethnicity, or social-economic situation, is not spiritually significant. Christ sanctifies the place they were in when he called them. Gordon Fee interprets the passage this way: "Under the theme of 'call' Paul seeks to put their 'spirituality' into a radically different perspective. They should remain in whatever social setting they were at the time of their call since God's call to be in Christ (cf. 1.9) transcends such settings so as to make them essentially irrelevant. . . . Thus one is no better off in one condition than in the other."[33] This is in contrast to the way the Reformers interpreted this verse.[34]

---

30. New Testament scholar Gordon Fee maintains that this strong distinction is not maintained by the original language. It is "each as God called" in verse 17 and "remaining in the situation in which he was called" in verse 20. Gordon D. Fee, *The First Epistle to the Corinthians* (Grand Rapids: Eerdmans, 1987), p. 307.

31. Luther translated the Greek *klesei* as German *Ruf* and *eklethe* as *berufen ist*.

32. Donald R. Heiges, *The Christian's Calling* (Philadelphia: United Lutheran Church in America, 1958), p. 49. Gustaf Wingren notes that non-Christians have a station *(Stand)* and office *(Amt* or *Stelle)* but only Christians have a *Beruf* or *vocatio*. "*Beruf* is the Christian's earthly or spiritual work." Gustaf Wingren, *Luther on Vocation*, trans. Carl C. Rasmussen (Philadelphia: Muhlenberg Press, 1957), p. 2, quoted in Heiges, *The Christian's Calling*, p. 49.

33. Fee, *The First Epistle to the Corinthians*, p. 307. Fee notes, "Although he [Paul] comes very close to seeing the setting in which one is called as 'calling' itself, he never quite makes that jump," p. 309.

34. On this point Paul Marshall observes, "The interpretation of calling as 'external conditions' would mean that Paul was using *klesis* in a sense used *nowhere else* in the New Testament. Indeed, it would be a usage without parallel in the Greek of the period. He would have to be coining a new term. . . . This means that the Bible does

Nevertheless, Paul envisions our ordinary work being taken up into the new order of things under Christ. In 1 Corinthians 15:58 he says, "In the Lord your labor is not in vain." Our activity is not just our own effort but is carried on "with a demonstration of the Spirit and of power" (1 Cor. 2:4-5). So rather than setting up a dichotomy of sacred and secular work, Paul sees all work directed to the new life in Christ and the advancement of Christ's kingdom. What makes such work Christian is not mere human striving but self-giving love, following Christ in dying and rising, in human weakness and yet resurrection power, in obedience to God and participation in the new order inaugurated through the death and resurrection of Christ.[35] I think Paul, if he were writing to businesspeople today, might say something like this:

> Stay in your business but go deep. Your work station, your office, your position will teach you everything and will be a means of growth in faith. Don't think that going into religious work will be a spiritual advantage. Your life is not a bundle of accidents. All the things that led you to where you are now — birth, education, interests, advantages, and opportunities — are part of God's providential leading in your life. Where you were when God called you is significant and is taken up into the all-embracing summons of God. Your life and daily work are significant and, if done not for yourself but unto the Lord, will not be in vain.

In summary, we do not find a textual basis in the Bible for speaking of business as a calling. There is not a single instance of a person

---

not contain a notion of vocation or calling in one of the senses in which these terms were used in Reformational theology." Paul Marshall, *A Kind of Life Imposed on Man: Vocation and Social Order from Tyndale to Locke* (Toronto: University of Toronto Press, 1996), p. 14.

35. In his study of human achievement and vocation in Paul's writing, W. A. Beardslee shows how the divine call may use and fulfill the human striving for achievement, which can only be frustrated unless it becomes a response to God's call. W. A. Beardslee, *Human Achievement and Divine Vocation in the Message of Paul* (London: SCM Press, 1961), pp. 19-20.

in the New Testament being called into a societal occupation by an existential encounter with God — not Paul the tent-maker, not Lydia the textile merchant, and not Peter the fisherman. Nor is there a single instance of a person being called to be a religious professional — not Timothy, not Barnabas, and not Priscilla. Nevertheless, scripture witnesses to people being led into positions of societal service where they could make a difference without a supernatural call: Joseph, Nehemiah, Daniel, Esther, Priscilla and Aquila.

The Bible shows us God as a vocational director, but he does not normally call people to service in various occupations in the same way he called people like Amos and Elijah to serve as prophets or Paul as an apostle. God may, of course, exceptionally give an existential call to individuals for any specific service. But normally God calls us to himself and *leads* us into particular expressions of service appropriate for our gifts and talents through our passions, abilities, and opportunities. And that work we do, whether international business or graphic art, becomes part of the all-embracing summons of God to belong to him, to live in a suitable manner, and to "do the Lord's work." So we can say that working in business is a calling in this general sense: It is one way in which we can do good work in the world and serve our neighbor — these being part of God's call. But is business a lower call than, for instance, being a pastor or a missionary? Here is a true story.

• **A HIGHER CALL?** •

"I'm counting on you, Murray, to set Robert straight and get him to accept his share of the company loan. I know he feels called to the mission field but that does not absolve him from his responsibility to me." As Murray listened in his home to these words he recalled how deeply he cared for both Bill and Robert, and how concerned he was that God's call would not divide these brothers. "We are business partners," Bill continued, "and we started this business feeling that God had called us to a business ministry together. I know Robert has arranged to see you later this morning and I thought I should see you first. You are a friend to us both and an elder of our church." Minutes after Bill left, the doorbell rang and Robert was on the doorstep. Murray wondered why he felt so much "in the middle."

Two weeks before in their regular mentoring time, Robert had dropped the bombshell to Murray, as he had to his brother Bill: "At the mission conference I got the call, and so did my wife. We are both sure that God is calling us to the mission field to work with students in Zambia." Murray recalled how ambivalent he felt about Robert's call as he invited him in and picked up the conversation again. "My wife and I," continued Robert, "were hoping the church would send us out and undertake a large part of our monthly support. We also would like *you* to consider becoming one of our prayer and support partners. The needs are tremendous." Robert could hardly have known that Bill had just left Murray's home, and he seemed to have forgotten what had happened three years ago.

Murray had met with both of them three years ago when they formed a business partnership and company, New Age Electronics, a high-tech assembly operation now employing twenty-five people. Bill, over fifty and much older than Robert, was the major shareholder and had guaranteed 75 percent of the company loan with his personal residence. Against Murray's advice Bill had not insisted that Robert sign a guarantee for his 25 percent share of the company loan. So legally, Robert could walk away from it — something he felt justified in doing in view of now having a higher call for his life.

"What about the loan?" Murray inquired.

"We were hoping Bill would take it on. He's so much better established than we are and is well able to handle it. This business is like a hobby to him."

"Can you sell your house?"

"We thought we should keep it and rent it so we have something to come back to."

"And the business?"

"I had hoped that it would yield enough to allow me to retire early and do something in the Lord's work, but it's been sheer survival and doesn't look like it will improve."

"Did you know that Bill was just here?"

"No! What did he say?"

"He said that you have 'peace' about all this and he has the 'pieces'!"

"This is certainly not turning out as I had hoped," Robert commented as he left the home.

Moments later the telephone rang. It was Bill asking Murray to set up a meeting with the elders with both of them to resolve the issue once and for all.

•   •

For Discussion

1. What are the issues in Murray, Bill, and Robert's dilemma?
2. Who is affected?
3. What biblical texts or principles could be of service to them in resolving this conflict?
4. How might Robert know that he was indeed called to overseas mission work?
5. Does the call of God override human obligations and duties? How does Paul's teaching in 1 Corinthians 7 speak to this?
6. What view of calling is implicit in the conversation these people are having?
7. How might the church help?
8. How might the church teach and minister to prevent such a conflict in the future?
9. How do you react to Martin Luther's statement: "How is it possible that you are not called? You have always been in some state or station; you have always been a husband or wife, or boy or girl, or servant." Martin Luther also said: "[If the Christian] is at a place where there are no Christians he needs no other call than to be a Christian, called and anointed by God from within. Here it is his duty to preach and to teach the gospel to erring heathens or non-Christians, because of the duty of brotherly love, even though no man calls him to do so. . . . [I]f he is at a place where there are

Christians who have the same power and right as he, he should not draw attention to himself. Instead, he should let himself be called and chosen to preach and to teach in the place of and by the command of the others."[36]

For Further Reading

Banks, Robert, and Kimberly Powell, eds. *Faith in Leadership: How Leaders Live Out Their Faith in Their Work and Why It Matters.* San Francisco: Jossey-Bass, 2000.

Chewning, Richard C., John W. Eby, and Shirley Roels. *Business through the Eyes of Faith.* San Francisco: HarperSanFrancisco, 1990.

Diehl, William. *Thank God It's Monday.* Philadelphia: Fortress Press, 1982.

Guiness, Os. *The Call: Finding and Fulfilling the Central Purpose of Your Life.* Nashville: Word, 1998.

Novak, Michael. *Business as a Calling: Work and the Examined Life.* New York: The Free Press, 1996.

Schuurman, Douglas J. *Vocation: Discerning Our Callings in Life.* Grand Rapids: Eerdmans, 2004.

Stevens, R. Paul. *The Other Six Days: Vocation, Work, and Ministry in Biblical Perspective.* Grand Rapids: Eerdmans, 2000.

36. Martin Luther, "That a Christian Assembly or Congregation has the Right and Power to Judge All Teaching and to Call, Appoint, and Dismiss Teachers, Established and Proven by Scripture," *Luther's Works* (Philadelphia: Fortress Press, 1966), vol. 39, pp. 310-11.

3

The Business Side of Ministry

Christ is not just the Lord of Christians; he is Lord of all, absolutely and without qualification. [Therefore] the entire membership of the Church in their secular occupations is called to be signs of his lordship in every area of life.

Lesslie Newbigin,
Unfinished Agenda: An Updated Autobiography

Richard Higginson in *Questions of Business Life* takes a hilarious look at various approaches to economic enterprise:

Feudalism: You have two cows. Your lord takes some of the milk.

Fascism: You have two cows. The government takes both, hires you to take care of them, and sells you the milk.

Communism: You have two cows. You must take care of them, but the government takes all the milk.

Capitalism: You have two cows. You sell one and buy a bull. Your herd multiplies, and the economy grows. You sell them and retire on the income.

Enron Capitalism: You have two cows. You sell three of them to your publicly listed company, using letters of credit opened by your brother-in-law at the bank, then create a debt equity swap with an associated general offer so that you can get all four cows back, with a tax exemption for five cows. The milk rights of the six cows are transferred through an intermediary to a Cayman Island company secretly owned by the majority shareholder, who sells the rights to all seven cows back to your listed company. The Enron annual report says the company owns eight cows, with an option on one more.[1]

There is no perfect system! Capitalism, though, is the best of several imperfect choices, for it has proved remarkably effective and durable. But, as Clive Wright notes in his penetrating study of business ethics, the Western form of it may not be suitable for all societies and cultures. He observes, "When terrorists crashed aircraft into the World Trade Center in New York in the name of Islam, that was a protest against the very model of democratic capitalism that [Michael] Novak so warmly commends. The terrorists were seriously misguided. But they fearfully demonstrated that the particular form of wealth creation which has proved so successful in the West is by no means universally regarded as acceptable."[2]

In the last two chapters we have met people wrestling with the significance of what they were doing or about to do in the system. Diane wanted to know if she was merely pandering to vanity in managing an upscale hair salon. Robert thought overseas service was meeting a deeper need than his business. Both were searching for meaning. One wanted to know how to function meaningfully within capitalism and the other sought a way out, though remaining dependent on others who worked in it. Is business a ministry, or can it be?

1. Richard Higginson, *Questions of Business Life* (Carlisle, Cumbria: Authentic Media, 2002), pp. 25-26.

2. Clive Wright, *The Business of Virtue* (London: SPCK, 2004), p. 70.

That is the question we will be addressing in this chapter. There is a long history of "No" as the answer.

The Long History of Anti-Business Attitudes

The Greek world had no concept of vocation. Work itself was a curse and the citizens of Thebes were even forbidden to work! The influence of the Greek world that surrounded and even enfolded the early church is well known.[3]

The Greek World and the Middle Ages

Plotinus, the single most influential philosopher of the ancient world, and one who profoundly affected Augustine and Western Christianity, defined the great opposites of spirituality and materialism. "The pleasure demanded for the Sage's life cannot be in the enjoyments of the licentious or in any gratifications of the body. . . . Let the earth-bound man [sic] be handsome and powerful and rich, and so apt to this world that he may rule the entire human race: still there can be no envying of him, the fool of such lures." The Sage, in contrast, will wear away the "tyranny of the body . . . by inattention to its claims."[4] Trade, for Aristotle, was essentially suspicious if not downright perverted: "Anybody who does anything for pay is by nature not a truly free person."[5] So profoundly did the Hellenistic world affect the people of God that the book Ecclesiasticus — written between the Old and New Testaments — continues to put manual work low on the hierarchy. While trades are needed for maintaining the fabric of this world (Ecclus. 38:34), the scribe and philosopher have chosen the better way.

3. See Lee Hardy, *The Fabric of This World* (Grand Rapids: Eerdmans, 1990).

4. Quoted in Max Stackhouse et al., *On Moral Business: Classical and Contemporary Resources for Ethics in Economic Life* (Grand Rapids: Eerdmans, 1995), p. 39.

5. Quoted in Gordon Preece, "Business as a Calling and Profession: Towards a Protestant Entrepreneurial Ethic" (paper presented at the International Marketplace Theology Consultation, Sydney, June 2001), p. 14.

Most of the early church fathers embraced this "upper and lower" approach to life: the higher for the monk, nun, priest, and pastor who reject ordinary work in the world, and the lower for the person who works in the world. Exceptionally, Clement of Alexandria (A.D. 150-215) seems to have been alone in taking a positive view of entrepreneurship and capital.[6] By and large the two-level regime was followed universally. Eusebius (about A.D. 315) put it this way:

> *Two* ways of life were thus given by the law of Christ to His Church. The *one* is above nature, and beyond common human living; it admits not marriage, child-bearing, property nor the possession of wealth, but, wholly and permanently separate from the common customary life of mankind, devotes itself to service of God alone in its wealth of heavenly love! . . . Such then is the perfect form of the Christian life. And the *other*, more humble, more human, permits men to join in pure nuptials and to produce children, to undertake government, to give orders to soldiers fighting for right; more secular interests as well as for religion; and it is for them that times of retreat and instruction, and days of hearing sacred things are set apart. *And a kind of secondary grade of piety is attributed to them.* . . .[7]

This division became evident in the supremacy of medieval monasticism, the way of Mary the contemplative, over and against secular life, the way of Martha the person active in the world. No wonder the subject of this book — doing God's business — seems to be an oxymoron, like fried ice or black light! By the fifteenth century only the monk, nun, and priest had callings. Ordinary Christians had no vocation. Karl Barth's summary is apt: "According to the view prevalent at the height of the high Middle Ages [secular work] only existed to free for the work of their profession those who were totally and ex-

---

6. B. Gordon, *The Economic Problem in Biblical and Patristic Thought* (Leiden: E. J. Brill, 1989), p. 87, quoted in Preece, "Business as a Calling," p. 15.

7. Quoted in W. R. Forrester, *Christian Vocation* (New York: Scribner's, 1953), p. 43, italics mine.

clusively occupied in rendering true obedience for the salvation of each and all."[8] This is not far from the contemporary idea that businesspeople in the church are simply "walking check books" needed to support the pastor.[9]

Martin Luther

Luther radically universalized calling to include all human occupations *except that of the monk* as a reaction against medieval monasticism and, at the same time, world-denying Anabaptism.[10] Luther based his thinking on a fundamental biblical truth: We do not choose; we are called. And all are called. In the medieval world, the monk *elected* a superior way of discipleship — a self-chosen path of poverty, chastity, and obedience. However, in true Christian discipleship, one does not elect; one is *called*. In one of his Christmas sermons Luther said, "I should rather be one of the shepherds tending the flocks in the field than to be canonized by the Pope."[11] Luther urged people to accept the position in which they found themselves. He was addressing a fairly stable society represented by the children's hymn:

> The rich man in his castle,
> The poor man at his gate;

8. Karl Barth, "Vocation," in *Church Dogmatics,* trans. A. T. Mackay, T. H. L. Parker, H. Knight, H. A. Kennedy, and J. Marks, III/4 (Edinburgh: T&T Clark, 1961), p. 601, quoted in Paul Marshall, *A Kind of Life Imposed on Man: Vocation and Social Order from Tyndale to Locke* (Toronto: University of Toronto Press, 1996), p. 22.

9. But in the late Middle Ages German mysticism challenged the monastic monopoly on having an "inner voice" or "feeling God's presence," and even Max Weber observed that Johannes Tauler held both spiritual and worldly callings as equal. Max Weber, *The Protestant Ethic and the Spirit of Capitalism,* trans. Talcott Parsons (New York: Charles Scribner's Sons, 1958), p. 212.

10. Klaus Bochmuehl, "Recovering Vocation Today," *Crux* 24, no. 3 (September 1988): 30-31.

11. Howard C. Kee and Montgomery J. Shroyer, *The Bible and God's Call: A Study of the Biblical Foundation of Vocation* (New York: Cokesbury — The Methodist Church, 1962), p. 11.

> God made them high and lowly,
> And ordered their estate.[12]

Every station in life offers opportunities for ministry or service with absolutely no expectation of reward either from God or people. Luther wrote, "A cobbler, a smith, a farmer, by means of his own work or office must benefit and serve every other, that in this way many kinds of work may be done for the bodily and spiritual welfare of the community, even as all the members of the body serve one another."[13] Vocation is given "structure by God through 'orders' and 'offices' which, because divinely decreed, serve good and necessary purposes even though some of them may involve evil men and seemingly evil actions."[14] Thus the Christian should remain in his or her station rather than try to escape it. Here Luther (and later Calvin) expounds on 1 Corinthians 7:17: "Each one should retain the place in life that the Lord assigned to him and to which God has called him." Only if a station is inherently sinful should it be abandoned.

> When I speak of a calling which in itself is not sinful, I do not mean that we can live on earth without sin. All callings and estates sin daily; but I mean the calling God has instituted is not opposed to God, as for example, marriage, man-servant, maid-servant, lord, wife, superintendent, ruler, judge, officer, citizen, etc. I mention as sinful stations in life: robbery, usury, public women, and, as they are at present, the pope, cardinals, bishops, priests, monks, and nuns, who neither preach nor listen to preaching.[15]

12. This quotation is from the hymn "All things bright and beautiful" by the Victorian hymn-writer Mrs. C. F. Alexander. The German word *Beruf* may have been generally used to describe someone's status or profession in society, but Luther was almost certainly the first to use the Latin word *vocatio* in this way. (See Lake Lambert III, "Called to Business: Corporate Management as a Profession of Faith" [Ph.D. diss., Princeton Theological Seminary; Ann Arbor: University Microfilms, 1997], p. 18.)

13. Martin Luther, "An Open Letter to the Nobility," quoted in Donald R. Heiges, *The Christian's Calling* (Philadelphia: United Lutheran Church in America, 1958), p. 53.

14. Heiges, *The Christian's Calling*, pp. 50-51.

15. *Luther's Table Talk*, trans. William Hazlitt (Philadelphia: Lutheran Publication Society, 1873), p. 447, quoted in Heiges, *The Christian's Calling*, p. 58.

Luther put it this way, "If you find a work by which you serve God or His saints or yourself and not your neighbor, know such a work is *not* good."[16] Thus, according to Luther, being a monk was not a calling and not even good work. It was not a ministry. While Christians may with equal confidence hold the lowest and the highest offices, certain offices in themselves are of greater significance than others.[17] The highest is pastor-preacher, then teacher, then worldly governor, then below these, physician, writer, secretary, and scholar of the liberal arts.

Nevertheless, scholars debate how relatively medieval or modern was Luther's attitude to business. For example, usury was a hot theological topic until a hundred years ago.[18] Along with medieval theologians, Luther saw usury as a sin. Also, Luther opposed the emerging mercantile system. Lake Lambert finds that he dismisses Christian involvement in trading companies, probably without understanding what he was condemning.[19] Here is what Luther said:

> This is why no one need ask how he may in good conscience be a member of a trading company. My only advice is this: Get out; they will not change. If the trading companies are to stay, right and honesty must perish; if right and honesty are to stay, the trading companies must perish.[20]

---

16. Martin Luther, "Church Postils," in *The Precious and Sacred Writings of Martin Luther*, vol. 10 (Minneapolis: Lutherans in All Lands Company, 1905), p. 27, quoted in Heiges, *The Christian's Calling*, p. 53.

17. Heiges, *The Christian's Calling*, p. 54.

18. Resources on the scholastic discussions of usury include Odd Langholm, *Aristotelian Analysis of Usury* (New York: Columbia University Press, 1984), Thomas Wilson, *A Discourse Upon Usury* (London: G. Bell and Sons, 1572/1925), and John T. Noonan, *Scholastic Analysis of Usury* (Cambridge, Mass.: Harvard University Press, 1957). A fine study of usury in scripture and business today is found in Richard Higginson, *Called to Account: Adding Value in God's World — Integrating Christianity and Business Effectively* (Guildford, Surrey: Eagle, 1993), p. 107.

19. Lake Lambert III, "Called to Business: Corporate Management as a Profession of Faith," Ph.D. dissertation, Princeton Theological Seminary, 1997, pp. 79-80.

20. Martin Luther, "Trade and Usury," *Luther's Works*, Jaroslav Pelikan, gen. ed. (Philadelphia: Fortress Press and St. Louis: Concordia Press, 1955), vol. 45, p. 272.

John Calvin

Calvin taught that calling is closely related to predestination. Your election is confirmed through your vocation.[21] 2 Peter 1:10-11 is the scriptural foundation for this: "Therefore, brothers and sisters, be all the more eager to confirm your call and election. . . . For in this way, entry into the eternal kingdom of our Lord and Savior Jesus Christ will be richly provided for you." Calvin and Luther agreed that all are called, that all stations enjoy divine approval, and that people should not lightly leave their callings. They disagreed, however, about the purpose of vocation. Luther said that God gives a vocation to encourage a life of loving service, while for Calvin it is for the proper ordering of the world, to prevent confusion. A passage in Calvin's *Institutes* illustrates this:

> The Lord bids each of us in all life's actions to look to his calling. For he knows with what great restlessness human nature flames, with what fickleness it is borne hither and thither, how its ambition longs to embrace various things at once. Therefore, lest through our stupidity and rashness everything be turned topsy-turvy, he has appointed duties for every man in his particular way of life. And that no one may thoughtlessly transgress his limits, he has named these various kinds of living "callings." Therefore each individual has his own kind of living assigned to him by the Lord as a sort of sentry post so that he may not heedlessly wander about throughout life.[22]

Unlike Luther, Calvin recognized the burgeoning world of commerce as an arena of legitimate activity for a Christian, and this had much to do with the direction vocation took in Reformed Protestantism, noticed of course by the followers of Calvin whom Max Weber studied.[23] In particular, Calvin read the Parable of the Talents (Matt.

21. Heiges, *The Christian's Calling*, p. 61.

22. John Calvin, *Institutes of the Christian Religion*, trans. Ford Lewis Battles (Philadelphia: Westminster Press, 1960), 3.11.6, p. 724.

23. Heiges, *The Christian's Calling*, p. 63.

25:14-30) in the more literal sense of *economic* stewardship. While lending for consumption at interest (usury) was a crime akin to murder, lending for production and enterprise with low rates of return (up to five percent) was acceptable.[24]

We will consider Calvin's influence on the Puritans and the capitalist spirit as observed by Max Weber in chapter 9.[25] Drawing on the thinking of the Puritans and of Deists like Benjamin Franklin, Weber argued that Calvin's view of the transcendence of God and his concept of predestination served to ratchet up the anxiety level of believers who were motivated to prove they were among the elect. But, with the closing of the monastery door as the most direct way to prove one's salvation, believers were thrust into this-worldly activity, especially in business, to which they gave themselves with a holy zeal.

The English Reformation and the Puritans

Calvin's sense of universal calling continued in the English Reformation. Joseph Hall said:

> The homeliest service that we do in an honest calling, though it be but to plow or to dig, if done in obedience and conscious of God's commandment, is crowned with an ample reward; whereas the best works for their kind (preaching, praying, offering Evangelical sacrifices) if without respect of God's injunctions and glory, are loaded with curses. God loveth adverbs and careth not how good, but how well.[26]

24. W. F. Graham, *The Constructive Revolutionary: John Calvin and His Socio-Economic Impact* (East Lansing: Michigan State University Press, 1987), p. 124, quoted in Preece, "Business as a Calling," p. 13.

25. See R. Paul Stevens, "The Spiritual and Religious Sources of Entrepreneurship: From Max Weber to the New Business Spirituality," *Crux* 36, no. 2 (June 2000): 22-33; reprinted in *Stimulus: The New Zealand Journal of Christian Thought and Practice* 9, no. 1 (February 2001): 2-11.

26. Joseph Hall, *Holy Observations* (London, 1607), quoted in Kee and Shroyer, *The Bible and God's Call*, p. 11.

The Puritans divided calling into two parts, the general call, which is the same for all, namely to invoke the name of Jesus and become his disciple, and the particular call, which is one's special contribution to serve God and the commonwealth, whether as a magistrate, homemaker, pastor, or businessperson.[27] Both the general and the particular are from God and each person has both.[28] All particular callings are holy. William Perkins, whose consummate work on calling is the epitome of Puritan reflection on the subject, says:

> The meanness of the calling does not debase the goodness of the work . . . for God looks not at the excellence of the work but the heart of the worker. And the action of a shepherd shearing a sheep, performed as I have said, in his kind, is as good a work before God as is the action of a judge in giving sentence . . . or a minister in preaching. . . . Now if we compare work with work, there is a difference betwixt washing dishes and preaching the Word of God; but as for pleasing God, there is no difference at all.[29]

When the Puritan commonwealth collapsed after the English Civil War, the particular call (to service) got separated from the general call (to salvation and discipleship) and the particular call became secularized, undermined as it were by war and wealth.[30] One's calling became simply an occupation, self-chosen and executed without an overarching commitment to faithfulness as a Christian called to discipleship.[31] As Weber has pointed out, certain aspects of Protestant

27. Notably in Calvin's teaching the "general" call is the invitation of God that goes out to all through the preaching of the Word, while the "special call," which God gives to believers alone, is the inward illumination of the Spirit, which enables the preached Word to dwell in their hearts. *Institutes* 3.20.8, p. 974.

28. See R. Paul Stevens, "Vocational Conversion: An Imaginary Puritan–Baby Boomer Dialogue," *Crux* 37, no. 4 (December 2001): 2-8.

29. William Perkins, *Collected Works* (London, 1612-13), quoted in Kee and Shroyer, *The Bible and God's Call*, p. 13.

30. Marshall, *A Kind of Life Imposed on Man*, pp. 48-53.

31. Gordon Preece notes that one who tried valiantly to resist the secularizing trend was the Puritan Richard Steele (1629-92) who wrote *The Religious Tradesman*. Preece comments, "Steele affirms business as a calling for a Christian if 'His devotion

theology, notably post-Calvinism, may have unwittingly contributed to the secularization of calling. Richard Higginson outlines some of the steps of secularization:

- It was difficult for people to fully accept God's grace; there was besetting temptation to seek assurance of salvation through their own efforts.
- Working hard came be taken to extremes; fear of idleness became obsessive.
- The motive of working for others gradually was replaced by a strong ideology of self-interest.
- The notion of stewardship remained strong, but when not carried through fully, stewardship became a disguised form of selfishness.
- With the gradual decline of religious belief and practice people no longer worked to glorify God. Calling was replaced by the notion of job or occupation.
- Where the word "vocation" survived, there was a gradual restriction in its application; the old medieval distinction reappeared. Business got lost to view.[32]

Thus, as Lambert summarizes, "While Luther and Calvin sacralized the secular by liberating vocation from the monastery, their later followers secularized the holy. The term 'vocation' now has only traces of a religious meaning, and its English equivalent, 'calling,' has been largely exiled to an ecclesiastical ghetto."[33]

As we saw in the case in the last chapter, the current situation in the Western world is not hard to read. "Calling" is reserved for those who are going into "full time ministry," even though a "part-

---

disposes him for business, and his business makes devotion welcome.' Although not strong on the Reformed meaning of vocation and simplistic in his criteria for selecting a calling ('lawfulness, suitability, advice, and interest of the soul'), Steele articulated a 'vision of the calling to business which many Christians had sensed and enacted.'" Preece, "Business as a Calling," p. 15. See also Lambert, "Called to Business," pp. 82-83.

32. Richard Higginson, *Questions of Business Life*, pp. 313-15.
33. Lambert, "Called to Business," p. 38.

time" option for discipleship is not available! Calling has been secularized in the world and clericalized in the church.[34] Ministry, then, is something one does in the church, and it is characterized by religious activity. But, as I will now seek to show, there is a business side to ministry.

The Inside Story of Ministry

The story of ministry has a beginning, a middle, and an ending.[35] Of the beginning we ask: What were God's basic intentions before the foundation of the world? The middle is where we find ourselves — confronted with the distortions sin has brought into the world, including the world of work; at the same time, we have the beginnings of salvation through the death and resurrection of Christ, the kingdom of God that has already come, though not yet in fullness. And the ending, as we have seen, is our final destiny and the world's ultimate end — the new heaven and new earth, the marriage supper of the Lamb, and the full consummation of the kingdom of God.

But the beginning of ministry goes even further back. It starts with the Triune God, Father, Son, and Spirit, one God in mutual ministry. There is ministry within God. Ministry went on before there was a world and before God-imaging creatures came to share in that ministry. The living God is not a solitary God, a lonely God, a needy God. The living God is the God of fellowship, completeness, contentment, infinite joy and love (Gen. 1:26-27; John 17; 1 John 1:3). Within the Godhead each serves the other and all are for the One. In the Trinity there is inclusiveness, community, and freedom. The Father is the source of its life but all three members act in a unified, loving, and harmonious

34. Michael Novak, *Business as a Calling: Work and the Examined Life* (New York: The Free Press, 1996), pp. 37-39. Novak argues that calling can be secularized. People speak of knowing themselves, finding what they ought to do, doing what they sense inwardly they are here to do and in so speaking, says Novak, they are witnessing to calling even though they may be uncomfortable with religious language.

35. Paul S. Minear, *To Die and to Live: Christ's Resurrection and Christian Vocation* (New York: Seabury Press, 1977), p. 136.

way. From the words of Jesus in John 17, we know that he prayed that the disciples might be one as the Son and Father are one — a ministry of unity and love. Ministry within the Godhead and from the Triune God is unitive and creative as well as restorative and curative. This has enormous implications: We are ministering not only when we reach out to the hurting and lost, or when we mend broken things; we minister when we create beautiful things, design new computer programs, or build community in the workplace.

Jesus is the minister par excellence. One of his messianic titles is "the servant" (Acts 3:13). In both the original languages of the Bible, Greek and Hebrew, "ministry" and "service" are the same word. Christ as servant-leader models both leading and following, as though these were two sides of the same coin. He passes on what is given; he does the will of the Father; he brings glory to the Father. At the same time he gives authority to the apostles and exercises kingly rule while serving on earth. As Robert Banks and Bernice Ledbetter note in their fine study of leadership, the trinitarian view "navigates between hierarchical (top down) and egalitarian (leaderless team) styles."[36] They suggest that leadership patterned after the Triune God involves shared authority; it is relational, being neither dictatorial nor egalitarian, and it cultivates mutual respect and dependence. Their analogy of geese in flight is apt, since the "lead" goose always gets tired and moves back to let another take the lead in the well-known "V" formation.

Nevertheless, ministry involves more than merely serving people or institutions, as popularized in the servant leadership concept. It is serving God and God's purposes. A servant is a person at the disposal of another. So a minister is a person at the disposal of God. More than that, a minister is a person through whom God serves and ministers. My colleague at Regent College, Darrell Johnson, summarizes the implications of a trinitarian approach to ministry in the following points:

36. Robert Banks and Bernice Ledbetter, *Reviewing Leadership: A Christian Evaluation of Current Approaches* (Grand Rapids: Baker, 2004), p. 70.

- Ministry is not something we do *for* God but God does *through* us (just as there is ministry/service within the Triune God).
- The call to ministry is the call to minister *with* God, not a call to minister *for* God.
- It is a call to enter into the creating and saving work of the Creator, a work initiated, empowered, and completed by God.[37]

Trinitarian ministry is especially illuminated by the theme of "the servant" in four poems of the prophet Isaiah in which God calls the servant "my servant" and speaks of the minister as "the servant of the Lord": Isaiah 42:1-9; 49:1-6; 50:4-9; 52:12-53:12. Initially God called the whole nation of Israel to be his servant on earth. But, in what has been pictured as an hourglass, the wide part — the people — narrows to an ideal Israel, a holy remnant that serves God. Then in Isaiah 52–53, at the neck of the hourglass, only one person embodies the servant. That individual is the Messiah Jesus. When the people did not function as God's servant on earth, God became his own servant on earth (Phil. 2:6-11). Now, in Christ, all the people of God are called into ministry — as the bottom part of the hourglass widens once again.

What does this have to do with business? Just this: All the ministry roles under the Old Testament — prophets, priests, and princes — specially appointed and anointed roles for a few people, are now fulfilled in the whole people of God. The Protestant Reformation emphasized the "priesthood of all believers" but scripture emphasizes as well, under the new covenant in Christ, the prophethood of all believers (Acts 2:17-18) and the princely rule of all believers in the kingdom (or rule) of God. And this ministry is not just in the gathered life of the sanctuary but in the dispersed life of the people of God in the world.

---

37. Darrell Johnson, "Authentic Ministry," notes from "Ministry and Spirituality" course, Regent College, September 2004. Johnson continues to show how God's ministry emerges out of God's trinitarian being. Christ's ministry is to the Father on behalf of the world ("I glorified you on earth by finishing the work that you gave me to do" [John 17:4]). Further, the call to ministry is the call to enter into Jesus' continuing ministry in and for the world (Acts 1:1) — prophetic, kerygmatic, evangelistic, priestly, shepherding, kingly, and diakonic. The Father is the source of the Trinity's life but all three members act in a unified and harmonious way.

Prophets, Priests, and Princes/ses

Prophets speak the word of God with immediacy. They explain the meaning of things, providing God's perspective (Pss. 127:1; 130:7; Isa. 35:1-4; Mic. 4:1-4; Rev. 21:1-4). They are visionaries. They point out where things are heading. They have the "big view." They declare what God is actually doing. They expose injustice and sin. In business they see that the right thing is done. They identify justice and fairness issues — compensation, executive remuneration, ruthless exploitation of the environment. And sometimes they blow the whistle.

Obviously one part of the prophet's role is bearing witness to Christ. We do this by being people who invite questions, by waiting and being ready when asked to give an answer for the hope that is within us. The integrity and excellence with which we work is part of bearing the word of God in word and deed.

Even in non-Christian or anti-Christian societies people respond positively to Christians and people of faith when they have work skills and character traits that are commendable. Often these people have unexpected access to power, people, and places.

Nicu Toader lived under the cruel and harsh communist dictatorship in Romania. During the height of the dictatorship, control was exercised over every aspect of life. During this time the local chief justice of the secret police of Timisoara called Nicu into his office.

Because he was an active leader in a very large underground Christian church, Nicu was expecting that this was the feared summons that would trigger the end of his freedom, and possibly his life. Almost worse than losing his freedom was the horrific pressure forcing cooperation with the secret police. It would often go like this: "Nicu Toader, we know you love your lovely daughter and handsome young son Emil. We also know there are terrible accidents with acid. You would not want anything to happen to them, would you? Tell us about your comrades' statements and beliefs and nothing will happen to your children."

On one occasion, Nicu was summoned to the secret police headquarters only to be told to go immediately to the chief's private apartment to fix his home appliances. "Here are the keys to my apartment.

I know — you know that we have spies everywhere — that you are engaged in illegal religious activities. But you are a serious Repenter [the term used for an evangelical Christian], I know that when you go to my apartment you will not go through my personal papers, take my food, or steal my valuables. And I also know that you are absolutely the best mechanic in the entire city of Timisoara. When you fix things they stay fixed! Your silly faith and your work skills bring you to my office this afternoon."

This was the first of several calls for personal help by the secret police of communist Timisoara. After the Christmas 1989 revolution in Romania, the chief admitted that his Bucaresti superiors had told him to arrest the leaders and crush the underground church in Timisoara. When Nicu's name appeared on the arrest list, the chief permanently deferred the order. It appears that God protected his church in Romania by the excellent work and public reputation of a skilled mechanic whose personal character convinced the chief to keep him around.[38]

Prophets may use the name of God in their ministry. But there are many dimensions of their ministry that can be undertaken without a verbal witness. Dan Jessen views ministry dimensions of daily work as a pyramid. At the bottom is the ministry of responsible service (meeting legitimate needs and wants). Then there is the ministry of competent service (something in which Nicu excelled). Higher in the pyramid is the ministry of deeds (working Christianly with love, honesty, and justice). At the top, and built on the others, is the witness of words. Jessen lists several kinds of word ministries: using positive, optimistic language; listening to someone who needs to talk about a problem; verbal witnesses during lunch hour or after work; raising questions about righteousness and justice when appropriate; and responding to questions about faith when asked.[39]

When I moved from working as a pastor to working as a carpen-

38. I am indebted for this story to Alec Woodhull, President of USA Affairs-Missio Link International that partners with Christians in Romania in a number of humanitarian and ministry enterprises.

39. Dan Jessen, "Ministry Dimensions of Daily Work," unpublished paper, September 1993, Charlotte, North Carolina.

ter, I thought I would have an opportunity almost daily to put in a good word for Jesus. But I worked six weeks on a particular construction job before the dry-wall taper turned to me and asked, "Paul, what happens when we die?"

Priests are bridge-builders. On most bridges, traffic flows two ways. So with the priest. He or she brings organizations, corporations, people, problems, and opportunities to God, lifting them up in intercession and prayer. But the priest also brings God's perspective and grace to people and places. Priests touch God on behalf of people and places, and they touch people and places on behalf of God.

Priesthood is not mere God talk. I will try to show this by suggesting that priestly ministry has three movements.

First, this ministry moves people *from hostility to hospitality.* This is a theme Henri Nouwen explores in his seminal book on hospitality, *Reaching Out.* Nouwen says, "Hospitality . . . means primarily the creation of a free space where the stranger can enter and become a friend instead of an enemy. Hospitality is not to change people, but to offer them space where change can take place."[40] Welcome and hospitality are desperately needed in the workplace.

The second priestly ministry is the movement *from space to place.*[41] Most workplaces are canned environments, raw space. But out of raw space a place can be created. It is priestly work, like that of Adam and Eve who were called to extend the sanctuary garden into the world, to trim the hedges, name the animals, and bring beauty, order, and safety to the rest of the earth. My grade four teacher was Miss Dickson. I don't remember anything she taught. But I clearly recall how she made out of the raw space of the classroom a beautiful place, graced with art and crafts, and tastefully arranged. The office, factory, and professional clinic can become such places. I recently visited a medical clinic in Kamloops, British Columbia. It was a place. The walls were decorated with beautiful photography created by the physicians themselves. The layout of the reception area, the personal

40. Henri Nouwen, *Reaching Out: The Three Movements of the Spiritual Life* (New York: Doubleday, 1975), p. 71.

41. I owe some of these thoughts to Robert Capon, *An Offering of Uncles: The Priesthood of Adam and the Shape of the World* (New York: Crossroad, 1982), pp. 18-23.

presence of a receptionist for each doctor, and the ordering of the examining rooms all created safety, beauty, and welcome. And it is precisely the priesthood of Adam and Eve and their descendents to extend the garden into the world by creating places of sanctuary, loveliness, and prosperity.

Third, priests create movement *from information to mystery*. Undoubtedly, we are now well into the information society. We are moving hell-bound into an age when words will be processed rather than fondled, when human work will be measured by bits of data stored on disks or magnetic tapes rather than goals met, and where people will be cataloged rather than cared for. More than ever the workplace needs a priesthood that lives on the edge of mystery.

Words, to take one important facet of business, are not mere vibrations in the air or data stored on a chip. Words are like people going out, actively revealing things. Out of the heart the mouth speaks, Jesus once said (Matt. 12:34). The person keeps coming out of the mouth. And if that person has integrity his or her words, like Samuel's, will not "fall to the ground" without result (1 Sam. 3:19). Priests treasure words and the people who speak them.

Princes and princesses rule. They coordinate and organize. They solve problems, provide resources, and integrate ideas. Speaking to this from the perspective of the banking industry, Sandra Herron says that good stewardship

> has to do with managing physical resources — such as money, facilities, and technology — as well as ensuring that the gifts and talents of my employees are effectively utilized. That requires, among other things, that I be conservative in my budgeting and frugal in spending company money. I look for ways to avoid waste. . . . But the clearest link between my work and the kingly ministry of Jesus Christ is in my role as a manager of human resources.[42]

---

42. Sandra Herron, "Reflecting Christ in the Banking Industry," in Robert Banks, ed., *Faith Goes to Work* (Washington, D.C.: Alban Institute, 1993), p. 86.

Rules assure that the structures in an organization bring justice. They exercise stewardship over the created order.

History gives some stunning examples where this has not taken place, often with serious consequences to the viability of a corporation. The 1984 Bhopal disaster in India was undoubtedly a major cause of the disappearance of Union Carbide as an independent corporation.[43] The Exxon Valdez oil spill in Alaska in 1989 had similar effects. On a positive note, Clive Wright recalls how in the early days of Shell's activities in Nigeria, when he was undertaking an internal audit on the exploration units in the region of Port Harcourt, he was justifiably proud of their careful work in minimizing the adverse effect of their exploration on the natural surroundings.[44] Princely work.

Obviously, each one of us is stronger in one area than another, but the whole people of God engaged in ministry in the workplace serves God and God's purposes as prophets, priests, and princes/ses in the church and the world. Business is indeed an arena for full-time ministry.

For Discussion

Reflect on Luther's comments as they relate to this chapter:

> When I speak of a calling which in itself is not sinful, I do not mean that we can live on earth without sin. All callings and estates sin daily; but I mean the calling God has instituted is not opposed to God, as for example, marriage, man-servant, maid-servant, lord, wife, superintendent, ruler, judge, officer, citizen, etc. I mention as sinful stations in life: robbery, usury, public women, and, as they are at present, the pope, cardinals, bishops, priests, monks, and nuns, who neither preach nor listen to preaching.[45]

43. Wright, *The Business of Virtue*, p. 155.

44. Wright also notes how thirty years later the standards had degraded (Wright, *The Business of Virtue*, p. 155).

45. *Luther's Table Talk*, p. 447, quoted in Heiges, *The Christian's Calling*, p. 58.

For Further Reading

Banks, Robert J., ed. *Faith Goes to Work: Reflections from the Marketplace.* Washington, D.C.: Alban Institute, 1993.

Chewning, Richard, ed. *Biblical Principles and Business: The Foundations.* Christians in the Marketplace, vol. 1. Colorado Springs: NavPress, 1989.

Higginson, Richard. *Called to Account: Adding Value to God's World: Integrating Christianity and Business Effectively.* Guildford, Surrey: Eagle, 1993.

Pope John Paul II. *The Vocation and the Mission of the Lay Faithful in the World.* Washington, D.C.: United States Catholic Conference, 1988.

Silvoso, Ed. *Anointed for Business: How Christians Can Use Their Influence in the Marketplace to Change the World.* Ventura, Calif.: Regal, 2002.

4

♦ ♦ ♦

A Praise-Worthy Form of Community

The purpose of a business firm is not simply to make a profit, but it is found in its very existence as a community of persons who in various ways are endeavoring to satisfy their basic needs and who form a particular group at the service of the whole of society.

John Paul II

The corporation is an expression of the social nature of humans. . . . It offers a metaphor for ecclesial community that is in some ways more illuminating than metaphors based on the human body ("the mystical body") or the family, the clan, the tribe, or the chosen people.

Michael Novak,
Toward a Theology of the Corporation

A company is a way of sharing bread. The word "company" comes from the Latin — *cum* (with or together) and *panis* (bread). Sharing bread (literally and figuratively) was something practiced by the first Christians in Jerusalem (Acts 2:42-47). I would argue that the modern business corporation follows the model of the early church, which pioneered a new pattern of mutual responsibility, accountability, structured authority, and voluntary participation that was neither *oikos* (household) nor *polis* (state). Max Stackhouse claims the church was the first "trans-ethnic and trans-national corporation."[1] The Benedictine monastic movement also was a precursor of the modern corporation since it gave the church a base that was neither *oikos* nor *polis* but was a disciplined, cooperative community outside traditional structures. And it was entrepreneurial.

In the Beginning and at the End — a Company!

Several theological reasons support the creation of companies. First, God created humankind "male and female" and "in [God's] image" (Gen. 1:27) — built for community, relationality, and love. God's purpose is to build on earth both the faith community and the human community. Thus the Bible faithfully records the cooperative endeavors of human beings, though often with humankind grievously failing, as they went about building families, ethnic groups, faith groups, nations, and ultimately a global community. The business corporation is part of this divine mission.

Furthermore, the vision of the new heaven and the new earth at the end of the Christian Bible is critical because it is the end toward which the joint work of God and humankind is striving — a transfigured creation with fully resurrected persons in community. Eschatology, the study of "end times," is central to the Judeo-Christian worldview since it shows us, as theologian Moltmann said so well,

---

1. Max L. Stackhouse, Dennis P. McCann, Shirley J. Roels, and Preston N. Williams, *On Moral Business: Classical and Contemporary Resources for Ethics in Economic Life* (Grand Rapids: Eerdmans, 1995), p. 113.

that we are placed not at sunset but at the dawning of a new day.[2] God originally had in mind the marriage supper of the Lamb, that powerful metaphor of people, place, and renewed creation that occupies Revelation 19–22. So he "thought up" the world, "thought up" a God-imaging creature, and even sent his Son to redeem people and creation to that end. Without a worthy end, humankind has no final meaning for tasks in this world. The end is a garden city, a community of all peoples experiencing the three-fold sabbath harmony of God, creation, and humankind. The end is really the beginning of it all. The mid-point we inhabit now, between creation and the new heaven and new earth, is also about community.

Business is, as Michael Novak rightly asserts, "a praiseworthy form of community."[3] The corporation is a community of shared life and enterprise, providing a relational context for ministry often deeper than the local church or neighborhood. "From its very beginnings," notes Novak, "the modern business economy was designed to become an international system, concerned with raising the 'wealth of nations,' *all* nations, in a systematic, social way. It was by no means focused solely on the wealth of particular individuals."[4] Whether pencils or automobiles, coffee or telephones, most goods cannot be created through the work of an isolated individual but require cooperation of several, often many, towards a common goal.

In the case study that follows we will explore how one business owner understood that mission and struggled to implement it.

• WHY IS BOB NOT FOR ME? •

Melinda Sanford, director of communications, came into Bob Thomas's office with an impish grin, signaling that something was brewing in the Ford division of Riverside Motors. "Cyril wants to know

2. Jürgen Moltmann, *Theology of Hope: On the Grounds and Implications of a Christian Eschatology*, trans. J. W. Leitch (New York: Harper & Row, 1967), p. 31.

3. Michael Novak, *Business as a Calling: Work and the Examined Life* (New York: The Free Press, 1996), p. 125.

4. Novak, *Business as a Calling*, p. 125.

why you are not *for* him." As she carefully delivered this message Melinda observed that her boss's desk was completely inundated with papers, letters needing a reply, the sales sheets for the week, and an advertisement for a special Seniors Day at the Lincoln dealership. But Melinda believed that Bob's busyness would pale into insignificance before the critical tension developing between her boss and his protégé, Cyril Miller, vice-president and manager of one of Bob's car dealerships. Melinda knew why this news would be painful.

She remembered how this traumatic day had begun. At the regular Monday breakfast meeting of the general managers of all the west coast Ford dealerships that Bob owned, Bob, with permission from Cyril, had used an example from Cyril's own division to teach and empower Bob's staff. Bob had said, "What I am trying to gain in these meetings is not merely 'ownership' of our mission and goals, but *enrollment.* I want you to function according to our agreed values by your *own* motivation, because you have embraced them for yourselves. That is how I understand empowerment: not giving you permission to create your own world in the organization but giving you a piece of the authority to fulfill our mission together." But this morning's meeting had taken an unexpected turn, one which Melinda had observed and now brought to Bob's attention.

The center of gravity for the meeting was a customer problem. Cyril had ordered an "impossible" customer, Jake Ellis, off the property. Cyril was defensive. "This difficult customer has driven my service representatives and technicians almost to distraction. Besides putting up with Jake Ellis coming back several times for nit-picky warranty work ranging from dissatisfaction with the paint job to rattles in the door, I had to show him fifteen different wheel-covers before finding the one he liked. None of us at Riverside wanted to see this man again."

In the managers' meeting Bob had invited the group to consider alternative ways to respond. Most of the managers concluded that Cyril had over-reacted. In the meeting Bob himself commented negatively on Cyril's response and used the situation to push harder for Riverside to become a corporation that defines world-class service in the car industry. "Our customers," Bob reminded them, "never have to *de-*

serve extraordinary service." Cyril left the meeting feeling wounded. Noticing his downcast expression, Melinda said to Cyril, "I am not too busy this morning. Why don't we have a coffee and talk?" Cyril confided, "I feel betrayed. Bob talks about empowering his senior managers, but I don't feel he is really *for* me. He doesn't stand behind me when I have a really difficult customer like Jake Ellis. Instead he ends up supporting the customer."

Bob had explained to the managers some of the background. This was Jake's first new car, bought in spite of his wife's objections. Jake had worked overtime at the mill for a whole year to save up the money for his life's dream. But when he took delivery, there was a flaw; the technician putting on the license plate had scratched the trunk. The body shop workers dabbed paint over the scratch but it didn't look right. Jake demanded and got a repaint, but it was not done well. One thing after another happened until Jake's discomfort was only surpassed by his wife's needling comment, reported later to Bob, "I told you, you should never have bought that car!" So one day, during another warranty repair, Jake unloaded on Cyril. Cyril, feeling that there have to be limits to extraordinary service, ordered the man off the property. "And don't come back!" On the way out, Jake demanded to speak with the president, so Bob struggled to listen to Jake's sad tale. "Is there anything I can do to make you a satisfied customer?" Bob. "No," replied Jake and walked out.

Melinda now pieced this all together in her mind. "Do you realize," Melinda asked Bob in the privacy of his office, "that most of our managers are not believers? How legitimate do you think it is to expect Christian standards of non-Christians? Do you think we have come to the limits of transformation? Can we help our employees find spiritual sources for motivation even before they become Christians?" Bob slumped into his chair thoughtfully. "We've got to do something, Bob, or Cyril will resign and it will blow this vision we have."

•   •

LET'S EXPLORE some of the dimensions of this case, in particular how organizational culture affects a business such as Riverside Motors, and how its owner, Bob, can affect the organizational culture. Every organization has a corporate "feeling" or environment that communicates to new and old members what is important and what is permitted. The minute people walk into the meeting room, the store, or the office they pick up a non-verbal message that is more powerful than mottos on the walls such as "The customer is number one" and "We exist to give extraordinary service." Culture turns out to be profoundly influential in determining behavior, expressing values, and enabling or preventing change.

Bob was completely committed to integrate his Christian faith with the mission, culture, and structures of the business he bought from his father ten years ago. Bob had invested a decade in transforming a car business into a ministry. He believed that every employee from the car washer to the CEO should be treated with equal dignity. Customers did not just buy their cars from Riverside. They joined the family, a family from which no one would ever be divorced. Bob's vision was to bring extraordinary service to the customer, doing even more than the customer expected, more than a customer would ever dare to request. The mission and goals of the business lined up with God's intention of humanizing the world and transforming people: facilitating personal development of every staff person, giving extraordinary service to the customer, and building community both inside and outside the business.

Bob also wanted Riverside Motors to make a difference in the city, so he invested heavily in local sports teams and contributed to community projects out of the profits of the company. He lived modestly himself, not taking the usual salary for many CEOs of one or two hundred times the salary of the entry-level employee. Bob's vision was that every human interaction and every contact with the structures of the business would be regarded as an opportunity for equipping. The organization would invite and evoke faith. To accomplish this the CEO and those beside him would primarily regard themselves as facilitators in their allocation of time, attitudes toward control and power, focus of investment, commitment to team-building, and willingness to work developmentally with people. The values foundational to the company were shaped by theological virtues:

faith, hope, and love translated into giving extraordinary service, developing people, and building community. The ultimate goal of the business is not making a financial profit but adding value to the customers, value for which customers will normally pay a premium that will result in profit. Melinda now reminded herself that Bob wanted to craft a corporation that would bring glory to God. But it was not clear to her today how God would be glorified when everything seemed to be on the verge of blowing up.

Understanding Organizational Culture

To understand Bob's situation we must explore the role of corporate culture.[5] Walter Wright explains it this way:

> Every organization has a hidden culture that has been developed over the years that controls what is actually done regardless of the values we espouse. The problem is that when the stated values of the church or organization are not in sync with the cultural beliefs and assumptions, it creates organizational dissonance and people get caught in the middle.[6]

People are sometimes frustrated, without understanding why, when they try to bring about change in an organization. Try to introduce women into an all-male kayaking club and one encounters almost irresistible forces, but none of them is rationally expressed or constitutionally codified. Further, some "successful" changes get reversed in a few months because they were not congruent with the culture of the organization; other changes are made easily for reasons that are not apparent unless one understands their invisible but all-pervasive impact on the organizational environment. To change the cultural climate itself is possibly the most substantial change that

5. Some of the following analysis is taken from R. Paul Stevens, "Organizational Culture and Change," in Robert Banks and R. Paul Stevens, eds., *The Complete Book of Everyday Christianity* (Downers Grove, Ill.: InterVarsity Press, 1997), pp. 713-18.

6. Walter C. Wright Jr., *Relational Leadership: A Biblical Model for Influence and Service* (Carlisle: Paternoster, 2000), p. 119.

can be made. It has a multiple impact on everything else. A man in a museum looking at the colossal skeleton of a dinosaur that once triumphantly roamed the earth turned to the woman beside him and asked, "What happened? Why did they die out?" She said, "The climate changed." At least that is one theory.

Motivation is primarily related to an organization's culture. We draw their best performance out of people in a healthy, life-giving organization. It is inspired, not compelled. Motivation is partly the result of a process in a group or system, and is not generated exclusively from within the individual. So motivation is only marginally increased by "trying to get people motivated" through incentives or threats. It needs to be considered culturally and systemically. In the managers' meeting, Bob put a drawing on the flip chart of an Olympic rowing boat with oars sticking out each side like an insect's legs. Then he put a second drawing of the same team with the same number of oars but in a boat that looked like a box with a square-ended bow and stern. "No matter how motivated they are, they just can't get that boat to move at more than a snail's pace," he told the managers. Privately Bob felt that in working with Cyril over the years he was trying to row a square boat.

Bob had high regard for Cyril as a hard-working and productive team member. They had a father-son type of relationship in spite of Cyril's being several years older. For ten years Bob had mentored this man, investing deeply in his development and his future. But Melinda also knew that asking Cyril to show unconditional love to Jake was possibly asking too much. Converting an organization is one thing; converting a man is another. When Bob took over Riverside he needed to bring about a change in the organizational culture. To do that he had, first of all, to understand it.

A classic study on organizational culture is Edgar H. Schein's *Organizational Culture and Leadership*. His central thesis is that much of what is mysterious about leadership becomes clearer "if we . . . link leadership specifically to creating and changing culture."[7] According

---

7. Edgar H. Schein, *Organizational Culture and Leadership: A Dynamic View* (San Francisco: Jossey-Bass, 1991), p. xi.

to Schein, culture includes each of the following but is deeper than any one of them: (1) *the observed behavioral regularities* in a group — for example, really good employees show up for work fifteen minutes early; (2) *the dominant values* of the group — for example, we keep our word; customers should receive their repaired vehicles when they are promised; (3) *the rules* or "ropes" of the group — for example, the usual way to climb the hierarchy is to engage in leisure-time diversions with your superior; and (4) *the feeling or climate* that is conveyed — for example, while not prohibited, it is also not acceptable to bring forward negative comments in staff meetings. Schein says that culture concerns the underlying assumptions and beliefs that are shared by members of the organization and that often operate unconsciously.[8]

The factors at work in an organizational culture can be pictured as three concentric circles. On the outside — the largest circle — are *the symbols, artifacts, and visible signs* of the culture, often expressed in logos, mottos, the appearance of a building, the way people dress, and the titles by which people are addressed. For instance, Riverside Motors had signs around the repair bays and sales areas stating their mission and commitment to service. Bob's door to his modest office was always open except when he had to deal with a confidential situation. The next smaller circle represents *the values* that underlie the more visible processes. Values are simply what is cherished by the organization. Often these are unexpressed and unconscious. Sometimes the stated values are incongruent with the real values that inform the culture. For example, a business may claim that it cherishes strong family life for its employees but actually requires the sacrifice of family for the corporation. One of the values cherished at Riverside is that every employee is to be prized and given the opportunity to develop his or her potential. The smallest circle (and the least visible) represents *the beliefs* that inform the values. Beliefs might include the equality of all people, regardless of race, religion, age, and education. A belief embedded in Bob's working philosophy is that a corporation has a social responsibility to all the stakeholders, including the sur-

8. Schein, *Organizational Culture,* p. 6.

rounding community. Beliefs are expressed in values, and values are expressed in symbols, cues, and visible patterns of behavior.

Some cultures can be toxic and death-dealing. A blaming culture is one example of this. In contrast, a culture built on strong beliefs and stated values can be fruitful and life-giving. A business with such a culture will also be, in the long run, more profitable. In a 1995 study, James Collins and Jerry Porras, who authored *Built to Last: Successful Habits of Visionary Companies,* discovered that visionary companies that had a strong core ideology (values plus purpose) and whose stated driving force was something other than maximizing shareholder wealth achieved growth in shareholder value twelve times greater than the general market between 1926 and 1990.[9]

Forming the Organizational Culture

Every organization or business has a hidden culture. In most organizations this culture is not formed overnight but through a long process. As Walter Wright notes,

> It is formed out of a shared history and experiences of the organization as it develops and survives. The founding leadership of our churches and organizations implant the first seeds of the culture. Then, over time, the community living together develops some unconscious ways of doing things. "The way things are done here" becomes automatic, reinforced over the years by what is valued and what is opposed.[10]

In a business it is often the founder who projects his or her own vision of what is "right" and "valued" and how people are to be treated. Riverside was founded by Bob's father, who took a traditional "top-down," hierarchical approach to leadership. It took Bob several years to change the culture for reasons we will soon explore. Values and priorities get embedded in something like the DNA of a business.

9. James C. Collins and Jerry I. Porras, *Built to Last: Successful Habits of Visionary Companies* (New York: HarperBusiness, 1994).
10. Wright, *Relational Leadership,* p. 120.

Years before I understood anything about organizational culture, I observed that each organization has something like a genetic code embedded at the time of conception that determines most of what it will become. The future of a person is in large measure the unraveling of his or her genetic code. In organizations, the founding moment, person, and principles are seeds planted in the organization that, over the years, develop. An organization that starts with certain assumptions about the nature of the community, its style of leadership, and its mission in society, will find it very difficult, though not impossible, to change its culture later.

As the group evolves, members take on the founder's assumptions, usually unconsciously. Some groups never allow their founder to die or leave, no matter how many successors have come and gone. Cultures tend not only to incarnate the strengths of founders but also their weaknesses. Some organizations would be helped if they could have a once-and-for-all funeral service for their founders! But whoever suggested this would be resisted by the organization's own culture. In fact, the opposite approach is usually more fruitful: finding out everything we can about the contribution our predecessors have made and appreciating their gifts to the organization. One thing is certain: Founders are influential. Schein's work is extremely helpful in elaborating what happens at various stages in a group's history and the importance of stories (about the "good old days") in transmitting the culture of a group.[11]

The mysterious quality of leadership called "charisma" enables a leader to embed his or her fundamental assumptions into an organization or group. A leader accomplishes this by whom he or she pays attention to, how he or she reacts to critical situations, whether he or she intentionally coaches other leaders, what criteria he or she uses for praising and rewarding others, and on what basis he or she recruits or rejects other leaders. Bob is a charismatic leader and he has been coaching Cyril since taking over his father's business, but Cyril was part of the former regime. And Bob's father's philosophy was "Get the job done, no matter how."

11. Schein, *Organizational Culture*, pp. 191, 241.

Reflecting Theologically on Organizational Culture

Whether in a church or business, the leader of an organization is in some sense the "minister of culture," or an environmental engineer. This task is implicit in the broad vocation of being human, through which we are called to be culture- and world-makers (Gen. 1:26-28). God created the first culture by fashioning the sanctuary garden for Adam and Eve, a garden with boundaries, structures, limits, challenges, work to do, and pleasures to enjoy. The first human culture was a sabbath culture featuring a three-fold harmony of God, humankind, and creation. But once human beings sinned, they created cultures that would not bring rest to people or the earth.

The men and women of Babel (Gen. 11:1-9) wanted to create a monolithic, homogeneous culture, and God judged that harshly. Imagine what would have happened if that arrogant, self-serving, and totally uniform culture had dominated the human enterprise for thousands of years! In place of Babel God crafted at Pentecost a colorful, pluralistic culture through which people of many languages and people groups heard the wonderful works of God in their "own native language[s]" (Acts 2:8). God wants a rich social structure on earth that is more unified because there are many.

In passing, we may note that the Old Testament gives us a few hints of God's grace in secular or pagan organizations. The culture of the Egyptian prison equipped Joseph to emerge as its leader (Gen. 39:20-23). As cupbearer to the pagan king Artaxerxes, Nehemiah was able to express his concern over the state of Jerusalem and be empowered to return to rebuild the walls (Neh. 2). Daniel was skilled in the culture of the Persians and in that context was able to play a seminal role in the destiny of his people (Dan. 1–6). God was at work in all these pagan organizational cultures.

In the New Testament Paul was continually "engineering" culture. His great, life-long vision was to create under God a church culture that embraced Jews and Gentiles as equal heirs, members, and partners in Christ. His grasp of the gospel meant that Jews did not become Gentiles in Christ; nor did Gentiles become Jews. Rather both were incorporated into a "new humanity" (Eph. 2:15) that transcended these profound distinctions without obliterating the differences. The same was true of men and women, slaves and free persons (Gal. 3:28). Central to Paul's ministry was a passion inspired by the gospel: God's community on earth must be richly diverse but, at the same time, it must treat all members as equal (2 Cor. 8:14). We can only speculate to what extent this carried over into his tent-making business in which he was essentially self-employed, though often working side-by-side with that marvelous tent-making couple Aquila and Priscilla.

The final image of organizational culture in the Bible is the most empowering. In the new heaven and the new earth described in the Revelation of John (21–22) every person's contribution is evoked in the fulfillment of the priesthood of all believers (1:6). Every nation, tongue, and tribe is preserved rather than being merged into one homogeneous uniformity. Our future in Christ is not to become angels but fully human beings in our resurrection bodies as we work and play in this fulfilled sabbath — the three-fold harmony of God, humankind, and creation. Even the kings of the earth bring their wealth and gifts into the Holy City (21:24). All human creativity finds perfect fulfillment, and every tear of frustration is wiped away (7:17).

Making Organizational Change

We are not fully in heaven yet. Indeed, all human organizations are only approximations of that perfection. Human organizations have fallen and been captivated by the "principalities and powers" (Eph. 6:12, KJV). Organizations are intransigent, resistant to change, and may make idolatrous demands. But these powers have been unmasked and disarmed by Christ (Col. 2:15), who brings in this life substantial though not complete redemption. So part of our public discipleship involves fostering organizational change. And changing the organizational culture is hard. Ask Bob.

Changing the artifacts — to use Schein's phrase — might involve having a staff meeting every Monday to improve communication. But unless the leader understands, cultivates, and gradually changes the fundamental assumptions of the organization, such equipping initiatives may be as effective as rearranging the deck chairs on the *Titanic* when the ship is going down. When the leader and the culture collide, the culture will probably win!

Schein's research shows, however, that culture-change mechanisms are at work in every stage of a group's history — birth, mid-life, and maturity. Significantly, he calls the end stage "maturity and/or stagnation, decline and/or rebirth."[12] He also shows that change becomes increasingly more difficult as a group becomes more established. While all change is motivated and does not happen randomly, "many changes do not go in the direction that the motivated persons wanted them to go" because those persons were unaware of other forces in the culture that were simultaneously acting.[13] So being the leader of this process of change is complex indeed.

Several strategies for leaders are useful here: First, understand the culture before you try to change anything. Give the culture its due. It influences everything. Second, recognize that the culture cannot be manipulated. While you can manage and control many parts of the environment of an organization — such as the president keeping his or her office door open all the time — the culture itself with its taken-for-granted assumptions cannot be manipulated. Third, good leadership articulates and reinforces the culture, especially those parts consistent with the vision of the organization. If this is not done, people are unlikely to accept any serious change. During a time of changing culture, leaders have to bear some of the pain and anxiety that is felt in the group, even while they seek to make the members feel secure. Fourth, sometimes direct change in a culture can be promoted by introducing new people in leadership, by promoting "maverick" individuals from within, and more especially people from outside, who hold slightly different assumptions. In fact, this is what happened when Bob took over from his father. But change takes time.[14]

When Bob took over his father's business, he did not try to change everything at once. He established his own goals and mission

---

12. Schein, *Organizational Culture*, p. 270.
13. Schein, *Organizational Culture*, pp. 300-301.
14. Schein, *Organizational Culture*, pp. 297-327.

and, in effect, changed himself. He established a relational basis of leadership by spending much of his day with key leaders in the organization, including Cyril. Over a period of several months, in the regular Monday meetings, he began to develop a mission statement for the business: customers should receive extraordinary service that is beyond what they might expect from a car business. When someone buys a car he or she joins the Riverside family. They will not be divorced. Bob noted at one of these meetings how a satisfied customer will tell several friends, who, through their recommendation to family and friends, may bring in generations of customers. An unhappy customer, according to some research, tells many more potential customers, and the loss of business is astronomical. Running a business is best understood as nurturing a system.

A Systemic Approach to Change

An organization is more than the sum of the parts in which each member, and each subsystem, is influenced by and influences the others. It can be easily pictured as a mobile; movement in one element requires adjustment in all the others. Edwin Friedman, a family systems therapist, has some additional insights on how a leader can bring change to a system. He uses the concept of homeostasis, that marvelous capacity of human bodies and social systems to regain their balance after a trauma. Every system has a natural tendency to maintain the status quo (homeostasis), just as a keel keeps a sailboat upright. The system does this whenever a threat, tragedy, or positive change requires new response patterns. Thus the system returns to the tried and tested rather than shifting to operate on a revised and improved basis (morphogenesis). A biblical example of homeostasis is the converted first-century Jews' less than full expression of Christian unity with Gentile believers, a hypocrisy that Paul fervently challenged (Gal. 2:11-21). A biblical example of morphogenesis is the extraordinary resolution of the Council of Jerusalem (Acts 15:1-29), in which the church changed the terms upon which Jews and Gentiles could have fellowship together.

To bring about systemic change, leaders must first join the existing system, become integral parts of the whole, and negotiate their places within it. The director or president must lead the way in this. In fact, this involves many stages of negotiation as the leader finds his or her place in the organization.[15] Then the leader might identify a problem and initiate a change that has a ripple effect throughout the system. Usually a problem will surface without provocation. But if a problem does not surface, something as inconsequential as changing the location of the water cooler, or removing it altogether, will do. How the leader responds to the ripple is crucial, because the response of the system will reflect all the systemic factors that make it stable, including multigenerational influences. The provoked or unprovoked crisis is an opportunity to explain what is going on and to appeal, as Barnabas, Paul, and Peter did in the Jerusalem Council (Acts 15:1-35), to systemic values that can be expressed in a more constructive way. The Chinese word for "crisis" is composed of two characters, one of which means "danger" and the other "opportunity." The systemic leader welcomes the opportunity of every crisis and sometimes will provoke one.

Using family systems theory, Friedman says we bring greatest change in a system by concentrating not on the dissenting or sick member but on the person or persons in the group who have the greatest capacity to bring change.[16] But the equipping leader must always remember that the only person completely open to definite and immediate change is himself or herself! A systems view encourages us to see that changing ourselves *can* make a difference to those with whom we are interdependently linked.

In the context of counseling families, Virginia Satir makes a remarkable statement about systems leadership that applies to all kinds of organizations. She says, "I consider myself the leader of the

15. See Mansell E. Pattison, *Pastor and People — A Systems Approach* (Philadelphia: Fortress Press, 1977); see also Philip Collins and R. Paul Stevens, *The Equipping Pastor: A Systems Approach to Empowering the People of God* (Washington, D.C.: Alban Institute, 1993).

16. Edwin H. Friedman, *Generation to Generation: Family Process in Church and Synagogue* (New York: Gilford, 1985), p. 22.

process in the interview but *not* the leader of the *people.*" This, she continues, "is based on the fact that I am the one who knows what the process I am trying to produce is all about. I want to help people to become their own designers of their own choice-making."[17]

So organizational leadership is not simply leading individual people in an organization. Leaders must work with the whole — culture and systems included. Process leadership asks questions, clarifies goals, orients people to their mission, maintains and explains the culture, and helps people and subsystems take responsibility for their own systemic life. In the end leaders are charged with the awesome task of creating an environment in which people change themselves.

What about Cyril?

Over the months and years of weekly consultations, Cyril had learned to recite the company creed from his head but it had not worked its way down to his heart. To use Schein's phrase, his underlying beliefs and the actual values by which he worked were incongruent. Bob had mulled this over many times. He pictured for himself a graph with agreement with values on the vertical axis (low to high) and performance on the horizontal axis (low to high from left to right). The ideal employee would be high in values agreement and high in performance. That, however, is rare. In reality most employees are higher in values agreement or higher in performance. As Bob thought about it, he felt he could work with any employee whose values were in sync with the company, even if that employee's performance was less than ideal. But, he asked himself, could he work with a person whose performance was high but did not actually agree with the cherished ways of behaving as an organization? And that was his struggle with Cyril — high performance, low agreement with the corporate values. Having invested so many years in this relationship, Bob wondered for the first time if he would have to let Cyril go.

17. Virginia Satir, *Conjoint Family Therapy,* rev. ed. (Palo Alto: Science and Behavior Books, 1983), pp. 251-52.

For Discussion

1. How would you feel if you were Cyril at the managers' meeting? How would you feel if you were in Bob's shoes?
2. What strategic role can Melinda play even though she is not in a "power position"?
3. What are the organizational and systemic factors at work in the case? How would releasing Cyril affect the company? How would retaining him affect the whole?
4. Should Bob release Cyril? If so, why? And how? If not, why not?
5. Melinda thinks Bob is expecting too much from his staff, many of whom are not people of faith. How far can one expect people to embrace and implement stated Christian values such as unconditional love, servant leadership, and interdependence?

For Further Reading

Collins, Philip, and R. Paul Stevens. *The Equipping Pastor: A Systems Approach to Empowering the People of God.* Washington, D.C.: Alban Institute, 1993.

Novak, Michael. *Toward a Theology of the Corporation.* Washington, D.C.: American Enterprise Institute for Public Policy Research, 1981.

Schein, Edgar H. *Organizational Culture and Leadership: A Dynamic View.* San Francisco: Jossey-Bass, 1991.

Senge, Peter M. *The Fifth Discipline: The Art and Practice of the Learning Organization.* New York: Doubleday, 1990.

5

◆ ◆ ◆

Marketplace Mission

The marketplace is the last mission frontier.

Ed Silvoso

The commercial business marketplace may well be
the primary mission field of the twenty-first century.

Charles Van Engen

B ob, who was introduced in the previous chapter, is a person on a
mission. He is convinced that his work in the car industry is as
much a life-giving mission as going to a primitive tribe to plant a
church or bringing medical help to a remote village in the developing
world. Can this be true? And, if it is true, what will it take for people
engaged in enterprise to view themselves that way and to be supported spiritually and emotionally by others in the Christian church,
in synagogues, and in other worship communities? My friend William

Diehl puts it this way in his book *Christianity and Real Life* written
when he was sales manager for Bethlehem Steel:

> In the almost thirty years of my professional career, my church
> has never once suggested that there be any type of accounting
> of my on-the-job ministry to others. My church has never once
> offered to improve those skills which could make me a better
> minister, nor has it ever asked if I needed any kind of support
> in what I was doing. There has never been an inquiry into the
> types of ethical decisions I must face, or whether I seek to com-
> municate the faith to my co-workers. I have never been in a
> congregation where there was any type of public affirmation of
> a ministry in my career. In short, I must conclude that my
> church really doesn't have the least interest in whether or how
> I minister in my daily work.[1]

Happily, a ground swell of renewed interest in mission in the marketplace is shown not only in the *Fortune* article quoted in chapter 1
but also in a number of popular and scholarly journals.[2] Most of these
articles and the seminars that serve as a public face for the movement start with the assumption that the marketplace is a mission
field, perhaps the most strategic one in the world today.[3] But in this
chapter we will be asking not only whether the marketplace is a location where mission work can be undertaken but also whether marketplace activity itself is part of the mission of God in the world. It is

---

1. William E. Diehl, *Christianity and Real Life* (Philadelphia: Fortress Press, 1976),
pp. v-vi.

2. See C. Neal Johnson, "Toward a Marketplace Missiology," *Missiology: An International Review* 31, no. 1 (January 2003): 87-97.

3. I acknowledge my indebtedness to an article by John Jefferson Davis who
traced the history of the interpretation of Matthew 28:18-20 from the early church to
the present, showing how the full meaning of the text was obscured by ecclesiastical
controversies over the missiological implications of the text that were first pointed
out by William Carey. Davis notes that "the marketplace implications of this crucial
text are just beginning to receive attention at the present time" (p. 1). Davis,
"'Teaching Them to Observe All That I Have Commanded You': The History of the Interpretation of the 'Great Commission' and Implications for Marketplace Ministries"
(South Hamilton, Mass.: Gordon-Conwell Theological Seminary, 1998).

certainly a hard mission field, characterized by greed, rapacious competition, sinful inequalities between the rich and the poor, exploitation, and idolatrous demands made on some workers.

Not surprisingly, the church has a long history of antipathy toward business, except for the value attributed to businesspeople who give their tithes and sit on church boards. For instance, consider Origen's criticism of people who did not sell their possessions and give to the poor, the condemnation of usury by the church councils and Luther, Pope Paul VI's condemnation of the "international imperialism of money," and the Argentinean Bonino's rejection of capitalism as "raising man's grasping impulse." These judgments lead Michael Novak to conclude that, if true, "this places the businessman [sic] in an intolerable position of being either corrupt or naïve."[4]

Business and Mission — How Are They Related?

Sunki Bang, who leads the Business Ministry Institute in Seoul, Korea, has helpfully suggested several ways of relating business and mission.

- Business *and* mission — two isolated activities.
- Business *for* mission — using the proceeds of business as a way of financing mission.
- Business *as a platform for* mission — work and professional life as means of channeling mission throughout the world (in Korea such people are called "Businaries").
- Mission *in* business — hiring non-believers and offering chaplaincy services with a view to leading them to Christ.
- Business *as* mission — business as part of the mission of God in the world.[5]

4. Quoted in Brian Griffiths, *The Creation of Wealth* (London: Hodder and Stoughton, 1984), pp. 9-11.

5. Bang notes that one of the dangers of taking the last position is the potential of minimizing evangelism. See Sunki Bang, "Tensions in Witness," *Vocatio* 1, no. 2 (July 1998): 17-18.

Bang was a university classmate of a person who intended to make a lot of money in business to devote to missions. Meanwhile, Bang himself intended to become a pastor. His friend became, in due course, the president of a large retail chain in Korea, and Bang became his theological and pastoral assistant, not merely to provide chaplaincy to his employees but to assist the president in the formation and development of company policies and culture. Would that more businesses would do this! In the process, the president moved from merely making money as a way of financing mission to seeing his business itself as part of God's mission.[6] We will explore that process in this chapter.

Toward a Holistic Theology of Mission in the Marketplace

Mission Starts with God

One misunderstanding that we must clear away is the notion that mission is essentially a human activity undertaken in response to God's love or as a duty to fulfill the Great Commission. In fact, mission starts not with human action but with the sending of God himself. The term "mission" comes from the Latin word *missio* meaning "send." It was used exclusively for the mission of God until recently.[7]

Augustine once said there is in the Triune God a Lover, a Beloved, and Love itself.[8] In the same way the Triune God is Sender, Sent, and

6. In his article "Toward a Marketplace Missiology," C. Neal Johnson outlines the many components of a new field of mission studies: marketplace missiology. Especially valuable is the list contained in note 3 of contemporary marketplace issues that are ripe for biblical research. The article, unfortunately, does not explore the question of whether marketplace activity itself is part of the mission of God in the world.

7. This truth has been developed most completely by George F. Vicedom, who writes: "Catholic dogmatics since Augustine speaks of sendings or the *missio* within the Triune God. . . . Every sending of one Person results in the presence of the Other." George F. Vicedom, *The Mission of God: An Introduction to a Theology of Mission,* trans. Gilbert A. Thiele and Dennis Hilgendorf (St. Louis: Concordia, 1965), p. 7.

8. Quoted in Jürgen Moltmann, *The Trinity and the Kingdom,* trans. Margaret Kohl (San Francisco: Harper and Row, 1991), p. 32.

Sending, as evidenced in the words of Jesus, who spoke of himself as the Son of God sent by the Father: "As you [Father] have sent me into the world, so I have sent them [the disciples] into the world" (John 17:18). Rather than sending, we could just as well speak of the "missioning" in God and by God. The Gospel of John uses "sending" more than thirty-one times for the out-going action of God within the Trinity or the sending forth by God of humankind. In other words, mission is God othering himself; this is *missio Dei* — the mission of God.

God's Mission Began with Creation

A second misunderstanding of mission is the tragic separation of the Great Commission (Matt. 28:18-20) from the Cultural Commission (Gen. 1:26-28). The first concerns the stewardship of the gospel; the second the stewardship of life and creation. Whole denominations of Christians line up after one or the other of these commissions as the mandate for their church's life. As I have indicated elsewhere, Adam and Eve (and their progeny) received three full-time jobs in Genesis 1 and 2: communion with God, community-building, and co-creativity with God. This tragic separation between the two commissions has led Christians to disagree about which type of work is most sacred and has fostered the unfortunate debate in the Western Christian world over the conflicting values of evangelism and social justice. (By and large in the developing world, there is not much debate.[9]) Far more helpful would be to speak of the *Greatest Commission,* found in John 17:18 and John 20, where Jesus says, "As the Father has sent me, so I send you" (20:21). He sends us into a fully incarnational mission

---

9. René Padilla comments: "Every human need . . . may be used by the Spirit of God as a beach-head for the manifestation of his kingly power. That is why in actual practice the question of which comes first, evangelism or social action, is irrelevant. In every concrete situation the needs themselves provide the guidelines for the definition of priorities. As long as both evangelism and social responsibility are regarded as essential for mission, we need no rule of thumb to tell us which comes first and when." C. René Padilla, "The Mission of the Church in the Light of the Kingdom of God," *Transformation* 1, no. 2 (April-June 1984): 19.

with all the resources of the Triune God into whose mission we are entering.

In creation God was already in mission, with his Word and Spirit as "missionaries."[10] God extends his mission by calling his first creatures to "fill the earth" (Gen. 1:28). As part of that "filling" Abraham and Sarah are sent to bless all the nations. It is a global mission — a subject to which we will return in the light of the globalization of commerce. Israel is called to be a light to the Gentiles — a model of creational stewardship and human community. And finally, Christ is sent from the Father, and the Son sends the church, the people of God.

Sin Has Marred Human Participation in the Mission of God

The issue in the Garden was lack of trust ("has God said?"). Behind it lay a questioning of God's goodness and the idea that to survive we must take matters into our own hands. So the root of Adam and Eve's sin was a desire for autonomy — living without communion with God, living independently.[11] The result was the curse (Gen. 3:16-19): women would deliver children in pain; the earth would resist cultivation; work would be tedious; relationships, especially between the sexes, would become politicized; and death would come. In business, sin appears as personal self-aggrandizement, what Richard Higginson has called the "Tower of Babel" syndrome: sexual alienation and exploitation, blame-shifting, moral ambiguity, and greed.[12] But the Fall also affects society and creation. The environment is destroyed, human existence is trivialized, workers are dehumanized and treated as machines, competition becomes predatory, and the developing world is exploited.

10. David Bosch, *Believing in the Future: Toward a Missiology of Western Culture* (Leominster Herefordshire, England: Gracewing, 1995).

11. See Ps. 1, Dan. 4, and Ezek. 31.

12. Richard Higginson, *Called to Account: Adding Value in God's World — Integrating Christianity and Business Effectively* (Guildford, Surrey: Eagle, 1993), pp. 70-95.

God's Mission Establishes God's Kingdom

The message Jesus came to announce, to embody, and to implement was the gospel of the kingdom. (The word appears 122 times in the gospels.) "The time is fulfilled," he said. "The kingdom of God has come near; repent, and believe in the good news" (Mark 1:15). During the forty days after his resurrection, Jesus was also "speaking about the kingdom of God" (Acts 1:3). Origen called Jesus the *autobasileia* — the kingdom embodied in his own person. The kingdom is the rule of the sovereign (God) and the response of the people. It is not a reign or a territory of land but a dynamic sovereign and saving rule. It is like a magnet pulling up iron filings. In contrast, Queen Elizabeth II of England reigns but does not rule — the citizens of England honor her but do not follow her commands — and indeed that is how many treat God!

In his classic study of the kingdom, Mortimer Arias describes how in our thinking and acting we have reduced the kingdom to a transcendent realm outside the world and the struggles of history, to the institutional and visible church, or to a catastrophic event precipitated by the second coming of Jesus in the future, the inner experience of salvation, the baptism of the Spirit, or a new social order created by revolution.[13] In contrast, the kingdom announced by Jesus was and is holistic: personal, social, intrapersonal, interpersonal, structural, political, and creational. This involves several things.

First, it brings the forgiveness of sins (Matt. 3:1-8; Luke 3:3-18). Second, the kingdom brings healing and recovery of full life: "the blind receive their sight, the lame walk, the lepers are cleansed, the deaf hear, the dead are raised, and the poor have good news brought to them" (Matt. 11:5; Luke 7:22). Third, the kingdom restores community by providing an open table for sharing meals with sinners, with poor and rich (Mark 2:15).[14] Arias says, "The act of eating and drinking was an act of proclamation. . . . The open table with public sinners

---

13. Mortimer Arias, *Announcing the Kingdom: Evangelization and the Subversive Memory of Jesus* (Lima, Ohio: Academic Renewal Press, 1984/2001), pp. 66-67.

14. See also Luke 7:36, 11:37, 14:1, 15:2, and 19:5.

and outcasts was Jesus' major and most provocative proclamation of the new order of the kingdom."[15] Finally, Jesus denounced collective, institutional, and structural sin (Matt. 23:4-25), especially for the effect it had on the poor and oppressed. He denounced the scribal system of religious bigotry and idolatry that was part of a social system of exploitation and oppression. Arias says, "The kingdom is the . . . relentless unmasker of all human disguises, self-righteous ideologies, or self-perpetuating powers."[16]

On one hand, the kingdom is grace and gift — not the creation of humankind. So, Arias notes: "It cannot be secured by fleeing from the world to a secluded life of 'purity' in the wilderness, as the Essenes attempted; it cannot be conquered by the piercing swords of the violent rebellion against Rome, as the zealots pretended."[17] On the other hand, the kingdom calls forth a human response to share in the inbreaking. David Bosch says, "Mission means the announcement of Christ's lordship over all reality and an invitation to submit to it. . . ."[18] This involves proclamation ("it is here"), annunciation ("it is coming"), denunciation (declaring what is unjust and opposed to the rule of God), embodiment (in the community of the King), compassion and consolation (to those sinned against), continuing conversion (like Peter's), and confrontation of the powers.

So kingdom mission includes creational stewardship, economic justice, community-building, a restored relationship with God, restored community, and care for neighbors. In business this calls for social responsibility, what is sometimes called the "triple bottom line" — profit, people, and the environment.[19]

The case of Bob in chapter 4 gives an example of kingdom work in dealing with injustice. In the car business, new car prices are usually

15. Arias, *Announcing the Kingdom,* pp. 24, 80.
16. Arias, *Announcing the Kingdom,* pp. 46-47.
17. Arias, *Announcing the Kingdom,* p. 17.
18. David J. Bosch, *Transforming Mission: Paradigm Shifts in Theology of Mission* (Maryknoll, N.Y.: Orbis Books, 1991), p. 148.
19. K. S. Alter, *Managing the Double Bottom Line* (Washington, D.C.: Pact Publications, 2000); see also E. Goodell, ed., *Social Venture Network Standards of Corporate Social Responsibility* (San Francisco: Social Venture Network, 1999).

determined through a process of negotiation between the dealer and the buyer. Bob researched this and found that the range of selling prices for the same vehicle was about six hundred dollars. Then he researched who was paying the top dollar and who the bottom. It turned out that the lowest price was paid by lawyers and executives with advanced negotiating skills, while the highest price was paid by women, young people, and minorities. He declared the situation to be unjust and developed a "one price-fair price" policy at his dealerships, giving incentives of time-saving services to lawyers and executives, to whom saving time was worth paying a little more to buy a car. That is kingdom work!

As René Padilla notes, "All human work that embodies Kingdom values and serves Kingdom goals can be rightly termed as Kingdom ministry. Gospel work and so-called 'secular work' are actually interdependent. Biblically we should speak of a single mission rather than prioritizing evangelism and social action/stewardship of creation."[20]

The Whole People of God Is Engaged in God's Mission

A further misunderstanding is the false notion that "mission is what missionaries do."[21] Thus, so it is thought, our participation in the mission of God is done representatively or vicariously by certain designated people called "missionaries." As John Davis has shown in his research on the interpretation of the Great Commission, it is not merely the apostles (and missionaries) who are called to preach, teach, and disciple, but the whole people of God.[22] Indeed, to say that the church does not *have* a mission but *is* one does not go far enough, though it underscores that all people of God are missionaries. The

---

20. Padilla, "The Mission of the Church," p. 19.

21. In the same way almost every theology of ministry published in the English language starts with the definition of ministry as what "the minister does" — proclamation of the Word and administering the sacraments. See R. Paul Stevens, *The Other Six Days: Vocation, Work, and Ministry in Biblical Perspective* (Grand Rapids: Eerdmans/Regent Publishing, 1999), p. 132.

22. See Davis, "'Teaching Them to Observe.'"

church itself is created through the mission of God and participates in the mission of God. And it does this not only in its gathered (ecclesial) life but in its dispersed (diaspora) life as members fan out into the world as agents of the kingdom of God Monday to Saturday.

God's Mission Is Not Finished

Salvation is a multi-stage matter. The kingdom is *here and now,* as Jesus proclaimed. It is also *coming now.* This is reflected in the Lord's Prayer ("Thy kingdom come") and the Beatitudes, in which the first and last statements are in the present tense and the rest are in the future tense.[23] And it is *coming fully in the future,* as indicated in the parables of the sower (Mark 4:3-8), the mustard seed (Mark 4:30-32), crisis and parousia (Matt. 24:40-44), the servant entrusted with supervision (Luke 12:41-46), the ten bridesmaids (Matt. 25:1-13), and the wedding banquet (Matt. 22:1-14). All mission done in and through business is partial and incomplete.

Mission is good news to the world. It is good news because it brings people into relation with Jesus. But it is also good news because it promises to bring *shalom* into the world. The ultimate goal of mission is the Sabbath shalom: the threefold harmony of God, creation and humankind, which will be fully obtained when Christ comes again and the kingdom of God is consummated. In the meantime we work towards that end, finding meaning in our imperfect and fragmented efforts on earth in view of the certain end, the full realization of the kingdom of God in a new heaven and earth.

What does this mean for business?

Business Is an Arena for Individual Witness

Before I tackle this much harder part of the question — whether business and marketplace activity in some sense engages the mission of

---

23. Arias, *Announcing the Kingdom,* p. 32.

God — I want to affirm that the marketplace is a mission field, an arena where the individual believer may, in appropriate ways, share her or his faith. This is the *kerygmatic* (proclamation) dimension. We are called to bear God's word and the good news of the kingdom in the marketplace as well as everywhere else. Every Christian is called to declare the wonderful deeds of God (1 Pet. 2:9-10). The marketplace is a mission field.

Reflect for a moment though, on the millions of believers who will never be able to cross an international frontier but who will spend most of their active waking hours in the workplace. It is estimated that the average North American Christian spends 88,000 hours in her lifetime in the workplace and more if one is a farmer or a professional. Indeed it is becoming more for everyone, with the whittling down of leisure time by more than 50 percent over the last three decades to a mere thirteen hours a month by some estimates. At the same time, these same believers spend fewer than 4,000 hours in the church building engaged in church-related activities. Perhaps with the whittling down of discretionary time we are reverting to the situation in the first two centuries when much of the work of evangelism was done by slaves working eighteen hours a day.

A gracious transformation in local church culture could be accomplished by refusing for fifty-two weeks to give "air time" in the Sunday service to returning missionaries, visiting clergy, and professors from theological colleges and, in its place, interviewing for five minutes an ordinary member of the congregation along these lines: "What do you do for a living? What are the issues you face in your daily work? What difference does your faith make in the way you deal with these issues? How can we pray for you in your ministry in the marketplace?"

In *The Equippers' Guide to Every Member Ministry*, I have suggested several ways of equipping "worker-priests for the marketplace": intercessory prayers for members working in the world; occasionally having lay marketplace preachers (who will always illustrate their message from their daily work); commissioning people who have a proven and enduring sense of call to serve God in some arena of society; teaching and preaching on work. I often ask my students when was the last time they heard a sermon on work. Usually only one or two out of a class of thirty have heard something in the last year or two. A further strategy is to develop a congregational learning curriculum that links small group study on key scriptures or marketplace issues with the Sunday teaching.[24]

The reasons for thinking that the marketplace is a key mission field are so obvious that one could only think that an enemy has blinded our eyes to the possibilities.

- *Access.* The marketplace gives access to people who work there while it denies access to outsiders, especially religious professionals, except in a few cases where industrial or corporate chaplaincy is accepted. My son works for a high-tech company. He has a security pass that allows him in but, when I have lunch with him, I cannot enter.
- *The relational context.* The corporation is a community of shared life and enterprise, providing a relational context for ministry often deeper than the local church or the neighborhood.
- *Sheer time.* Most working adults spend most of their waking hours in this community.
- *Intrinsic issues and values.* The marketplace itself raises issues that are openings for the gospel and pastoral care: identity, relationality, priorities, credibility, life-purpose, success and failure.
- *Life-centeredness.* The opportunities abound for relational evangelism in which a person may hear the gospel not only by word but in the lived-out behavior of the witness, far surpassing the openings created by parachuting people into a new neighborhood in door-to-door visitation or short-term missions. In this context note Paul's emphasis on people observing "my way of life" (1 Cor. 4:17; 2 Tim. 3:10). As R. F. Hock has indicated in his study of Paul's tentmaking, far from being at the periphery of his life "Paul's tent-making was actually central to [his life] . . . and his trade was taken up into his apostolic self-understanding, so

24. R. Paul Stevens, *The Equippers' Guide to Every Member Ministry* (Vancouver: Regent College Publishing, 2000), pp. 91-111.

much so that, when criticized for plying his trade, he came to understand himself as the apostle who offered the message free of charge."[25]

- *Proximity to people in need and crisis.* When trouble and hardship hit, a worker is more inclined to share this with a colleague at work than a religious professional in the church. The opportunities for pastoral care in the marketplace, that is caring for the whole person — body, soul, and spirit — are enormous, so much so that several theologically trained people known to me have gone into pastoral ministry in business rather than the church. Instead of a few hours of direct pastoral care one can have in church leadership one has forty or more hours a week in the marketplace.

I have a proposal to make: Every theological student preparing for pastoral ministry should spend a semester in the workplace listening and learning how to empower people for full-time service in the marketplace. Every pastor should spend one day a week with members of her church in the workplace setting, listening and praying. Every professor of theology in a seminary should spend two weeks each year in a professional office or a factory. Every theological faculty should include people who model full or part-time ministry in the world, since education is essentially an imitation process and students become "like" their teachers (Luke 6:40). Every local church that has members traveling to other countries for business should pray for them and "send them off" as missionaries in the same way as we currently pray for short-term mission teams to Mexico. Every church should open its pulpit, at least occasionally, to thoughtful business people to speak God's Word from the integrative perspective of being a business person, a school teacher, or a lawyer.

Along the lines of my earlier suggestion — commissioning and honoring ordinary members for their work in the world — one church did something right. A village church in Yorkshire recently

---

25. R. F. Hock, *The Social Context of Paul's Ministry: Tentmaking and Apostleship* (Philadelphia: Fortress Press, 1980), p. 166.

honored one of its members with a $90,000 stained glass window. The parishioner was Thomas Crapper, a plumber born in the nearby village of Thorne in 1836. As reported in *The Globe and Mail,* "the window incorporates a tastefully rendered silhouette of a toilet as part of a celebration of local achievements." Mr. Crapper was the inventor of the flush toilet.[26]

Business Can Be a Means of Church-Planting

There is a long history of such missionary activity in the context of trade. Well before William Carey's time, Nestorian Christians, though regarded by some as heretics, carried the gospel eastwards as the silk roads to India and China developed. Nestorian Kurd George M. Lamsa says, "The coincidence of the opening up of the trade routes into Farther Asia — with the ascendance of the Nestorian Church — offered a ready outlet for missionary efforts."[27] In the sixth and seventh centuries these merchant-missionaries dominated the silk roads and built Nestorian chapels all along the roads.

Significantly William Carey, the so-called founder of modern missions, envisioned the gospel going into the entire world through the means of international trade. He drew on the text in Isaiah 60:9: "Surely the islands look to me; in the lead are the ships of Tarshish, bringing your sons from afar, with their silver and gold, to the honor of the Lord your God, the Holy One of Israel, for he has endowed you [Zion] with splendor."[28] In Carey's view it was inexcusable not to go into the entire world to preach the gospel now that we have the mari-

26. *The Marketplace: MEDA's Magazine for Christians in Business* (January-February 2001): 2.

27. George M. Lamsa and William Chauncey Emhardt, *The Oldest Christian People* (New York: Macmillan, 1926), p. 64, quoted in Tetsunao Yamamori and Kenneth A. Eldred, *On Kingdom Business: Transforming Missions through Entrepreneurial Strategies* (Wheaton, Ill.: Crossway, 2003), p. 184.

28. William Carey, *An Enquiry into the Obligations of Christians to Use Means for the Conversion of the Heathens* (Leicester, 1792), p. 68. Carey says, "This seems to imply that in the time of the glorious increase of the church, in the latter days, commerce shall subserve the spread of the gospel."

ner's compass and can safely cross any sea and indeed do so for trade.[29] International trade, whether on a small scale of entrepreneurial import-export businesses or the grand scale of multinational corporations, represents an unprecedented opportunity for believers to be present in the world God loves, to make contacts with people, to earn the right to speak and to share the wonderful good news of Jesus.[30] It is being done today by thousands of believers in places where the formal missionary is not welcome. Even in so-called "open countries," such as post-Christian Europe and Canada — truly "hard-to-reach" though not "closed countries" — trade brings the business person into contact with people who would never darken the door of a church.

Steve Rundle and Tom Steffan ask, "Could globalization [the subject of the next chapter] be God's way of bringing business people — perhaps the largest and most underutilized segment of the church — back into missions?"[31] In their book, *Great Commission Companies,* Rundle and Steffan note that while Christian companies may unintentionally forward the Great Commission in making Christ known, "Great Commission Companies" are driven by the mission of God. They are not merely Christian companies that have a reputation for integrity and high-quality work. They exist for mission. A similar approach is taken by Tetsunao Yamamori and Kenneth A. Eldred in *On Kingdom Business: Transforming Missions Through Entrepreneurial Strategies.* Rundle, an economist, and Steffan, a missiologist, define a "Great Commission Company" in these words:

---

29. "As to their distance from us, whatever objections might have been made on that account before the invention of the mariner's compass, nothing can be alleged for it, with any colour of plausibility in the present age. Men can now sail with as much certainty through the Great South Sea, as they can through the Mediterranean, or any lesser Sea. Yea, and providence seems in a manner to invite us to the trial, as there are to our knowledge trading companies, whose commerce lies in many of the places where these barbarians dwell." Carey, "An Enquiry," p. 67.

30. See Michael C. R. McLoughlin, "Back to the Future of Missions," *Vocatio* 4, no. 2 (December 2000): 1-6.

31. Steve Rundle and Tom Steffan, *Great Commission Companies: The Emerging Role of Business in Missions* (Downers Grove, Ill.: InterVarsity Press, 2003), p. 25.

A Great Commission Company is a socially responsible, income-producing business managed by kingdom professionals and promoting the growth and multiplication of local churches in the least-evangelized and less-developed parts of the world.[32]

Some remarkable implications that are drawn from this definition are these: first, drawing people into the family of God is central to the organization's purpose; second, there is a clear link between the business plan and the mission goals of the business; third, the business has a global perspective. Rundle and Steffan recognize that not all Christian business leaders will agree with them that their companies should *intentionally* draw people into faith in Jesus. They cite and analyze several companies that fit their description of companies that exist for mission: Silk Road Handicraft Company, Pura Vida Coffee, Global Engineering and Management Solutions, and Gateway Telecommunications Services. A central tenet of their thesis is that "globalization is part of God's plan to integrate the whole body of Christ into his global plan (mission)."[33]

One can hope that such businesses will be multiplied even more widely provided that they undertake their corporate activity as work that has intrinsic value (as explored in the four previous chapters) and not merely a means of being present in a restricted-access or closed country to traditional missionaries. It goes almost without saying that the church has been influenced by the contemporary prioritization of the professional ministry and the professional missionary as the highest calling, aided and abetted by Calvin's doctrine of a "secret call"[34]

---

32. Rundle and Steffan, *Great Commission Companies*, p. 41.

33. Rundle and Steffan, *Great Commission Companies*, p. 47.

34. "I pass over that secret call, of which each minister is conscious before God, and which does not have the church as witness. But there is the good witness of our heart that we receive the proffered office not with ambition or avarice, not with any other selfish desire, but with a sincere fear of God and desire to build up the church. That is indeed necessary for each one of us (as I have said) if we would have our ministry approved by God" (*Institutes* 4.3.11, p. 1063). Calvin's concern was to prevent "noisy and troublesome men [from] rashly tak[ing] upon themselves to teach or to rule" (*Institutes* 4.3.10, p. 1062).

and by medieval dualism. One practical implication of this dualism in the modern and post-modern worlds is that tent-making mission, often deemed to be the future of the global mission of the church, normally depreciates the actual work which people perform to gain entry to a restricted-access country. Tent-making is often, though not always, a disguised form of clericalism. The ministry is all important. The work itself, whether it is business or teaching English, is considered not to have any intrinsic value. Its value is only extrinsic — access. Not surprisingly, converts aspire to what is modelled — professional Christian service.[35] As we have shown already, business is worth doing and is a concrete way of loving neighbors, even though it is so often mixed with sin. This leads us to explore another dimension of marketplace mission.

Business as a Means of Societal Service

This is the *diakonic* (service) role. We are serving God and God's purposes in the marketplace as we release talents, create community, and serve our neighbor through providing goods and services. Businesses also have a social and creational responsibility sometimes spoken of as a double or triple bottom line.

The Body Shop was one of the first companies to undertake a serious commitment to social responsibility and to conduct a social audit. Originally a U.K. cosmetic company, they declared and evaluated themselves on the following holistic criteria: against animal testing; support community trade; activate self-esteem; defend human rights and protect our planet.[36]

35. See Siew Li Wong, "A Defense of the Intrinsic Value of 'Secular Work' in Tentmaking Ministry in the Light of the Theological Doctrines of Creation, Redemption, and Eschatology," master's thesis, Regent College, Vancouver, April 2000. In the course of researching this thesis, Ms. Wong interviewed executives in most of the tent-making missions based in North America and found only one that indicated that the work that tent-making missionaries do had any intrinsic value. For most it was merely instrumental (pp. 6-11).

36. Cited in Allan Bussard, Marek Marcus, and Daniela Olejarova, *Code of Ethics and Social Audit Manual* (Bratislava, Slovakia: The Integra Foundation), p. 19.

The Johnson & Johnson Company has published their social commitment in the form of a creed, here reproduced in abbreviated form:

> We believe our first responsibility is to the doctors, nurses and patients, to mothers and fathers and all others who use our products and services. . . . We are responsible to our employees, the men and women who work with us throughout the world. . . . They must have a sense of security in their jobs. Compensation must be fair and adequate, and working conditions clean, orderly and safe. We must be mindful of ways to help our employees fulfil their family responsibilities. . . . We are responsible to the communities in which we live and work and to the world community as well. . . . We must encourage civic improvements and better health and education . . . protecting the environment and natural resources. Our final responsibility is to our stockholders. Business must make a sound profit. . . . Reserves must be created to provide for adverse times. When we operate according to these principles, the stockholders should realize a fair return.[37]

Recently General Electric, under the leadership of Jeff Immelt, said it would take four things to keep a company on top. The first three were predictable: execution, growth, and great people. The fourth was unexpected: virtue. Commenting on this new level of corporate responsibility in a giant corporation, Marc Gunther says, "As an old-line manufacturer, GE tended to view environmental rules as a cost or burden. Now Immelt sees growth opportunities in cleaning up the planet. He wants GE to be known as one of the few companies with the scale and know-how to tackle the world's toughest problems."[38]

37. www.jnj.com/home.html.
38. Marc Gunther, "Jeff Immelt Wants to Instill Values in Everything the Company Does — Without Compromising the Profit Principle," *Time,* 15 November 2004, p. 2. See also Wilfried Luetkenhorst, "Corporate Social Responsibility and the Development Agenda," *Intereconomics* 39, no. 3 (May/June 2004): 157-66.

Business as a Means of Community-Building

This is the *koinonic* (fellowship and partnership) role. We build community by caring for our neighbor in the workplace and creating corporate and professional cultures that reflect in some measure the presence of the kingdom: people-affirming, interdependent communities that give people significance, that release talents and help people learn to love. Indeed many feel that the marketplace is the last community left for reasons we have elaborated above. Some go so far to say it is the "corporate cathedral"!

The word "community" is used in many different ways. It can refer to a specific group of people (people in a certain geographical locale, a religious congregation, co-workers) or it can describe a quality of relationship. For example, many people are familiar with a unique phenomenon that emerges between individuals during a crisis like a hurricane or flood. In such situations, people tend to drop their pretences, overcome obstacles, and reach out to help or emotionally support one another. In the process, they find surprising strength, tolerance, and acceptance.[39]

The Foundation for Community Encouragement defines a community this way: "A community is a group of two or more people who have been able to accept and transcend their differences regardless of the diversity of their backgrounds (social, spiritual, educational, ethnic, economic, political, etc.) This enables them to communicate effectively and openly and to work together toward goals identified as being for their common good."[40] There are multiple factors that militate against community in modern and post-modern society: urbanization, transience and mobility, unsafe streets, specialization, lack of time, and the overwhelming individualism of the North and West of the planet.

Peter Mogan consults with businesses in order to facilitate com-

---

39. I am indebted for these thoughts to Peter Mogan in a presentation on "Community: Where Can I Find It?" in the Integra Staff Conference, Sofia, Bulgaria, May 2004.

40. Quoted by Peter Mogan in the Integra Staff Conference, Sofia Bulgaria, May 2004.

munity-building. Some of the building blocks for community in business he outlines are having a core ideology (purpose and values), facilitating connectors, telling stories, rituals, time spent together, and, surprisingly, conflict. Peter was retained as a consultant with a high-quality printing business. To begin with he joined the system (as we explained in the last chapter). When he started he found the employees were insecure about the future of their jobs; the culture was highly politicized; there was a wall between the white collar and blue collar workers; values were held only at the top and productivity was moderate. He developed a process of community-building that involved identifying core values both corporately and individually. Then he established a community development team that set about building community. Finally he implemented a program of leadership development that focused on character, knowledge, skills and dealt with the "baggage" that people bring to their leadership. The company started to have family events, company-wide training, frequent recognitions and celebrations. The result, years later, has been that the "wall" has come down; politics has been reduced; staff turnover has become minimal; conflict is out in the open and walked through in a feedback environment; and there is higher productivity. This is marketplace mission.

Business as a Means of Grappling with the Powers

This is the *prophetic* (discernment) role. We serve God by calling the marketplace to accountability for injustice, rapacious competition, for idolatrous demands made on workers, for unjust and unfair remuneration patterns, and for participation in global inequities. In this way we engage not only individual but systemic evil, what Paul called "the principalities and powers." We also work prophetically by pointing to the final consummation of history and the new heaven and new earth, giving meaning to this-worldly activity.

A significant micro and medium size economic development program in Central and Eastern Europe is the Integra Foundation. Understandably they face critical issues with corruption in government and business. One of their main programs is an initiative in "coping with corruption" which aims at building transparent and ethical corporate cultures in the former communist countries. Commenting on the context, Bussard, Marcus, and Olejarova, authors of their *Code of Ethics and Social Audit Manual,* note: "Some companies consciously violate their stakeholders, but these do not survive long. . . . It is well-known, and increasingly well-documented, that corruption in Central and Eastern Europe decreases competitiveness, frightens away needed foreign investment, perpetuates unemployment, and robs the vulnerable in these societies of needed social and public services."[41] They note that exceptional companies are aware that they are part of a larger picture and so invest in their communities, in arts, education, and community projects. In so doing they are moving well beyond "public relations" into mission and service to the communities in which their stakeholders live and work. This is holistic mission.

So it is not either-or, either mission field or mission, but both-and.[42] Viewing the marketplace as "mission field" serves to build the *faith community;* regarding the marketplace as "mission" serves to build the *human community.*

Steve Brinn, a self-proclaimed "sinful capitalist," asks,

Why shouldn't Christians be up to their ears in tough stuff — and aren't most of our reasons for shying away from it shallow or false? From the time I entered business more than 22 years ago, Christ to me has been a model of engagement. Dangerous engagement in life, where there was high exposure with questionable people and complicated issues, entailing prospects for great conflict and trouble. Christ's invi-

41. Bussard, Marcus, and Olejarova, *Code of Ethics,* p. 5.

42. The Mennonite Economic Development Associates have as their mission statement: "As Christians in business our mission is to honor God in the world of business and economics by extending his reign to all our activities. With Jesus as Lord of the marketplace our task is to love, serve, preach, and heal. We use our faith, skills, and resources to correct inequities, work toward economic justice, seek righteousness, bring hope where there is no hope, and make all things new." Quoted in Bang, "Tensions in Witness," p. 17.

tation to be like him led me, in the business context, from safe harbors to open water.[43]

For Discussion

Stephanie (introduced in chapter 1) is a pastor of a large church in Toronto. She knows that the majority of her congregation is composed of professionals, university professors, and business men and women. Last week one of the executives said to her: "I don't believe the church really validates what I do in business — except as a means to another end. What I do is considered of Christian significance insofar as I evangelize or witness at work, earn a good income and contribute generously to my church. All these validations are only instrumental. I've received no inherent validation from the church for what I do as a Christian in business."

1. What is she to do? How can she serve the church she loves in equipping the people for their service Monday to Friday? Review some of the suggestions made in this chapter. A major research study on this has been made by Laura Nash and Scotty McLennan, *Church on Sunday, Work on Monday* (San Francisco: Jossey-Bass, 2001).
2. What can members of her church do to facilitate integration of faith and work?

For Further Reading

Bosch, David J. *Transforming Mission: Paradigm Shifts in the Theology of Mission*. Maryknoll, N.Y.: Orbis Books, 1991.

Carroll, Vincent, and David Shiflett. *Christianity on Trial: Arguments Against Anti-Religious Bigotry*. San Francisco: Encounter Books, 2002.

43. Steve Brinn, "Tough Business: In Deep, Swift Waters," *Vocatio* 2, no. 2 (July 1999): 3-6.

Gibson, D. *Avoiding the Tentmaker Trap.* Hamilton, Ont.: WEF International, 1997.

Humphreys, Kent. *Lasting Investments: A Pastor's Guide for Equipping Workplace Leaders to Leave a Spiritual Legacy.* Colorado Springs: NavPress, 2004.

Myers, Bryant. *Walking with the Poor: Principles and Practices of Transformational Development.* Maryknoll, N.Y.: Orbis, 1999.

Oliver, E. H. *The Social Achievements of the Christian Church.* Reprinted Vancouver: Regent Publishing, 2003.

Rundle, Steve, and Tom Steffan. *Great Commission Companies: The Emerging Role of Business in Missions.* Downers Grove, Ill.: InterVarsity Press, 2003.

Stark, Rodney. *For the Glory of God: How Monotheism Led to Reformations, Science, Witch-Hunts, and the End of Slavery.* Princeton, N.J.: Princeton University Press, 2003.

Yamamori, Tetsunao, and Kenneth A. Eldred, eds. *On Kingdom Business: Transforming Missions Through Entrepreneurial Strategies.* Wheaton, Ill.: Crossway, 2003.

6

◆ ◆ ◆

Globalization

Globalization is . . . gradually undermining the nature of "national places" and creating a borderless world in which everyone belongs equally everywhere but nobody is at home in community.

Paul S. Williams

We can say with confidence that there is no unavoidable reason why all the six billion human beings on planet Earth should not have their essential material needs met and why they should not move on to the unlimited wealth offered by the weightless economy.

Clive Wright

H ardly any subject can generate more heat than that of globalization. As the two quotations above indicate, people line up on two (or more) sides. On the left are those who hold that capitalism is a system of oppression.[1] On the right are those who maintain that capitalism is the only system capable of providing economic development, creating wealth, and ensuring political freedom.[2] In the middle are those who give a modest endorsement of capitalism while critiquing some of its cultural and political ways of functioning.[3] What cannot be denied is the moral and spiritual challenge to all people engaged in what is now irrevocably a global business.[4] Here is a true situation.

• A MULTINATIONAL DILEMMA •

Sitting among the other bleary-eyed, early-morning commuters Tom Campbell had still not found the peace of mind he had hoped for when he went to bed the night before. As the train made its way painfully slowly down the Northern Line of London's Underground he allowed himself a slight smile as he reflected on how the dilemma facing him today was essentially the same one he had been presented with nine years ago when, as an idealistic, fresh-faced eighteen-year-old, he had started out in the world of work. He couldn't help thinking

1. This view is taken substantially by Christian thinkers Ron Sider, Jim Wallis, Samuel Escobar, Andrew Kirk, and most liberation theologians.

2. This is the view of Christian thinkers Michael Novak and Brian Griffiths. For a development of this view, see Craig Gay, *With Liberty and Justice for Whom? The Recent Evangelical Debate over Capitalism* (Grand Rapids: Eerdmans, 1991), p. 162.

3. This is the view of neo-Calvinists and authors such as Abraham Kuyper and Bob Goudzwaard. See Michael Novak, "Human Dignity, Personal Liberty: Themes from Abraham Kuyper and Leo XIII," in *Journal of Markets & Morality* 5, no. 1 (Spring 2002): 59-126. See Craig Gay's critique of Novak in *Journal of Markets & Morality* 5, no. 1 (Spring 2002): 127-134.

4. Other resources are Thomas L. Friedman, *The Lexus and the Olive Tree* (New York: Farrar, Straus and Giroux, 1999); "Globalization and Christian Ethics," *Center for Applied Ethics* 8, no. 1 (Winter 2001) — the Ron Sider/Michael Novak debate; Stanley Grenz, "Community as Theology Motif for the Western Church in an Era of Globalization," *Crux* 28, no. 3 (September 1992): 10-19; Bruce Nicholls, *Contextualization: A Theology of Gospel and Culture* (Downers Grove, Ill.: InterVarsity Press, 1979); Vinay Samuel, "Evangelical Response to Globalisation: An Asian Perspective," *Transformation* (January 1999); Loren Wilkinson, "One Earth, One World, One Church," *Crux* 28, no. 1 (March 1992): 28-36.

that perhaps God was giving him a second chance to make the right decision; the only dilemma was that now, nine years down the line, the right decision was no clearer to him.

While he was still in high school Tom had been awarded a lucrative sponsorship from a highly respected firm of consulting engineers. The package was extremely generous: In return for a year's work prior to going to university and an annual six-week summer internship during which time he would be earning a good salary, not to mention gaining invaluable practical experience, he would secure a sponsorship worth £6,000 (= $12,000 US) over the course of his four years of undergraduate study. With no obligations to work for the company upon graduation the offer had sounded almost too good to be true and Tom had not been slow in accepting it.

Tom could not remember much about his first day in the office; even at the time it had all seemed a blur. He was introduced to various people and pieces of office hardware. He viewed a presentation on the work the firm was doing now and in the future. He met the team to which he was to be attached for the year and, to his consternation, he was introduced to the work that they were doing. The company was a large firm of consulting engineers and he, along with two other interns, had been placed in their Industrial Projects division. The project group to which he had been attached was working on the renovation of a number of factories in Uzbekistan, part of the former Soviet Union. The factories, all in various states of disrepair, had been bought by an Anglo-American tobacco multinational corporation that was planning, after renovating them, to put in their machine lines and start producing cigarettes to sell to the local Uzbek population.

At the time, it had been only four months since Tom's grandfather had passed away. The doctors had thought it highly likely that the lung cancer that had killed his grandfather was a direct result of the smoky atmospheres of the clubs in which he had worked during his career as a band leader. Tom recoiled from the idea that by working on these factory projects he might now, albeit in an indirect way, contribute to the death of others' loved ones. Yet he saw no way out. He had signed a contract. He was sure that God had opened the door for him into the company, and he knew that over the coming years of undergraduate study he would desperately need the sponsorship money to avoid going into debt. At the time, seeing no other option open to him, he had accepted the situation, admittedly begrudgingly at first, and spent the year doing odd jobs for the various engineers on the team.

A lot of water had passed under the bridge since those days and Tom, having returned to the company as a graduate structural engineer, was now recently chartered and leading a small team of engineers in the same Industrial Projects division he had worked in nine years before. Only last week he had been called into his director's office and asked to lead the company's bid for a second phase of the tobacco company project in Uzbekistan. It would involve the design of a new production plant allowing the tobacco firm to triple their current output of cigarettes. Tom knew that heading up such a project would provide a fantastic opportunity for him to demonstrate his leadership potential. If his firm were to win the competition for the job, it would provide much-needed work for the company, which was currently experiencing something of a downturn. And, in Uzbekistan, it would directly create at least 150 jobs, not to mention innumerable benefits to the local economy.

Tom spent the week wrestling with his thoughts. He knew that he could turn down his boss's offer. The firm had plenty of other competent engineers who could lead the bid, yet he felt that in some way he owed the company a debt of gratitude for the generous treatment he had received over the years. Although Tom was aware that the project would certainly benefit the fledgling Uzbek economy, he was also conscious of the hidden cost to people's health years down the line. Having taken part in a number of direct action protests against globalization during his time at university, Tom was no fan of multinationals — particularly those that sold a product that obviously harmed the health of those who used it. Tom had tried to imagine "What would Jesus do?" in this situation, but he had only ended up thinking that perhaps Jesus had it rather easier than he, living in first-century Palestine.

The train was already at Camden Town, only three more stations before his stop. His boss, David, was expecting an answer this morning.

• •

Working in One World

Before most of us in the Western world have finished breakfast, we have put on clothing from half a dozen countries and eaten our way around the world. The signs of this global phenomenon are all around us: ubiquitous travel, urbanization, a global economy, international job transfer, the information age, and the English language medium. Sadly, there is at least one more sign — the globalization of violence.[5] In terms of economic realities it has been said that when the stock market in Tokyo itches the rest of the world scratches. We are linked together. Don Lewis, my colleague at Regent College, says "Globalization can . . . be defined as the intensification of worldwide social relations which link distant localities in such a way that local happenings are shaped by events occurring many miles away and vice versa."[6] This includes international development agencies (the United Nations Development Program, World Bank, International Monetary Fund, and so on), weaponry and war technology, information technology (such as cable TV and the World Wide Web), international pop culture (such as MTV), brand-name products, the global dominance of the market economy (rather than state control), and the global interchange of goods and services.

Convinced that globalization is fundamentally driven by economics, Paul Williams, a British economist and business consultant, says, "Globalization can be defined as the process by which market economies, governments, and cultures are becoming increasingly inter-linked across the globe."[7] Most large companies are doing multinational business, and even small companies are purchasing raw materials or finished products from other countries, especially where there is cheap labor. Except for a few resistant pockets left on earth, capitalism and the free market system have taken over. The results spill over into every area of human world-making. Recently, I went to

5. Robert D. Kaplan, "The Coming Anarchy," *Atlantic Monthly,* February 1994, pp. 44-76.

6. Don Lewis, public lecture, Regent College, 2000.

7. Paul Williams, lecture in "Marketplace Ministry" course, Regent College, February 2004.

Bangkok for a conference, hoping to be immersed in Thai culture and, instead, I was confronted with frenzy around Michael Jackson's visit.

Globalization has produced some benefits: it has transferred information technology to smaller countries, it has provided non-agricultural employment in countries formerly dominated by subsistence farming, and it has created new industries and services in countries with stagnant economies. In the last ten years, by the 2003 reckoning of the World Bank, the percentage of people in the world living in poverty has dropped from 29.6 to 23.2 percent. This means, it is estimated, that four hundred million people, while still desperately poor, no longer face starvation daily. Consumer purchasing power worldwide has nearly tripled. Infant mortality is down 42 percent since 1970, and worldwide, rural families' access to safe water has increased five-fold.[8]

But there is another side to the picture. Employment has been lost in both industrialized countries (through outsourcing) and in less industrialized countries. The damage to the biosphere is potentially catastrophic. It is well known that if the whole populated world were to adopt the high-consumption lifestyle of the West and North, it would take at least three planets of resources. Faced with globalizing cultures, ethnic groups struggle to maintain their identity, and perhaps some of the Balkanization of various nations around the planet can be attributed to this struggle for identity in an increasingly merged world order. One cannot belong to the whole human race. Economically the poor are getting poorer and the rich richer, even though there has been, overall, some increase in wealth world-wide. Jeremy Rifkin in *The End of Work* forecasts world-wide unemployment through technology, even in the so-called service sectors. "Just outside the new high-tech global village lie a growing number of destitute and desperate human beings, many of whom are turning to a life of crime and creating a vast new

8. World Bank, *Global Economic Prospects and the Developing Countries* (Washington, D.C.: The World Bank, 2003), p. 30, quoted in Steve Rundle and Tom Steffan, *Great Commission Companies: The Emerging Role of Business in Missions* (Downers Grove, Ill.: InterVarsity Press, 2003), p. 47.

criminal subculture."[9] On top of this, Third World debt is at a punishing level.[10]

The *New York Times* noted that the three richest people in the world have more than the combined GNPs of the forty-eight poorest countries; that the richest 20 percent of the world's people consume 86 percent of all goods and services, while the poorest 20 percent consume 1.3 percent of all goods and services; that Americans and Europeans spend seventeen billion dollars a year on pet food, this being four billion more than what is needed to provide basic health care and nutrition for everyone in the world; and that Americans spend eight billion dollars a year on cosmetics, two billion more than needed to provide basic education for everyone in the world.[11]

John Morrow, a marketplace student at Regent College and a banker, says, "Economic integration . . . tends only to increase the economic growth rates of those countries, typically of the West, with sufficiently strong and diverse economies to attract investment and rapidly increase their exports." He qualifies President John F. Kennedy's well-known phrase, "a rising tide floats all boats," by adding that for those who do not own boats or who have leaky boats it appears only to exacerbate inequality.[12]

And who benefits? Some countries have benefited immensely from globalization, notably Singapore. Other countries have found most of their basic services — water, electricity, and telecommunications — taken over by foreign companies. The result of this is often increasing poverty for most and increasing wealth for the rich few in those countries. William McGurn, writing for Canada's *Financial Post*, says, "Though the West is not to blame for the poverty of the undevel-

9. Jeremy Rifkin, *The End of Work: The Decline of the Global Work-Force and the Dawn of the Post-Market Era* (London: Penguin, 2000), pp. xvii-xviii.

10. See James H. Ottley, "The Debt Crisis in Theological Perspective," in Max Stackhouse, Tim Dearborn, and Scott Paeth, eds., *The Local Church in a Global Era: Reflections for a New Century* (Grand Rapids: Eerdmans, 2000), pp. 39-47.

11. *New York Times*, 27 September 1998, p. 16.

12. John Morrow, "The Global Economy and Global Free Market Capitalism: Towards a Christian Perspective," paper for Marketplace Ministry Seminar, Regent College, 2000.

oped world, the Pope is right to wonder about a globalization mentality, still prevalent in all too many negotiations, which seeks to stack the decks of openness. For years the United States insisted that poor countries open their markets to our high-end goods while we maintain quotas in one of the few industries where developing nations might compete: textiles."[13]

Ultimately the issue is a spiritual challenge. Is there an ethic strong enough to direct and discipline capitalism? Os Guinness says, "Capitalism, having defeated all challenges, such as socialism, now faces its greatest challenge — itself, because it devours the very virtues it needs to thrive."[14] As we have already seen, the Protestant ethic, however it was understood, did have a moral and spiritual foundation. Thus Guinness observes, "Originally the menace of unrestrained economic impulse was held in check by the Protestant ethic — people worked in response to their calling. But now, with this ethic dissolved, including its moral attitudes toward hard work and saving, only hedonism remains."[15]

It is critical that we gain a theological understanding of the globalization phenomenon, especially since the study of economics and business has, in the West, been largely secularized.

The Christian Foundation of Wealth Creation

While the secularization of the study of economics and business is now virtually complete in the Western world, it is important to realize that the democratic capitalist form of wealth creation emerged in a culture largely shaped by the Christian faith.[16] The great explosion of wealth creation took place after the Protestant Reformation, but the church

13. William McGurn, "Globalization Gospel Reaches the Eternal City," *Financial Post*, 23 December 2000, p. D11.

14. Os Guinness, *The Call: Finding and Fulfilling the Central Purpose of Your Life* (Nashville: Word, 1998), p. 135.

15. Guinness, *The Call*, pp. 134-35.

16. See Clive Wright's development of the Judaic and early Christian perspectives on wealth creation, *The Business of Virtue* (London: SPCK, 2004), pp. 4-12.

progressively retreated from providing ethical perspectives and a systematic theology of wealth creation. Representative of this is the work of R. H. Tawney. In his *Religion and the Rise of Capitalism* (1926), Tawney makes a starkly negative assessment of the process: "Compromise is as impossible between the Church of Christ and the idolatry of wealth, which is the practical religion of capitalist societies, as it was between the Church and the State idolatry of the Roman Empire."[17] Of course, Christians have discussed the Protestant work ethic and its affirmation of labor and diligence at length, but this is not a substitute for a deeper integration of religion's ethical teachings on economics.[18] Generally Christian comment on capitalism has assumed that wealth is a temptation; it is limited (there is insufficient to go around) and wealth creation is a zero-sum game (one person's wealth is another's loss). To begin with we must understand what we mean by the creation of wealth.

Wealth creation, as Clive Wright defines it, is "the process whereby needs and wants are satisfied."[19] We create wealth by identifying and meeting more needs and wants. Wright notes that "the capacity to add value is, it would seem, unique to the human species. By the stimulation of desire we are metaphorically, and almost literally able to turn dross to gold. It is an act of creation. And it would appear to be of infinite potential."[20] Business exists not mainly to make a profit but to meet needs and wants and to do so profitably.[21]

Wright develops in outline a Christian theology of wealth creation through the following affirmations, which I offer in summary form:

- The Old Testament is generally positive about wealth, seeing it as a blessing of God and imposing on it an economic morality. (We will take up this matter later in discussing the Jubilee.)

17. R. H. Tawney, *Religion and the Rise of Capitalism,* rev. ed. (London: Penguin, 1990), p. 280, quoted in Wright, *The Business of Virtue,* p. 23.

18. Wright, *The Business of Virtue,* p. 14. Wright offers an excellent summary of the history of economic thinking in both the Jewish and Christian eras.

19. Wright, *The Business of Virtue,* p. 47.

20. Wright, *The Business of Virtue,* p. 48.

21. See Wright's careful discussion of "wants and needs," *The Business of Virtue,* p. 49.

- The Old Testament also warns against the danger of wealth leading to autonomy and self-sufficient arrogance (Deut. 8:17-18).
- While Jesus warns against the idolatry of wealth as mammon (Matt. 6:24, KJV) he does not deny the world of business but accepts it as part of everyday life. Jesus draws many of his teachings from the world of the marketplace.
- God's act of creating the universe and declaring it good affirms the essential goodness of the material world and the worthiness of exploring and developing it.
- Human beings have a part to play in the continuing process of creation.
- In creating God-imaging creatures, God has endowed humankind with freedom of choice (albeit limited freedom) and creativity, qualities essential to wealth creation.
- Undoubtedly, sin plays into our understanding of wealth creation. Meeting needs and wants can easily turn into covetousness and greed. Also, the distribution of wealth is unequal and no system has been devised to obtain perfect equality without restricting freedom of choice. Capitalism, like democracy, is the best of all imperfect systems. Winston Churchill is famous for describing democracy as "the worst form of government — except all the other forms that have been tried from time to time."[22]
- God's concern for the whole of life and the whole person suggests that even wealth creation, though it may be abused and misdirected, is not beyond the reach of God's forgiveness and redemption.
- In particular, we are called to service and especially to be servants of the poor, both by caring for the poor and by eliminating poverty. Wright puts it this way: "Wealth is created only by serving the needs and wants of our fellow human beings. At the same time we serve them we exercise the option for the poor because we create the only means by which poverty can be alleviated — wealth. As in so much of the human condition there is a paradox here. We deploy dubious motives such as greed as the means to

22. Quoted in Wright, *The Business of Virtue*, p. 74.

overcome poverty. For the Christian, the paradox can be resolved when the motive of greed is replaced by that of service."[23]

- Before the Industrial Revolution wealth was limited. One person's meal was at the expense of someone else's hunger. But with the changes since that revolution humankind's capacity to produce goods is no longer a zero sum game, especially with the application of technology in the new "weightless economy." Regrettably, however, the ability to distribute goods effectively for all humankind has not matched humankind's ability to produce.[24]

So the secularization of wealth creation occurred within a culture shaped by Christian thought, including key tenets derived from Christian faith. Wright lists these:

> the autonomy of the individual and his or her responsibility for personal decisions; the awareness that the material conditions of existence in this world are not fixed but can be shaped to improve the standard of living; the creative instinct that can be fostered in each person; the concept of service to others as a special duty upon each member of the community. Secularization did not eliminate these concepts: indeed it integrates them into the economic system.[25]

So wealth creation is an essentially good human activity. But it is part of the purpose of God on a very large scale.

God's Global Plan

God is on a global mission. God's original command to Adam and Eve was to "fill the earth." They were supposed to extend the sanctuary garden (Eden) into the world. They sinned and were forced out of the garden. Then, as recounted in Genesis 11, the people of Shinar built a

23. Wright, *The Business of Virtue*, p. 81.
24. Wright, *The Business of Virtue*, pp. 46-83.
25. Wright, *The Business of Virtue*, p. 206.

tower to try to reach heaven and to solidify their autonomous and uniform culture (for they had one language). So God came down and scattered them physically and culturally. This act was both judgment (a condemnation of their self-made autonomous world and lifestyle) and fulfillment (by forcing them to get on with the job of filling the earth).

This filling, however, was not meant to be in the bland uniformity of the people of Shinar. The reason has to do with the God in whose image we have been made. God is one God in three persons who relate without merging. The Greek term for this is *perichoresis*. It means interanimation, interpenetration, not a bland homogenization of "one God" but a rich community of Father, Son, and Holy Spirit with each for the other and all for the one. Dallas Willard says, "The ultimate reality [is] an interpersonal union too 'one' to be many and too 'many' to be just one."[26]

God made humankind a duality (male and female), insisting that human life should not be a bland uniformity but a rich co-humanity through the creation of diverse cultures, lifestyles, and languages. It was to this mission — blessing all the nations — that Abraham was called, and all children of Abraham through faith in Jesus Christ. The antithesis of God's global mission is the tower of Babel. The prototype of this global mission is the day of Pentecost — the vision of which inspired Paul in his apostolic mission and his letters — a rich unity through diversity. The consummation of this global mission is in the New Jerusalem — an international, inter-racial community that is heterogeneous with all tribes, peoples, languages, and cultures, integrated "perichoretically," without merging, around the throne of God and Jesus the Lamb.

Globalization as experienced in the world today is a largely homogenizing phenomenon that is forcing people to find their identities in smaller racial and ethnic groups, ironically, at a time when we are living for the first time in a global village. Yet, at the same time, a rich intercourse of cultures and gifts flows between nations in the emerg-

26. Dallas Willard, *The Divine Conspiracy: Rediscovering Our Hidden Life in God* (San Francisco: HarperSanFrancisco, 1998), p. 246.

ing world economy that even the Fathers of the church long ago likened to the members of Christ's body — arms, eyes, mouths, and feet — a lovely unity through diversity in which we can genuinely say "I need you." Michael Novak notes, "Commerce, as several of the Eastern fathers of the Catholic Church wrote, notably St. John Chrysostom, is the material bond among peoples that exhibits, as if symbolically, the unity of the human race — or, as he dared to put it in mystical language, shows forth as a material sign the 'mystical body of Christ.'"[27]

One implication of this is that world trade can contribute substantially to world peace. Robert Richards, an economist, asks, "Can you today in your most bizarre thought-process or most wild, outlandish thinking even imagine the Japanese bombing Pearl Harbor? Of course not. Even raising the question seems nonsensical for one simple reason: they would be declaring war on their best customer. The well-being of the typical Japanese family is directly related to the well-being of the United States and vice versa."[28]

But, as I have said, the Old and New Testaments include a moral economic correction about wealth creation.

The Jubilee

Paul Williams, mentioned above, is convinced that there is a "distinctively Christian economics, applicable to modern society, and rooted in the fundamental relational nature of God and the biblical revelation. The relational objectives that shape market processes in the biblical approach constitute a Christian paradigm for the socio-economic organization of society in distinction to either the right or left-wing politics of capitalism currently on offer."[29] This Christian economics is based primarily on the Old Testament legislation about the Jubilee in

27. Michael Novak, *Business as a Calling: Work and the Examined Life* (New York: The Free Press, 1996), pp. 46-47.

28. Robert Richards, *God and Business: Christianity's Case for Capitalism* (Fairfax, Va.: Xulon Press, 2002), pp. 378-79.

29. Paul S. Williams, "Hermeneutics for Economists: The Relevance of the Bible to Economics" (master's thesis, Regent College, 1995), p. iv.

Leviticus 25, the pronouncements of the prophets about social and economic justice, the fulfillment of the Jubilee vision announced by Jesus in his inaugural sermon in Luke 4:18-19, and the ultimate vision of the kingdom of God in the New Heaven and New Earth (Rev. 21–22). We are to see in this Old Testament legislation a paradigm of the form of life we are now invited to live under the New Covenant inaugurated by the coming of Christ. Thus, as Chris Wright proposes, "paradigms provide us with objectives without requiring literal transposition of ancient Israelite practice."[30]

The prophets pointed out that Israel had betrayed intimacy with God and trusted in idols, foreign gods, or other nations; further, they had failed to live by God's laws and so had failed to become a model nation. This happened through unjust decrees, oppression of the poor, corrupt and dishonest practices.[31] The prophets addressed several concerns:

- The oppression of the poor
- The manipulation of currency — This is the real concern of the "accurate weights and measures" statements, which are not about fair prices but reliable and fair currency.
- The selling of discarded grain swept up from the threshing floor
- The accumulation of land by a few (Isa. 5:8 — "join house to house" and "add field to field")
- The defrauding a man of his home and inheritance (Mic. 2:2)

Ezekiel saw the renewal of the Jubilee as part of the restoration of the glory of the nation (46:16-18). In particular the Jubilee provisions

---

30. Christopher J. H. Wright, *Living as the People of God: The Relevance of Old Testament Ethics* (Leicester: Inter-Varsity Press, 1998), p. 89. Further, developing the *typological* interpretation — the land typifies our share in fellowship and life in Christ as believers. The socio-economic dimensions of the Jubilee were expressed in the communal sharing expected of believers (Acts 2:44-45; 1 Tim. 6:18; Rom. 15:26-27). However, the Jubilee is fundamentally and gloriously a type of Christ's whole ministry (Luke 4:18-19) — the release from bondage and the restoration to relationship with God and others (Eph. 2:11-12). The *eschatological* interpretation points to the New Creation (Mic. 4:4; Zech. 3:10; John 14:2-3).

31. Isa. 10:1-4; Jer. 2:34; 5:1; 5:26-29; 7:1-11; Amos 2:6-8; 4:1-3; 5:7-13; 8:4-7.

of Leviticus 25 provide a paradigm for envisioning an economic way of functioning not only for the church but the world.[32] The central thrust of this legislation is as follows:

- God trusts the land to families who do not own the land (God does) but can profit by the land even if there is economic hardship.
- If the land must be "sold" all that can be sold is the lease-hold right (based on the number of years to the next Jubilee) and eventually it must be returned to the family.
- Those that fall into debt or who have been forced to work as wage laborers are released and restored to their property.

Williams comments: "Far from representing an abandonment of the laws of supply and demand or enforcing economic loss on those dispossessed of land on the Jubilee Year, these provisions actually create a perfectly transparent leasehold market in land."[33] Williams critiques Ron Sider, who says this means abandoning the laws of supply and demand. In contrast Williams asserts, "What is at the same time prohibited by this text is a freehold market in land, because God owns the freehold. . . . Fundamentally, the Jubilee laws would prevent the accumulation of land ownership in the hands of a few wealthy farmers and the permanent alienation of any Israelite families from the economic and social foundations of their society."[34] A dramatic example of this is the ruling that Zelophehad's daughters must marry within the clan (Num. 36:1-12).

What did these provisions do? First, they guaranteed the centrality of the extended family in Israelite life. Second, they limited economic inequality by banning interest and preventing the permanent break-up of the relation between a family and their land. Third, the ban on inter-

32. The chapter has four parts: (1) 1-7 sabbatical year; (2) 8-13 jubilee year; (3) 14-34 land ownership; (4) 35-55 hired labor. If a man is forced to work for someone else he is not to be treated as a slave but as a hired worker. In the Year of Jubilee he is free to return to the family land.

33. Williams, "Hermeneutics for Economists," p. 143.

34. Williams, "Hermeneutics for Economists," p. 143.

est discouraged lending outside the kinship group. "Those with surplus capital would have no economic incentive to lend outside their kin group, (1) because they would get no return and (2) because they risk losing the capital entirely in the year of debt cancellation."[35] In contrast, Sider advocates state-sanctioned transfers of wealth through the tax system, and this would result in those who received transfers essentially receiving a state-enforced handout. But, says Williams, this would also be a disincentive to the work of the rich.[36]

The key assumption of capitalism is the economics of choice. Individuals optimize choice to maximize their utility. For this to work there must be a free market for labor and capital, and free trade. In contrast to capitalism, the economic provisions of the Old Testament (and what Israel was to model to the nations) were founded on God's ultimate ownership, the strong link between an extended family and the means of production, the reinforcement of community and kinship through prohibiting lending at interest (since there would be no incentive to lend outside the kinship group if there were nothing to be gained by it), and the provision of release and renewal for those who had experienced economic hard times. Old Testament economic provisions are fundamentally relational and communal.[37]

Going still further, Williams proposes that biblical economics is based on stewardship. He contrasts biblical economics with the prevailing model of capitalism in the North and West. Economic activity must be fruitful, must care for creation, and must support a God-honoring culture, in contrast to Western capitalism's clear objective of the maximization of wealth, which leads to rising social and environmental costs.[38] Biblical economics works for relational peace, in

---

35. Williams, "Hermeneutics for Economists," p. 147.

36. Williams, "Hermeneutics for Economists," p. 150.

37. In his treatment of the Jewish perspective on wealth, Clive Wright concludes, "prosperity is a sign of God's blessing. But the wealth we create carries with it an obligation to use it for the benefit of the community as a whole." Wright, *The Business of Virtue*, p. 6.

38. Williams, "Hermeneutics for Economists," p. 138. See also see Craig Gay's critique of Novak on responsibility rather than rights. *Markets and Morality* 5, no. 1: 127-34.

contrast to capitalism's vision of individual freedom. Instead of seeking the good of the whole, as biblical economics proposes, capitalism is concerned with individual utility, which leads to the justification of greed and idolatry of wealth. Whereas modern capitalism emphasizes the importance of complete mobility in order to maximize wealth generation, the Bible restricts the mobility of capital, particularly to maximize social relationship and stability (which includes relative labor immobility). Even more fundamentally, whereas modern capitalism prioritizes the freedom of the individual over the cohesion of the community, the Bible is willing to sacrifice elements of individual freedom (for example, whom you can marry) and wealth generation in order to secure the freedom to relate.[39]

Does Jubilee have direct application to the local and the global economy? Williams asserts that it does in three areas: First, Jubilee speaks to land ownership. "A whole range of modern laws tend to undermine the possibility of a long term relationship between a family, a community, and a place. . . . Reform of inheritance laws and the enablement of family trusts would help in this regard."[40] Second, Jubilee has current application in the ban on interest. Williams suggests the value of local credit unions, community banks, and programs to capture regionally produced savings to be available for regional investment projects. And third, Jubilee champions the centrality of the extended family. Western economics has, by and large, undermined the role of the extended family "in favor of the state (as the provider of welfare), the company (as the context for economic activity), the nuclear family (as the main source of allegiance), and the individual (the basic unit of society)."[41]

But implementing kingdom economics along these lines and bringing transformation to business, whether locally or globally, is bound to face resistance.

---

39. Williams, "Hermeneutics for Economists," pp. 151-52.
40. Williams, "Hermeneutics for Economists," p. 154.
41. Williams, "Hermeneutics for Economists," p. 155.

The Powers

In scripture the terms "powers," "principalities," "thrones," and "authorities," used mainly by the apostle Paul, cover a series of realities that profoundly affect our life in the here and now. They range from "visible" social structures, economic systems (like capitalism), ideologies, and judicial and governmental systems, to "invisible" spiritual forces and personages that cause resistance: death, mammon, the demonic, and Satan. Amazingly, these powers were originally created by God and for God; that is, they were made good and made for our good (Col. 1:15-17). We were meant to live in an ordered universe — a cosmos, not a chaos. The powers are like dikes that hold back the chaos. But the powers have been colonized by Satan; they have taken on a life of their own; they have become resistant and godlike in influence. Yet, according to Colossians 2:13-15, Christ did three things with the powers when he died on the cross and was resurrected: He disarmed them; he showed how their strength is pretentious and puny; and he triumphed over them. They still have an effect on us, but essentially they have met their match. One writer describes them as chained beasts kicking themselves to death.[42]

Capitalism and globalization are powers. Further, the person working in the world has to encounter other dimensions of resistance, including greed, predatory competition, unjust practices, systemic unemployment, exploitation of labor, and sometimes the demonic. Speaking to the soul-grabbing appeal of the powers, Max Stackhouse says: "The really compelling powers, after all, are not im-

---

42. See a more extended treatment of the powers in R. Paul Stevens, "Principalities and Powers," in Robert Banks and R. Paul Stevens, eds., *The Complete Book of Everyday Christianity* (Downers Grove, Ill.: InterVarsity Press, 1997), pp. 795-801. Other resources include Peter L. Berger, *The Sacred Canopy: Elements of a Sociological Theory of Religion* (Garden City, N.Y.: Doubleday, 1967); H. Berkhof, *Christ and the Powers*, trans. John Howard Yoder (Scottdale, Penn.: Herald, 1962); D. G. Reid, "Principalities and Powers," in *Dictionary of Paul and His Letters*, ed. F. F. Hawthorne, R. Martin, and D. G. Reid (Downers Grove, Ill.: InterVarsity, 1993); H. Schleir, *Principalities and Powers in the New Testament* (New York: Herder & Herder, 1964); Walter Wink, *Naming the Powers: The Language of Power in the New Testament* (Philadelphia: Fortress Press, 1984); John Howard Yoder, *The Politics of Jesus* (Grand Rapids: Eerdmans, 1972).

personal dynamics, or morally or spiritually neutral forces like gravity. They grab after people's souls, they shape mass perceptions; they
form an ethos and shape the habits, mores, and range of possible institutions and life plans that persons and groups can imagine or extend."[43]

How are we to relate to them? Historically the church has related
to the powers in four ways, depending on their metaphysical explanation. If the problem is seen as demonic, the solution is to intercede
and to practice exorcism. If the problem is assessed to be structures
colonized by Satan, then the solution is to approach them with suffering powerlessness as the Anabaptists and Mennonites have generally done. If the problem is diagnosed as broken, fallen, and sinful
structures, then the solution is to get in there as regents and make a
difference in politics, business, economics, government, and the media. If, however, the assessment is that evil structures are unredeem-
able, as the Marxist analysis of capitalism assumes, then there should
be a just revolution and the replacement of the evil structures.

Globalization is a power that can be redeemed through all the
strategies of grappling with the powers: prayer, suffering powerlessness, transformative participation, and in some cases, replacement.
Max Stackhouse was asked, Is God in globalization? His answer: Yes
and no! Yes, God is in globalization, knitting together nations in trade
and a community of enterprise, nations that might otherwise be war-
ring against each other. God is in globalization helping some nations
increase their wealth and lifting the poor. Max Stackhouse argues
that God is in the process providentially and that the social-cultural
forces most often identified as globalization were formed in societies
fundamentally stamped by Christian theological ethics; that is, Christianity is largely responsible for it![44] And no, God is not in globalization where it increases dependence on and debt owed to the rich
North and West, where it dehumanizes people in sweat factories,
where it rapes the earth instead of being a steward.

43. Max L. Stackhouse, "Is God in Globalization?" paper presented at Regent
College, 1999.
44. Stackhouse, "Is God in Globalization?" p. 16.

Is globalization the kingdom of God? No. But can we work in the global economy and do so as agents for the kingdom of God? Yes. Is globalization an opportunity to work and serve towards the vision of the New Jerusalem? Yes, if we work and serve in transformative service, in fellowship, in prophetic discernment, and in proclamation. As Stackhouse says, "Christ is bringing these principalities, authorities, and dominions under the laws of God for the purposes of God as part of the mercy of God, and . . . all believers are called to be agents of this reconciliation process for the glory of God."[45]

Economic globalization holds both peril and promise. Christians need to *understand* the phenomenon, something that is seldom evidenced in pronouncements from church pulpits.[46] Christians need to have a *theology of wealth creation* and to understand what God's purpose and promise are in relation to creating and satisfying needs and wants. Christians need *not shrink from participating* wholeheartedly in the economic order, even in multinational corporations, with all the attendant difficulties, where they can "make a difference." Christians must also *see the incredible possibilities of the expansion of the kingdom of God* through the expansion of world trade (as we saw in the last chapter) in the same way that Carey envisioned the gospel going everywhere at the beginning of the modern era. And finally Christians must *take the lead in caring for the poor,* especially providing the means of their own wealth creation mainly though not exclusively through micro- and medium-sized economic development.[47] Ralph McCall, a Swiss entrepreneur who has worked in multinational companies, says that Europe may well be the "needy people group" and the multinational corporation "the lost tribe" that should be reached.

45. Stackhouse, "Is God in Globalization?" p. 19.

46. Robert Richards has a very practical section on "implications for the clergy" in Richards, *God and Business,* pp. 420-41.

47. The record of the church in providing substantial transformation of society is stunning. Edmund H. Oliver in *The Social Achievements of the Christian Church* (Vancouver: Regent College Publishing, 2004) records this story from the first to the twentieth centuries.

For Discussion

Consider Tom Campbell's dilemma.

1. What thoughts and feelings might Tom have as he ponders the boss's offer?
2. What "powers" is he grappling with?
3. What opportunities will he have, if he accepts, to implement a positive mission?
4. Who will be affected by his decision either way?
5. To whom might he turn for advice and support as he wades through this decision?
6. Would "doing more good than harm" be a sufficient reason to proceed?
7. How might Tom influence his company, and their Uzbek client, towards a holistic and humane practice of business?

For Further Reading

Friedman, Thomas L. *The Lexus and the Olive Tree.* New York: Farrar, Straus, and Giroux, 1999.

Gay, Craig. *With Liberty and Justice for Whom? The Recent Evangelical Debate over Capitalism.* Grand Rapids: Eerdmans, 1991.

Richards, Robert. *God and Business: Christianity's Case for Capitalism.* Fairfax, Va.: Xulon Press, 2002.

Rifkin, Jeremy. *The End of Work: The Decline of the Global Work-Force and the Dawn of the Post-Market Era.* London: Penguin, 2000.

Stackhouse, Max, Tim Dearborn, and Scott Paeth, eds. *The Local Church in a Global Era: Reflections for a New Century.* Grand Rapids: Eerdmans, 2000.

Yoder, John Howard. *The Politics of Jesus.* Grand Rapids: Eerdmans, 1972.

———— ◆ ◆ ◆ ————

PART TWO

MOTIVATION
Towards a Marketplace Spirituality

7

Going Deep

No man [sic] can afford to live in the marketplace who does not also live in the desert.

Archbishop Hume

Someone asked Abba Anthony [the founder of Eastern monasticism], "What must one do in order to please God?" The old man replied, "Pay attention to [these three things]: whoever you may be, always have God before your eyes whatever you do; do it according to the testimony of the holy Scriptures; in whatever place you live, do not easily leave it."

The Sayings of the Desert Fathers

We turn now from theology to spirituality, from meaning to motivation. Spirituality is "in" today. But often it is the search for the divine being inside the person. So a spate of books and seminars encourages us to take not only our hands, minds, and hearts to work — but also our spirits. Personally, I welcome the recognition that human beings at work are not merely thinking machines or heartless computers but persons with spirits. We bring our whole person to work, body, soul, and spirit. But there is a more critical reason for us to explore the spirituality of business.

Busy, But Not Deep

Business is stressful. The sources of stress are not hard to find: shifts in the work world — sometimes a weekly paradigm shift, technology, relational pressures at work and home, the 24-7 work week, cultural shifts that press us to be politically correct and wary of possible litigation, and the pressure of the global economy. But the most pernicious source of stress is drivenness within ourselves, which makes us constantly busy. Not surprisingly the word "business" is close to the word "busy-ness."

The symptoms of "busy" people are all too visible: They live compulsive, habitual lives. They have no time for friends, are too preoccupied to keep Sabbath, feel guilty when resting or doing nothing, and fill up every open slot in their date book or Palm Pilot. They are consistently "overbooked." The teacher in Ecclesiastes describes it well: "Then I saw that all toil and all skill in work come from one person's envy of another" (4:4). Commenting on this compulsive money-maker, Derek Kidner says "he has surrendered to a mere craving and to the endless process of feeding it. . . . Such a man [or woman], even with a wife [or husband] and children, will have little time for them, convinced that he is toiling for their benefit although his heart is elsewhere, devoted and wedded to his projects."[1] Mary Baechler, cofounder and president of Racing Strollers, in an article entitled "Death of a Marriage," said: "There was a fundamental moment when I chose the business over the marriage." Baechler asks reflectively,

---

1. Derek Kidner, *The Message of Ecclesiastes: A Time to Mourn and a Time to Dance* (Downers Grove. Ill.: InterVarsity Press, 1976), p. 47.

"How does someone who is obsessed live peacefully with someone who isn't?"[2]

Often the source of such busy-ness is the desire to find approval for one's accomplishments. But the busy person may be unaware of the deep well of this negative motivation within. Such people do not know themselves. Many leaders, whether in business, politics, or church, are trying to escape from themselves. They have what psychologist Eric Fromm called "market-oriented personalities"; they are people who sell themselves to purchase signs of acceptance.

Good questions for people like this to ask are: Why am I so sensitive to criticism? Why am I compelled to fill up the gaps in my date book? Why do I find it hard to give up places, positions, and ministries? Why am I so competitive? Why is it so important for me to succeed? Why am I unable to let go of the pain of others? Why am I afraid to be alone, always seem to need people? Why am I so discontent? Why do I need to control others? Why am I so busy? Why do I burn out relationships? Why am I sometimes so unmotivated?

Christian Spirituality

Christian spirituality is a way of life for disciples of Christ. It is the lived experience of God, rooted in the revealed word of God, grounded in community, and illuminated by the rich tradition of the church. It is concerned with all of life, not merely piety and not exclusively prayer. It is both individual and corporate, churchly and worldly, inward and outward, concerned with personal relationship with God and with justice in the world. Furthermore, Christian spirituality is biblical and trinitarian.

Biblical spirituality is characterized by the irruption of God in the thick of life, seeing *through* life, issues, situations, and places, as though we were looking through a Kodachrome transparency. Open the Bible and we see God at work in the world. More than that, the Bible "reads" us — tells us who we are and reveals what we are doing.

2. Mary Baechler, "Death of a Marriage," *INC,* April 1994, p. 76.

Eugene Peterson puts it this way: "'Biblical' means an orientation and immersion in the large, immense world of God's revelation in contrast to the small, cramped world of human 'figuring out.'"[3]

A fully Christian spirituality is also trinitarian. That is, the lived experience relates to the Triune God — Father, Son, and Spirit. Trinitarian spirituality has five dimensions: First, it means that our fellowship and community is not just with other seekers and disciples; we are actually taken into the fellowship and love-life of Father, Son, and Spirit (1 John 1:3). Speaking to this with great eloquence, Thomas Torrance says that the doctrine of the holy Trinity is "the fundamental grammar of our knowledge of God. . . . Through his self-revelation in the incarnation God has opened himself to us in such a way that we may know him in the inner relations of his divine Being and have communion with him in his divine life as Father, Son, and Holy Spirit.[4] Second, a trinitarian spirituality means that the God whom we know is not distant in heaven but immanent and present, not only in sacred places and sacred times but in the warp and woof of everyday life. The incarnation of God in Jesus and the empowering presence of the Holy Spirit mean that God is with us in even the grittiest business situation.

Third, our lived experience of God is like the interpenetration but not the merging of Father, Son, and Spirit. The Greek word used for this is *perichoresis*. We are becoming truly ourselves in the context of a love relationship. It is communion with God, not being swallowed up in God like a drop of water in the ocean. The apostle Paul spoke of this as "I in Christ" and "Christ in me." Paul was still Paul, but he was in communion with God. Fourth, the concern and purpose of the Triune God into which we are immersed is not merely redemptive and curative (saving souls and mending people) but also unitive and creative (making things beautiful and bringing things and people together).

And finally, the Trinity helps us pray. Prayer is not easy. But as my colleague Edwin Hui says, "Paul has anticipated our difficulties and

---

3. Eugene Peterson, lecture at Regent College, Vancouver, B.C., 1990.

4. Thomas F. Torrance, *Trinitarian Perspective: Toward Doctrinal Agreement* (Edinburgh: T&T Clark, 1994), p. 1.

has reminded us of the most fundamental experience or reality of the life of prayer (and there is no other life than the life of prayer . . .): first, even as 'we do not know what we ought to pray for, but the Spirit himself intercedes for us with groans that words cannot express' (Rom. 8:26 [NIV]), and second, 'Christ Jesus . . . is at the right hand of God and is also interceding for us' (Rom. 8:34 [NIV])." So, continues Hui, "In this praying event, the person who prays has an unmistakably three-facets 'experience' of the Triune God as she is being incorporated by the 'Spirit' into the life of the 'Son' towards the 'Father.' It is an experience of . . . being invited into the conversation of God to God in and through the one who prays."[5]

"I have no time to pray," says a busy executive. But it is not just executives. Recently I went for two days of prayer to a Benedictine monastery near Vancouver. But the guest master, whom I have known for thirty years, said to me: "How I would love to go to a monastery to have two days of quiet. The phone rings. There are endless e-mails and letters and the constant duties of my work!" Not a few business people feel "burned out" after a few decades in the commercial world and think that they want to do something "significant" by getting out of business. But the solution is in another direction. It starts with recognizing that God is not absent from the marketplace. Ironically, this message is coming largely from people outside the church.

Spirituality without Religion

Among the flood of books and articles on "the new business spirituality" is *New Traditions in Business: Spirit and Leadership in the Twenty-First Century* edited by John Renesch.[6] Coordinating the ideas of

---

5. Edwin Hui, presentation on Spiritual Theology at the Regent College "Whirlwind Tour of the Faculty," Vancouver, B.C., 2000.

6. Authors taking up this challenge include L. Bolman and T. Deal, *Leading with the Soul: An Uncommon Journey of Spirit* (San Francisco: Jossey-Bass, 1995); Denis Breton and Christopher Largent, *The Soul of Economics: Spiritual Evolution Goes to the Marketplace* (Wilmington, Del.: Idea House Publishing Co., 1991), who reinterpret the law, Beatitudes, and Lord's Prayer as a mythical structure for rethinking economics;

twelve leading thinkers about business tomorrow, Renesch and others propose a new concept of business:

- The company is a community, not a corporation, a system for being, not merely a system for production and profit.
- The new image of the manager is that of a spiritual elder.
- Employees are members of the body working interdependently for the common good.
- While mission statements, vision, goals, and values will continue to *push* a company, a "Higher Purpose" (parallel to the "Higher Power" made popular by Alcoholics Anonymous) will *pull* a company forward.
- The corporation is an equipping (learning) organization that provides an environment for every-member service (ministry) so each person will become more human, more creative, and more integrated with the Higher Purpose.

Renesch and his associates are not alone. In 1997 the British economist Charles Handy wrote eloquently in *The Hungry Spirit* about the need for a recovery of spirit in business. An annual corporate leadership and ethics forum at Harvard University involving key corporate leaders in North America, including Canadian psychologist Martin Rutte, is currently exploring the recovery of spiritual values in the marketplace. The *Vancouver Sun* recently carried an article on Tanis Helliwell, a Canadian New Age therapist and business consultant, who offers a seminar entitled "Take Your Soul to Work." There

---

Jack Canfield and Jacqueline Miller, eds., *Heart at Work: Stories and Strategies for Building Self-Esteem and Reawakening the Soul at Work* (New York: McGraw Hill, 1996); Gilbert Fairholm, *Capturing the Heart of Leadership: Spirituality and Community in the New American Workplace* (Westport, Conn.: Praeger, 1997); Charles Garfield et al. with Michael Toms, *The Soul of Business* (Carlsbad, Calif.: Hay House Inc., 1997); Emilie Griffin, *The Reflective Executive: A Spirituality of Business and Enterprise* (New York: Crossroad, 1993); Os Guiness, *Winning Back the Soul of American Business* (Washington, D.C.: Hourglass Publishers, 1990); Ian Percy, *Going Deep* (Toronto: Macmillan Publishing Co., 1998); and John Renesch, ed., *New Traditions in Business: Spirit and Leadership in the Twenty-First Century* (San Francisco: Berrett-Koehler Publishers, 1992).

is indeed a host of authors, conferences, seminars, and traveling gurus promoting something that is neither simply traditional religion (though it draws heavily on it) nor simply New Age spirituality (though there are affinities).

My thesis student, Jeff Sellers, has helpfully summarized three aspects of this mixture of New Age and traditional religious spiritualities:

- Corporate aspect: higher purpose more than higher profit, ecological sensitivity.
- Personal aspect: self-actualization, autonomy, creativity, spiritual motivation.
- Cosmic aspect: cooperation, harmony, spiritual evolution, and global synergy.[7]

The language used today by many businesspeople taken up with the spirituality movement seems like a return to the revival tents of frontier Christianity: caring, love, spiritual, the human spirit, awakening, backsliding, new heresy, inner resources, inner authority, inner wisdom, soul, the search for a deeper sense of life purpose, co-creation, the pursuit of unconditional love, *metanoia* (repentance), the business leader as a spiritual elder, the need for transcendence, relationship with God, wonderment, evoking spirit, celebration, the corporate cathedral, the Higher Purpose, communion, spiritual values, disciplines, and, remarkably, tradition. One of Renesch's authors analyzes the reason: "The basic positivistic and reductionistic premises of scientific materialism are being replaced by a new set of beliefs that include increased faith in reason guided by deep intuition. In other words, a 'respiritualization' of society is taking place that is more experiential and less fundamentalistic than most of the historically familiar forms of structured religion."[8] The alleged paradigm

7. Jeff Sellers, "New Age or Kingdom Come? Description and Critique of the 'New Business Spirituality' in Light of a Biblical Spirituality of Work" (master's thesis, Regent College, Vancouver, B.C., April 2000), pp. 18-103.

8. Willis Harmen in Renesch, ed., *New Traditions*, p. 16.

shift of the century is not a return to religion but to spirituality without religion.

The corporation again has a soul and a calling. Vision is replacing profit as the raison d'être of a company. A corporation exists to make a long-term contribution to society, indeed to the globe. As older social cultures, cities, neighborhoods, and churches have become atomized, business cultures will be the new tribes, the new neighborhoods. Corporations *are* our new communities. One indication of this change of focus is the reminted mission statements of large corporations to show that they are "not mainly for profit" but "for good." Samples include:

Du Pont: "A new partnership with nature"
Mary Kay Cosmetics: "To give unlimited opportunity to women"
Merk: "To preserve and improve human life"
Sony: "To experience the joy of advancing and applying technology for the benefit of the public"
Wal-Mart: "To give ordinary folk the chance to buy the same things as rich people"
Walt Disney: "To make people happy."[9]

Crucial to this respiritualization of business is the role of intuition and awakening of will, joy, strength, and compassion through the liberating power of relating to a higher purpose that inspires creativity and a calling. Thus we are challenged with soul work, not merely remuneration or the challenge of a career. Most commonly this higher purpose is not thought of as a being or power outside the system, because nothing is outside the system! The new business spirituality affirms "inner wisdom, authority, and resources, challenging the scientific materialism that was dominant in the earlier part of the [twentieth] century."[10] The private corporation, these thinkers claim, has the potential of providing spiritual eldership for

9. Charles Handy, *The Hungry Spirit: Beyond Capitalism — A Quest for Purpose in the Modern World* (London: Hutchinson, 1997), p. 78.
10. Harmen in Renesch, ed., *New Traditions*, p. 15.

the young and of extending creation across geographical, cultural, and political boundaries — the potential to become the most powerful institution on earth. So the church of Max Weber's study *The Protestant Ethic and the Spirit of Capitalism* has been reinvented as the corporate cathedral.

Who would have thought that post-Protestant Calvinism, which fired one generation of entrepreneurs, would be replaced after several decades of spiritual wilderness with business spirituality without religion? Many of the concepts of the New Business Spirituality are entirely congruent with historic Christianity and Judaism: co-creativity, spirit, love, service (the same word as "ministry" in Greek), interdependence, community, relationality, global concern, ecological sensitivity, vocation or calling. The New Business Spirituality movement reflects, on one hand, the insatiable hunger of the human being for Someone beyond humankind, for authentic community, and for significant service. On the other hand, this New Business Spirituality needs to address some presuppositional questions.

For example, the New Business Spirituality assumes the intrinsic goodness of human beings without any consideration of the brokenness and sin of people, this latter being the only Christian doctrine that has been empirically verified! "Human transcendence," one of the buzzwords of the movement, is an oxymoron. Human beings cannot transcend themselves, though the attempt to do so is the tree of the knowledge of good and evil extended into the twenty-first century (Gen. 2:17; 3:5). Nor can humans save themselves. So there is new life without new birth, repentance without turning to God, hope without a substantial and worthy end for the whole human story, god without God, and faith without a transcendent divine being.[11] It was only a

11. One presupposition at issue is anthropology, the implicit view of the human person. Much of the New Business Spirituality deifies the person in speaking of the "the limitless potential of the individual," and the "Divinity that is at our deepest core" (William Miller in Renesch, ed., *New Traditions*, p. 71). Authors in the field of business spirituality use "transcendence" for the Buddhist experience of transcending all distinctions so that emptiness equals fulfillment (Herman B. Maynard in Renesch, ed., *New Traditions*, p. 42). A second issue is soteriology or redemption. The New Business Spirituality appeals to the intrinsic goodness of humankind without

few decades ago that psychiatrist R. D. Laing, ahead of his time, said that Amos had prophesied that there would be " not a famine of bread, or a thirst for water, but of hearing the words of the LORD" (Amos 8:11). That time, Laing prophesied, has come.[12] The New Business Spirituality addresses the God-shaped vacuum in the souls of people in the workplace, a gap that has unfortunately been left unattended by the religiously occupied church and the secular humanism of Western culture. But there is another way, and it is one rooted in the long tradition of the Christian faith.

The Mixed Life

In *One Minute Wisdom* Anthony de Mello relates the following conversation: "Said the Master to the businessman: 'As the fish perishes on dry land, so you perish when you get entangled in the world. The fish must return to the water, you must return to solitude.' The businessman was aghast. 'Must I give up my business and go into the monastery?' 'No, no. Hold on to your business and go into your heart.'"[13] In the history of Christian spirituality, this has been called the "mixed life." It is a life of active engagement mixed with withdrawal to know God and ourselves — John Calvin's famous "double knowledge," which he said was the heart of true religion. The mixed life was expounded brilliantly by Walter Hilton, a fourteenth-century Augustinian canon, in *Letters to a Layman*. Responding to a business-

---

dealing with human brokenness, disorder (sin). Theory X and Y wrestles with these double truths about humankind (see Lee Hardy, *The Fabric of This World: Inquiries into Calling, Career Choice, and the Design of Human Work* [Grand Rapids: Eerdmans, 1990]). While human beings cooperate with God in the process of redemption, ultimately humankind cannot save itself. A third issue is epistemology and ontology. The acceptance of the subjective principle of epistemology — we invent what we know; what we believe is what is — leads to a multiverse.

12. R. D. Laing, *The Politics of Experience and the Bird of Paradise* (Harmondsworth, England: Penguin Books, 1967), p. 118.

13. Quoted in Elizabeth A. Dreyer, *Earth Crammed with Heaven: A Spirituality of Everyday Life* (New York: Paulist Press, 1994), p. 89.

person who wanted to leave business to know God better, Hilton wrote:

> You ought to mingle the works of an active life with spiritual endeavours of a contemplative life, and then you will do well. For you should at certain times be busy with Martha in the ordering and care of your household, children, employees, tenants, or neighbours. If they do well, you ought to comfort and help them in this; if they do badly, then teach them to amend themselves and correct them. And you should regard and wisely know how your property and worldly goods are being administered, conserved, or intelligently invested by your employees, in order that you might, with the increase, the more bountifully fulfil the deeds of mercy to your fellow Christians. At other times you should, with Mary, leave off the busyness of the world and sit down meekly at the feet of our Lord, there to be in prayer, holy thought, and contemplation of him, as he gives you grace. And so you should go from one activity to the other in maintaining your stewardship, fulfilling both aspects of the Christian life. In so doing, you will be keeping well the order of charitable love.[14]

This is precisely what Jesus did. As I read the gospels I am convinced that Jesus did not live a "balanced life," with everything scheduled and poised, as some have proposed. At times he could not eat because of the press of activity. But Jesus did live a disciplined life. He had times of fasting, whole nights given to prayer, and special times of intercession (Luke 22:32). But most evident is his rhythm of engagement and withdrawal — what we are here calling the mixed life. In John 6:15 we have a brief reference to this practice when people were about to take him by force and make him king. Luke tells us that "[Jesus] would withdraw to deserted places and pray" (Luke 5:16). In Mark 6:45 we have the strange, even shocking words, "he dismissed the crowd." The crowds did not leave on their own accord. He sent

---

14. Walter Hilton, *Toward a Perfect Love,* trans. David Jeffrey (Portland, Ore.: Multnomah Press, 1985), pp. 8-9.

them away, saying "no" to the sick, wounded, guilt-ridden, and demon-possessed while he went to be alone with the Father. For Christians the need of the world is not the call of God. The call comes from God and we will need to withdraw frequently and regularly from compulsive need-meeting in order to hear the voice of God.

Critical to living the mixed life is knowing that we are beloved of God, that God takes delight in us, and that we do not have to do anything to gain God's love and approval. My colleague Darrell Johnson puts it this way, "Jesus played to an audience of one (the Father)." This contrasted with the Pharisees. "How can you believe," Jesus said to them, "when you accept glory from one another and do not seek the glory that comes from the one who alone is God?" (John 5:44). Many leaders in business, politics, and religion are deeply insecure, and out of that insecurity they base their leadership on the search for one of three things: power, intimacy, or status. The ultimate solution for this is living in the delight of God (Isa. 42:1). We will not know this deep within ourselves without reflection, prayer, and hearing the word of God.

Can this be done in the context of work? Today praying and reflecting in the workplace itself present many problems. Before the information age, work days had "down" and "in-between" times. But now with cell phones and Blackberries attached to our belts or in our purses, and hands-free phones in cars, we hardly have a moment left to be contemplative. We have to create those moments and turn off the phones and personal digital assistants. We need to go for short walks and sometimes be unavailable. Most of our work, though, demands our total attention, unlike the repetitive work that seventeenth-century monk Brother Lawrence enjoyed in the monastery kitchen in that delightful book, *The Practice of the Presence of God.* Many of our prayers in the workplace will be "arrow prayers" like that of Nehemiah in the high pressure of court life: "So I prayed to the God of heaven. Then I said to the king . . ." (2:4-5). We will also experience charismatic moments with an "aha," a celebration of something new and great. And we can relate to our co-workers sacramentally: They are image bearers.

A difficult assignment presents an opportunity for prayer. Brother Lawrence used to say to the Lord at the beginning of a task, "I cannot do this unless you help me." When he made a mistake, he would turn this into a prayer: "Lord, I will never do otherwise unless you mend what is amiss in my life." But we also need longer seasons of withdrawal to pray, celebrate, and refresh ourselves in priorities. Here are some time-tested disciplines that require a block of time at the beginning or end of the day, and sometimes a whole day of withdrawal:[15]

First, we can practice *invocation* and commendation habits at the start or end of the day. Steve Brinn speaks about "simmering" in the morning rather than bounding out of bed.

Second, we can employ *lectio continua,* the continuous reading of scripture to saturate mind and heart with the wide world of God's presence and activity. When we read the Bible from the perspective of life in the world we make several discoveries. The Bible describes ordinary people working and being apprehended by God in the context of everyday life. God reveals himself not mainly in the tent, temple, and church but in the workplace and neighborhood. The Bible shows us how to live in the marketplace with justice, faith, and even shrewdness. Ministry can take place in the context of marketplace activity, as it did with tent-makers Paul, Aquila, and Priscilla. We discover that the marketplace is a metaphor for the kingdom of God that inspires many of the parables of Jesus. We get refreshed in vision and perspective. Personally, I follow a plan of Bible reading that takes me through the Old Testament once a year and the New Testament and Psalms twice a year by reading four chapters a day, two from each testament.[16]

Third, we can practice *lectio divina,* the slow, meditative reading of scripture accompanied by prayer. This involves both meditation on a specific text and memorization of certain texts.

Fourth, by *journal-keeping* we can record our feelings, emotions, longings, and prayers in the presence of God, without self-criticism, by means of a written record. Psalm 42:5-6 is a journal entry: "Why are you cast down, O my soul, and why are you disquieted within me?

15. I acknowledge my indebtedness for some of these suggestions to my colleague Bruce Hindmarsh, "A Mixed Life or a Mixed Up Life?" (paper presented at Regent College marketplace cohort meeting, Knoxville, Tenn., May 2004).

16. *McCheyne's Calendar for Daily Readings* (Carlisle, Pa.: Banner of Truth Trust).

Hope in God; for I shall again praise him, my help and my God." David is talking to God about his own depression in the light of something greater than his experience. In his *Confessions,* Augustine said, "For it is better for them to find you and leave the question unanswered than to find the answer without finding you."[17]

Fifth, we can practice *fasting* — from food — being quiet for God; from things — giving control to God; from people — being alone with God.

Sixth, through *confession* we can express to God with complete candor and honesty a Spirit-born brokenness not only for inappropriate behavior and thoughts, but also for the breach in our relationship with God (1 John 1:9). Augustine said, "I will confess therefore what I know of myself, and what I do not know: for what I know of myself, I know through the shining of your light; and what I do not know of myself, I continue not to know until my darkness shall be made as noonday in your countenance."[18] Confession to another believer is being honest with God in the presence of another (James 5:16). The benefits are a free conscience, inner healing, and sometimes physical healing. Bonhoeffer, in his classic *Life Together,* comments deeply on this: "He who is alone with his sin is utterly alone. . . . The final breakthrough to fellowship does not occur, because, though they have fellowship with one another as believers and as devout people, they do not have fellowship as the undevout, as sinners. The pious fellowship permits no one to be a sinner. So everybody must conceal his sin from himself and from the fellowship." Bonhoeffer continues, "Many Christians are unthinkably horrified when a real sinner is suddenly discovered among the righteous. So we remain alone without sin, living in lies and hypocrisy. The fact is that we are sinners!"[19]

Finally, we can practice *Sabbath.* The word "Sabbath" means to cease, to desist from work and striving, preferably for a complete day each week. We do not "keep" Sabbath; Sabbath keeps us — keeps us focused on God as the ultimate reality, keeps us rightly ordered in terms

17. St. Augustine, *Confessions* (trans. Pine-Coffin) 1.6.

18. St. Augustine, quoted in Kenneth Leech, *True Prayer: An Invitation to Christian Spirituality* (San Francisco: Harper & Row, 1980), p. 123.

19. Dietrich Bonhoeffer, *Life Together* (San Francisco: Harper & Row, 1954), p. 110.

of priorities, and keeps us mindful that we are not accepted by the most important person in the universe because of our performance. My friend Justyn Rees is right when he suggests that more people have died by not keeping this law in the Ten Commandments than by not keeping the "thou shalt not commit murder" law. Stress takes its toll and lots of people die because they do not have a mixed life. And if we are not keeping one day for play, prayer, worship, and contemplation, then we are probably taking ourselves too seriously. Worse than that, we are hurting ourselves. We were made for this weekly celebration, and church worship may well be part of it, but not if Sunday becomes a day of church-related meetings and, in effect, one more work day.[20]

Living the Tension Well

"Going deep" will not eliminate tension. Jacques Ellul puts it this way, "The Bible tells us that the Christian is in the world, and that there he or she must remain. . . ."[21] Some try to disconnect the spiritual life from the material one. Ellul says others moralize and "Christianize" life in the marketplace "covering it up with an ethical glaze." Yet we cannot deny the tension: We live in a sinful world and we cannot change it, or at least not much of it; at the same time we cannot accept it as it is.

> He has sent us into the world, and just as we are involved in the tension between sin and grace, so also we are involved in the tension between these two very contradictory demands. It is a very painful, and a very uncomfortable, situation, but it is the

20. In scripture, Sabbath is a law to be kept, a law not rescinded but fulfilled by Jesus (Exod. 20:8-11; Mark 2:28). It is a blessing, a gift, as we celebrate creation (Exod. 20:8-11) and redemption (Deut. 5:12-15). It is a calling, a vocation; even God rests (Gen. 2:2). It is a sacrament in time and a sign of our relationship with God (Exod. 31:12-13, 17). It is a metaphor of salvation (Heb. 4:9; Matt. 1:18) and a prophecy and foretaste of the New Heaven and New Earth when there will be a continuous Sabbath of threefold harmony among God, creation, and humankind.

21. Jacques Ellul, *The Presence of the Kingdom,* trans. Olive Wyon (New York: Seabury Press, 1948), p. 7.

only position which can be fruitful for the action of the Christian in the world, and for his [sic] life in the world. . . . We must accept — in a spirit of repentance — the fact that our life in the world is necessarily 'scandalous.' . . . To be honest, we must not accept this tension of the Christian, or of the Christian life, as an abstract truth. It must be *lived,* it must be realized, in the most concrete and living way possible.[22]

For Discussion

• A VOICE IN THE WILDERNESS •

As the door gently shut behind Tom Simpson, his partner and long-time friend, Brandon O'Malley, looked over the desk and considered how to fit in Tom's "urgent" request. With telephone message lights flashing, unanswered e-mails running down the full length of his computer screen, and papers all over the office "screaming" for attention, Brandon felt a curious mixture of excitement and anxiety. Tom's client, an unsophisticated Korean businesswoman, was about to be evicted by an unscrupulous landlord from her store space at a prestigious shopping center after having invested thousands of dollars in improvements. The familiar sense of outrage about an injustice rose in Brandon, and he knew this was a case perfect for his skills as a litigation lawyer and his penchant for the underdog. Yet at a deeper level in him a small voice longed to be heard.

This was year twenty-five in Brandon's practice, the first twenty spent working for the Colorado Department of Lands and the past five years working as a member of Imago Law Group — a firm of ten lawyers united by their shared Christian faith and their desire to be in mutually supportive and disciplined relationships. The son of an immigrant alcoholic father and a very dependent mother, Brandon sought all of his life to prove himself and to care first for his mother and siblings and then for others, especially those who were unable to fight for

22. Ellul, *The Presence of the Kingdom,* p. 17, italics his.

themselves. It fit in well with his theology of Jesus as champion of the poor, homeless, and oppressed. Brandon's accomplishments were impressive: top of his class in his school days and a remarkable trial record as a lawyer.

After years of listening to Tom's "gentle" suggestions to leave government and work at a private practice, Brandon had decided to take the risk of starting a practice with the inception of the Imago Law Group. Now, five years later, Brandon had a practice that was bursting at the seams but was struggling financially. He worked with a blend of Tom's commercial clients (who usually paid him handsomely for his services) and downtrodden clients (who were often difficult to deal with and who were challenging when time for collecting fees came around). Despite the busy-ness, making money at the practice was difficult for Brandon because he lacked many of the disciplines essential to the business side of law. Life was chaotic at most times. Calls would go unanswered. Deadlines would not be met. Bills would not go out on time. Retainers would not be obtained. Always available to meet with fellow lawyers and staff, Brandon found himself working twelve to fifteen hours a day and many weekends. Rarely did he say no to a request for services, either from a member of Imago or from a needy prospective client. His wife, Ann, and their children had learned to expect little in the way of time from Brandon and were happy with what they could get. At the bottom of his list were personal times of reflection, prayer, and recreation. Brandon's once intimate relationship with God was distant, only occasionally did Brandon sense the call of his Lord, and even more rarely did he notice the deep cry of his own heart for "home."

So it was strange that today Brandon would notice that a voice that raised questions about whether to take on one more case would keep him at the office until midnight and force him to yet again juggle his overwhelming work load. The new case was perfect: a great injustice that cried out for his unique skills as a litigator and negotiator; another chance to speak for the disempowered. So why the unease? Perhaps just indigestion, and yet. . . .

•　　•

1. What is the surface issue?
2. What are the deeper issues?
3. What factors will influence Brandon in his decision?
4. What resource does Brandon have for making the decision?
5. What does the Bible and Christian faith have to say about issues of identity, significance, loving ourselves, and boundaries?

For Personal Reflection

Review the questions posed in this chapter. Which ones apply to you?

1. Why am I so sensitive to criticism?
2. Why am I compelled to fill up the gaps in my date book?
3. Why do I find it hard to give up places, positions, and ministries?
4. Why am I so competitive?
5. Why is it so important for me to succeed?
6. Why am I unable to let go of the pain of others?
7. Why am I afraid to be alone, always seem to need people?
8. Why am I so discontent?
9. Why do I need to control others?
10. Why am I so busy?
11. Why do I burn out relationships?
12. Why am I sometimes so unmotivated?

For Further Reading

Bolman, L., and T. Deal. *Leading with the Soul: An Uncommon Journey of Spirit.* San Francisco: Jossey-Bass, 1995.

Green, Michael, and R. Paul Stevens. *Living the Story: Biblical Spirituality for Everyday Christians.* Grand Rapids: Eerdmans, 2003.

Handy, Charles. *The Hungry Spirit: Beyond Capitalism — A Quest for Purpose in the Modern World.* London: Hutchinson, 1997.

Hilton, Walter. *Toward a Perfect Love,* trans. David Jeffrey. Portland, Ore.: Multnomah Press, 1985.

Stevens, R. Paul. *Seven Days of Faith.* Colorado Springs: NavPress, 2001.

$\blacklozenge$ $\blacklozenge$ $\blacklozenge$

Cultivating Integrity

Hire and promote first on the basis of integrity; second, motivation; third, capacity; fourth, understanding; fifth, knowledge; and last and least, experience. Without integrity, motivation is dangerous; without motivation, capacity is impotent; without capacity, understanding is limited; without understanding, knowledge is meaningless; without knowledge, experience is blind. Experience is easy to provide and quickly put to use by people with the other qualities.

Dee Hock, President of Visa

An amoral approach to business, as for any other human activity, is not sustainable in practice. All human behaviour is governed by some set of moral understandings, even if they are not necessarily articulated in any coherent manner.

Clive Wright

The ethical meltdown in business has been so great that many cynically charge that the term "business ethics" is an oxymoron. Moral failures in financial reporting hit the news almost weekly. Nevertheless, people working in almost every field — politics, business, and religion — desire integrity. James Kouzes and Barry Posner, in their book *Credibility: How Leaders Gain and Lose It, Why People Demand It,* maintain that only with credible leaders can innovation flourish. In this chapter we will consider the spiritual motivation for consistent ethical decision-making. Business ethics has to do with three things: the moral value of the actual services and goods produced by business activity, the way in which businesspeople and organizations conduct themselves, and the consequences that business activity has on society.[1]

It is important to know what is right and wrong. It is also important to know what would motivate us to do the right thing and, when there seems to be no "simple right thing" to do, to be able to live with integrity with ourselves and our God. We make ethical decisions every day. Let's look at some in particular:

Working in the Gray Areas

• BRIBERY: JULIUS •

Julius's dream is just about to come true. For five years he has been preparing a new business project — the first quick muffler and brake repair service station in an African country. He is in the process of acquiring all necessary permits and licenses in order to start construction as soon as possible. But, after facing all kinds of obstacles, he now confronts a new problem — an official who must approve a high-voltage power supply connection has asked for a kickback to allow Julius to continue on schedule.

Julius has worked for an organization that helps entrepreneurs to start and grow their small businesses so they can contribute to the

---

1. Clive Wright, *The Business of Virtue* (London: SPCK, 2004), p. 119.

economic, social, and spiritual transformation of their communities. Julius loved their vision, and it was this organization that helped him put together the new business plan and resources for the muffler and brake repair station. He overcame many obstacles on the way. A previous investor pulled out from the project so he had to find a new group of investors. When a promising negotiation to lease land for the station came to a dead end, Julius had to buy a piece of land on the other side of the town. Despite these and many other problems, a new company, Instant Muffler, finally took shape with three partners — Julius, the development agency, and a group of Christian businesspeople from the United Kingdom. The total investment to start the new business would be $230,000 US. Julius and his project received great encouragement after all those years of hopes and disillusions from the surprising "Best Business Plan of the Year" award through a nation-wide competition. Through this award the project received a highly beneficial investment loan from the biggest commercial bank in the country. The bank was eager to see the project up and running as soon as possible. The other investors wanted to see some tangible results as well, especially the British, who had invested a large amount and were expecting a good return.

Julius is working with a Christian friend, Mololo, an architect who runs his own small engineering and planning company, CLG. CLG is now in the process of getting all approvals for the project and licenses for construction. The office of the Electric Power Supply (EPS) Company advises the people from CLG that the new building would be connected to a high-voltage source four hundred meters down the road. It seems strange to CLG engineers that the connection is so far away. After a short investigation, they identify a high-voltage connection cable just next to Julius's construction site. The engineering firm proposes this option to the power company official responsible for the project, but he replies with a counter-proposal: Instant Muffler can use the closer connection, but he wants a kickback of 10 percent from the value of the savings made. Mololo investigates further and finds that the more remote connection requires additional approvals and bureaucratic red tape because the underground cable would cut across three pieces of land owned by different people. As there would likely be other hidden problems in the ground — such as the need to relocate other utilities — estimated net savings by connecting to the closer supply would be at least half. His recommendation is to pay $1,000 USD to the EPS official with a condition that the project can fully account for this cost based on a proper invoice.

Julius thinks about the ambiguity of the situation. We are able, he reasons, to discern corruption clearly when we use public power for private gain, or when we receive something for doing nothing, or do something that should not be done, or when we bend the law. But when corruption facilitates business in situations that are not conducive, like business-hindering environments in many developing countries, how can we draw meaningful lines between right and wrong?[2]

But Julius is not sure what to do, and his friends in the development agency are also puzzled. The United Kingdom investors are asking for an update on the construction schedule by the beginning of next week. He can't wait much longer to make a decision.

• •

• **FINANCIAL MISREPRESENTATION: ANGELA** •

As the CFO of a software development company, Angela had a dilemma. During the process of obtaining pre-IPO private, third-stage funding for the company, the core team was putting together a final eighty-page business plan, which would include a five-year financial forecast. The first two years of revenue forecasts resulted in lower numbers than during the prior round of financing. One reason for the difference was the issue of revenue recognition. Briefly, revenue recognition in the software arena involves a United States law that says a software company may show the amount of the revenue being generated by a customer purchase only when the software is "fully installed and functional." For Angela's company, software implementations took anywhere from six to fourteen months, but the sales

2. See Bernard Adeney, *Strange Virtues: Ethics in a Multicultural World* (Downers Grove, Ill.: InterVarsity Press, 1995).

team usually sold the packages on the premise of a three- to six-month implementation. In a late-night drafting session to finalize the numbers for publication in the business plan, two board members and the CEO asked that the revenue numbers for the last quarter (which had not yet officially been closed) and the numbers for the first two years be bumped up significantly. "Keep in mind," they said, "that these are forecasts, not actuals, and that in a private financing round, actual financials usually are unaudited." Angela was not sure what to do.

• •

ADD TO THE dreary situations in the preceding cases the following common ethical challenges in business: false advertising, sexual discrimination, affirmative action, unfair compensation, nepotism, theft of time, theft of products, defamation, price fixing, industrial espionage, lying, destructive products or services, executive salaries, insider trading, and business bluffing.

Business bluffing, in particular, received a respectable public face years ago in an article by Albert Carr. When the law as written gives a person a wide-open chance to make a killing, argued Carr, that person would be a fool not to take advantage of it. If he or she doesn't, someone else will. Carr likens such behavior to the bluffing of a poker player who seizes every opportunity to win, as long as it doesn't involve outright cheating. "And no one thinks any the worse of you on that account.... And no one would think any the worse of the game of business because its standards of right and wrong differ from the prevailing traditions of morality in our society."[3]

Business is tough. So, for that matter, is church leadership, being a parent, and just existing with integrity in the world. The "Western" moral consensus has broken down. In the North and West we live in a largely post-Christian world. It is a seemingly valueless society, but in reality a new set of values prevails — choice, self-gratification, and

---

3. Albert Z. Carr, "Is Business Bluffing Ethical?" (1967), in *Beyond Integrity: A Judeo-Christian Approach to Business Ethics,* ed. Scott Rae and Kenman Wong (Grand Rapids: Zondervan, 1996), p. 55.

relativism. And we work in a global marketplace where varying ethical standards clash. How are we to make moral decisions in the marketplace, and what would motivate us to do so? These questions are a matter of marketplace spirituality — our lived experience of God in the context of everyday life both individually and communally.

Traditionally, ethics has been approached in one of three ways.

- The *command* approach. Technically known as the deontological perspective, this approach takes categorical imperatives like the Ten Commandments as guides.
- The *consequences* approach. The formal name for this is the teleological perspective (from the Greek word for "end" — *telos*). This utilitarian approach asks, What is the best outcome for the greatest number?
- The *character* or virtue approach. This says that ethical behavior flows from a character that is virtuous.[4] Virtues are praiseworthy or desirable traits of character and intellect.

All three approaches find support in scripture, as we shall see.[5] But there is no single, simple way of responding biblically and in a Christian way to ethical challenges.[6]

Commands — Categorical Imperatives

Clive Wright shrewdly observes that in our society we are more comfortable speaking about "good" and "bad" than "right" and "wrong" because in business people are generally uncomfortable with abso-

4. I acknowledge my indebtedness to Dr. Gordon Preece of the McQuarrie Christian Studies Centre for these alliterative headings.

5. The deontological (command) approach is found in Lev. 10:1-2; Num. 15:32-36; 2 Sam. 6:6-7; and 1 Cor. 6:9, 15ff., 20. The teleological (consequences) approach is found in Deut. 24:5; Exod. 20:12; Prov. 6:17; Exod. 1:19; 1 Sam. 16; 2 Kings 6; Mark 2:23-26; 3:4; and 1 Cor. 10:23. The character (virtue) approach is found in the Beatitudes (Matt. 5:3-10).

6. Wright, *The Business of Virtue*, pp. 113, 129.

lutes.[7] While many in our society will say that absolutes are obsolete, we are still under the summons of a moral God who has clearly declared how we are to live. The Ten Commandments are an example of this. The Decalogue, applied to the marketplace, exhorts us:

1. to put God first and to have no other gods. We are not to consider anything — not even consumerism or our careers — as of ultimate concern except the One who is ultimate;

2. not to be idolaters, creating our own images of God (read sex, money, and power) and making these images our ultimate concern — that is, worshipping them;

3. not to misuse God's name, taking it as a vain and empty thing by manipulating God, twisting God's arm to get our own way, or manipulating people; not to misuse God's name by guaranteeing votes or sales through association with the dominant form of Christianity in our culture;

4. to keep the Sabbath and not allow work to consume us seven days a week, thus letting it become our identity;

5. to honor our elders, maintaining respect and love for family, which is indeed part of our calling before God, and not to replace older workers with younger ones because they are cheaper;

6. not to commit murder either directly by eliminating people or indirectly by denying them the dignity of God-imaging beings or harming them with products and services;

7. not to commit adultery but to be chaste and sexually faithful to our spouses; not to use sexually seductive images and fantasies to sell products or services;

8. not to steal, taking what rightly belongs to another, by not paying the wages of employees and debts to creditors;

9. not to give false testimony but to tell the truth even in advertising and sales; not to add the words "new" and "improved" to the label without changing the contents simply to create a competitive edge;

10. not to covet — the most inward of the Ten Commandments —

7. Wright, *The Business of Virtue*, p. 103.

which means loving God enough to be content with what we are and have; not to stimulate inordinate and unhealthy desires through advertising.

Should we follow the Ten Commandments?[8] Lewis Smedes claims they are "survival guidelines for the human community."[9] John Lach in an article in *The Christian Century* suggests, "Following a code — the Ten Commandments, for instance — does not guarantee that the right thing will be done in every case. But it does insure that the person who unflinchingly acts by the code will do the right thing much more often than if he acted out of instinct or private inspiration."[10]

Turning to the New Testament, we find that Jesus summarized the whole law in the two great commandments: "'Love the Lord your God with all your heart, and with all your soul, and with all your mind.' This is the greatest and first commandment. And a second is like it: 'You shall love your neighbor as yourself.'[11] On these two commandments hang all the law and the prophets" (Matt. 22:37-40). "Do not think," Jesus said, "that I have come to abolish the law or the prophets; I have not come to abolish but to fulfill" (Matt. 5:17). The deontological/command approach to ethics is still compelling. Further, Jesus said, "In everything do to others as you would have them do to you; for this is the law and the prophets" (Matt. 7:12). It is well known that Jesus taught us

8. A recent book takes the approach that the Ten Commandments are foundational not only for Christians and Jews but also for society. David W. Gill, *Doing Right: Practicing Ethical Principles* (Downers Grove, Ill.: InterVarsity Press, 2004).

9. Lewis B. Smedes, *Mere Morality: What God Expects from Ordinary People* (Grand Rapids: Eerdmans, 1983), p. 15, quoted in Gill, *Doing Right*, p. 55.

10. John Lach, "Dogmatism in Disguise," *The Christian Century*, 16 November 1966, p. 1402.

11. This is not a commandment to love yourself but rather the commandment requires the Christian to aim at his or her neighbor's good just as unswervingly as one by nature wishes his or her own good, thus inverting love for self! This is not merely applying love we have or ought to have for ourselves to our neighbor. Luther said, "God's command drives us to our neighbor . . . faith snatches us away from ourselves and puts us outside ourselves." Martin Luther, "Treatise on Christian Liberty," in *Luther's Works*, trans. W. A. Lambert, ed. James Atkinson (Philadelphia: Fortress Press, 1966), vol. 2, p. 342.

to internalize these commandments by stressing our motives — not looking lustfully, letting our word be our bond, and not hating.[12]

But is love enough? Are there two categorical imperatives or one? Love, or love and justice?[13] Love is disinterested service to another.[14] Justice involves fairness and equity, doing the right thing.[15] Lewis Smedes, in *Mere Morality,* centers his ethical reflection on the so-called "moral" half of the Decalogue and argues for both love and justice:

> Justice and love are the two absolute moral commandments. They cover every conceivable human situation. There is no nook or cranny in our lives together in which we may ignore the demands of justice and love. Everything we do must be fair; if it is not fair, it is not right. And everything we do must be helpful, or at least not hurtful; if we mean it to hurt and not help people, it is not right. . . .

Smedes continues:

12. Sprinkled throughout the New Testament are other categorical imperatives. But it is not the only way the New Testament has been read by people seeking ethical guidance. See Richard Longenecker, *New Testament Social Ethics for Today* (Grand Rapids: Eerdmans, 1984), pp. 2-8, 15.

13. "To do the loving thing in each situation is highly laudatory. But while love must always motivate and condition every human action if such actions are to be truly ethical, love as the sole criterion for ethical decision making is highly suspect . . . love as a moral criterion is an easily adjustable norm." Longenecker, *New Testament Social Ethics,* p. 8. Longenecker cites Joseph Fletcher's *Situation Ethics* as an example of how contextualizing love disregards human egoism, stupidity, and cruelty. Love for God and neighbor includes righteousness, concern, and all the forces and structures that affect our neighbor's well-being.

14. "With whatever is relevant to actual need, love changes its tactic; against what is irrelevant love stands firm. When all fellow-feeling and natural affection wither, when there are no grounds for love in the neighbor's apparent worth, when his response is not appreciative but the contrary . . . when otherwise there is not foundation or justification for love, a Christian loves on in faith." Paul Ramsey, *Basic Christian Ethics* (Chicago: University of Chicago Press, 1977), p. 90.

15. In Christ, justice is simultaneously ethical (telling us what conformity to God's will requires), redemptive (making things right, the supreme example being God's justice in Jesus on the cross), and imputed (the alien righteousness that is given to believers when they are in Christ).

Justice tends to urge us to keep the rules, especially the "Thou shalt not's." Love translates the negative commands into positive invitations to creative helpfulness. Justice and love are the absolutes of life to which the other commandments point....[16]

Why obey the categorical imperative? What would motivate us to do so? Paul Ramsey notes, "Whoever imagines that religion adds to ethics only the threat of supernaturally administered punishment has simply never read the Bible."[17] In both the Old and New Testaments the motivation to obey is our relationship with God. It is a question of spirituality. We are accountable to God and empowered by God to conform our lives and behavior to the way of being that is in God himself.[18] "Be holy," God says, "for I am holy" (Lev. 11:44). Even under the Old Testament this is not merely a crushing demand. Jeremiah prophesied that God would write his law on our hearts or motivation (Jer. 31:33) and Ezekiel prophesied that God would put his Spirit in us and "make [us] follow [his] statutes and be careful to observe [his] ordinances" (Ezek. 36:27).

The command approach has the strength of time-honored and tested signposts. Imperatives provide stability and constancy. The weakness of this approach is that sometimes it offers conflicting rules.

But there is a second way of approaching ethical decisions.

Consequences — The Goal or End

In the teleological, sometimes called "utilitarian" approach, the consequences, generally the greatest good, determine moral rightness.

16. Smedes, *Mere Morality,* p. 240.

17. Ramsey, *Basic Christian Ethics,* p. 12.

18. The "command" to love takes us beyond principle and law because it casts us on God himself. It is gospel, not law. "The love with which man loves God and his neighbour is the love of God and no other; for there is no other love; there is no love which is free or independent from the love of God. . . . Loving God is simply the other aspect of being loved by God. Being loved by God implies loving God; the two do not stand separately side by side." Dietrich Bonhoeffer, *Ethics* (London: SCM Press, 1976), p. 176.

The Old and New Testaments often show us people making ethical decisions based on the end in view. Some of the stories are deeply challenging. Take Abraham, for example. God commanded him to take his son up Mount Moriah and offer him up like the pagans did. Abraham faced two conflicting commands: not to commit murder and to sacrifice his son. It was complicated by the fact that Isaac, his son, was the only visible means of fulfilling God's promise to him of having a large family. But Abraham obeyed. He obeyed with an end in view since, on the way up the mountain, he said to the servants who remained behind that "we" will go up to worship and "we" will return, somehow anticipating that God was able to raise up from stones a child to Abraham or to bring him back from the dead, a matter noted expressly in the New Testament (Gen. 22:5; Heb. 11:19).

Then there was Rahab the prostitute in Jericho who lied to her king and his men about the whereabouts of the Hebrew spies. She had hidden them on the roof of her house because she could see God's work and presence in the coming of the Israelites. Her actions were guided by the coming kingdom. For this she is noted as a hero of faith in Hebrews chapter eleven.

Jacob schemed against his father-in-law Laban to get what his family needed after serving Laban for fourteen years as an indentured slave for the bride price of his two wives. Clearly, Jacob shrewdly planned how to take "nothing" from Laban (Gen. 30:31) but at the same time, by clever breeding, and through a God-inspired dream, got what he needed from his father-in-law's flocks and herds (31:10-13). His actions were, as Laban noticed (31:30) and as the narrative demonstrates, dominated by the sense of destiny he had — his desire to return to the land that God had promised him. Was this a holy shrewdness? Similarly, was his mother's scheme to get Jacob blessed in spite of his father Isaac's pathetic favoritism of Esau a holy shrewdness — in view of the end (Gen. 27)?[19]

And then there is the extraordinary parable of Jesus in Luke 16 where the master commends his dishonest manager for his shrewd-

---

19. I have explained the story of Jacob in *Down-to-Earth Spirituality* (Downers Grove, Ill.: InterVarsity Press, 2003).

ness in providing for himself when he was going to be laid off (Luke 16:8). What does Jesus mean by his exhortation to "be as wise as serpents and innocent as doves" (Matt. 10:16)?

Clearly, the New Testament calls us to consider the end of our actions when making them. Do those ends contribute to the inbreaking of God's life-giving rule? Do they reflect God's purpose on earth? Do they bring justice into society (Col. 4:1-2; 1 Pet. 1:15)?

Reflecting the consequences approach, Peter Chao of Eagle Communications offers some tests of moral action that are based on personal outcomes:

- *Sleeping test* — If I do this, can I sleep at night?
- *Newspaper test* — Would I do this if it were splashed on the front page of the morning paper?
- *Mirror test* — If I do this, will I feel uncomfortable with myself when facing the mirror?
- *Child test* — If I do this, would I mind telling my teenage child?[20]

Ultimately, the best "end" or *telos* of our actions is that which expresses love. *Caritas* (in Latin), or *agape* (in Greek), is not mere physical passion or emotional affection. It is unconditional caring and doing the best for the other. Clive Wright commends love as one positive thing that the Christian faith offers to the moral quest because it is both a unifying principle that would seem to be unique to the human species and a concept that can appeal beyond the Christian community.[21]

The consequences approach to ethics has the strengths of dealing with reality, emphasizing the need to take responsibility, and being concerned to increase human happiness and well-being. The weakness of this approach is that we are often unable to calculate definitively the likely consequences of certain actions.

20. Peter Chao, Eagle Communications, in an address delivered at the Marketplace Theology consultation, Sydney, Australia, July, 2001.

21. Wright, *The Business of Virtue*, p. 131.

Character — Virtue Ethics

The third approach to ethics is the way of virtue or character. A person who follows this approach assumes that right action is the by-product of a righteous and virtuous character. Most businesses today talk about values. Many publish their organizational values in a prominent place as motivating guidelines. But values do not easily have opposites. "I have my values and you have yours; it's all a matter of what's important to you." Virtues, in contrast, have opposites: vices. Virtues are habitual tendencies to do the good. They are absolute, not relative. "Virtues," as Al Bussard notes, "do not ignore the reality of sin, but they do not submit to cynicism about the possibility of transformation."[22] And they focus on character, not rules.

The ancient philosopher Aristotle identified nine intellectual virtues — technical skill, scientific knowledge, prudence, intelligence, wisdom, resourcefulness, understanding, judgment, cleverness — and twelve moral virtues — courage, temperance, liberality, magnificence, magnanimity, proper ambition, patience, truthfulness, wittiness, friendliness, modesty, righteous indignation.[23] The long church tradition has emphasized four of the classical Greek virtues — justice, prudence, moderation, and courage — and has added the "theological virtues" of faith, hope, and love — three virtues to which we will return in a later chapter.

Justice deals with fairness. It aims to balance rights and claims and to treat people and organizations with dignity. Clive Wright says, "In the context of business, the virtue of justice affirms the principle of conformity to the law, both in spirit and letter. But it goes well beyond requiring legitimacy in this formal sense. It also demands that 'a proper balance of conflicting interests be sought.'"[24]

Prudence is habitually choosing to learn from the past. Wright

22. Al Bussard, "The Classical Virtues and Their Application to Integra," a paper given at the Integra staff conference, Sofia, Bulgaria, May 2004.

23. Wright, *The Business of Virtue,* p. 116.

24. Wright, *The Business of Virtue,* p. 140. Wright goes on to outline characteristics of a "just business": service, legitimacy, proportionality, trustworthiness, and reciprocity (pp. 142-46).

notes that prudence "is the ability to defer gratification from the immediate to the longer term . . . the capacity to think beyond the immediate consequences of an act. . . ."[25] Wright continues, "Prudence is perhaps at the root of one of the most fundamental requirements in business: the need for trust, fidelity, and probity. These qualities or virtues may be summed up in the concept of honesty. . . ."[26]

Moderation or *temperance* means living within the limitations God has placed on us, avoiding the excesses of self-indulgence and greed, and not taking on projects we cannot complete. Wright comments on an important business application of this virtue: "Where a wealth-creation activity involves consumption of a finite natural resource, temperance calls for moderation in that exploitation and some degree of just balance between the good achieved and the resource consumed."[27]

Courage or *fortitude* is willingly taking risks, a virtue needed for whistle-blowing.[28] Wright says, "Courage means the ability to withstand temptation despite the pressures of abuse, ridicule, or misunderstanding — in other words to adhere to principle. In the business context, courage . . . enables anxieties over the inevitable uncertainties and risks to be kept in perspective."[29]

Faith involves including God in our planning and believing that people can change. *Hope* means not being ruled by cynicism as we anticipate the blessing of God. And *love* shows caring loyalty to people and organizations; it gives people one more chance to hurt you and sees people as God sees them.[30] In many ways the theological virtue of love unifies and embodies all the other virtues. And while love is the ultimate motivation behind the virtues, integrity is the expression of that virtuous life. Integrity is not mere honesty but the inte-

25. Wright, *The Business of Virtue*, p. 139.

26. Wright, *The Business of Virtue*, p. 140.

27. Wright, *The Business of Virtue*, p. 141.

28. John E. Richardson, "Whistle-Blowing," in Robert Banks and R. Paul Stevens, eds., *The Complete Book of Everyday Christianity* (Downers Grove, Ill.: InterVarsity Press, 1997), pp. 1114-16.

29. Wright, *The Business of Virtue*, pp. 141-42.

30. As developed by Bussard, "The Classical Virtues."

gration, wholeness, and soundness of a person who is free from moral corruption.

While the Bible does not give us a list of virtues, or even tell us ten steps to becoming virtuous, it does point in the direction of God-like righteousness as an all-encompassing character trait.[31] As children of a loving and holy God who is conforming us to his character, we find the spiritual motivation to grow in virtue.

In the prophetic tradition of the Old Testament this was clearly the case. People are called "to do justice, and to love kindness, and to walk humbly with your God" because God is just (Mic. 6:8). In the case of Hosea, God's self-sacrificial love motivates the prophet to redeem his unfaithful wife because there is *hesed* (covenant love) in the heart of God. So in the Old Testament righteous living and working are rooted in thanksgiving to God and conformity to God's character of love and justice.[32]

Turning to the New Testament, we find that Jesus calls people to an extraordinary ethical life. The Beatitudes (Matt. 5:3-12) are statements of what life is like in the kingdom Jesus announced and embodied. "Blessed are the poor in spirit, for theirs is the kingdom of God." Applied to business the Beatitudes might look like this:

- Blessed are the poor in spirit — those who think much of God and others, and little of themselves.
- Blessed are those who mourn — who admit when they are wrong and grieve for sin in persons and organizations.
- Blessed are those who yield rights for the betterment of others — the meek shall inherit the earth.
- Blessed are those who passionately desire that the right thing be done — hungering and thirsting for righteousness.

31. Significantly, the Bible seldom uses the word "virtue" except in 2 Pet. 1:5-7: "Make every effort to support your faith with goodness [*arête* — virtue], and goodness with knowledge, and knowledge with self-control, and self-control with endurance, and endurance with godliness, and godliness with mutual affection, and mutual affection with love." The "list" in Philippians 4:8 is ad hoc.

32. See Alexander Hill, "Business Ethics," in Banks and Stevens, eds., *Everyday Christianity,* pp. 90-96.

- Blessed are the merciful — those who show kindness and grace when others let them down.
- Blessed are the pure in heart — those who cultivate "a single eye" and focus all their life on God and God's kingdom.
- Blessed are the peacemakers — those who bring together factions and people, building community among those who are at odds with one another.
- Blessed are those who "take" the pain of doing the right thing — who are persecuted because of righteousness.

Can we live by the teaching of Jesus? He does are not give us much wiggle-room. He also makes it clear that he is not simply announcing a character quality that will be applicable when he comes again and establishes his kingdom fully on earth. He means *now*. The person who hears his words and puts them into practice is the house built on the rock (Matt. 7:24). And there is a promise attached to it — not achieving worldly wealth and acclaim, but being a full participant in the life of the kingdom, seeing God, and ultimately inheriting the earth. This is a radical ethic. Can it be lived? So demanding is this ethic that philosopher Alfred North Whitehead said, "As society is now constituted a literal obedience to the moral precepts scattered throughout the gospels would mean sudden death."[33] What if we all were meek, turned the other cheek, did not resist evil, spoke the truth to our harm, and denied ourselves? But surely this is one more case where Christianity has not been tried and found wanting but found difficult and left untried.[34]

The character approach has its strengths as well. In his superb

33. Alfred North Whitehead, quoted in Edward L. Long, *Conscience and Compromise* (Philadelphia: Westminster Press, 1954), p. 18. Paul Ramsey says something similar. "The beatitudes are thoroughly eschatological (Matt. 5:3-12; Luke 6:20-23). Jesus was not so naive as to suppose that by the power of their meekness the meek would sooner or later inherit the earth. To be realistic about the forces which triumph in the present age, if the meek ever inherit the earth, the not-so-meek would promptly take it away from them. Meekness and inheriting the earth are entirely separate matters; only the approaching kingdom brings them into connection." Ramsey, *Basic Christian Ethics*, p. 26.

34. Hill, *Just Business*, p. 11.

treatment of virtue ethics, *The Business of Virtue,* Clive Wright says virtue ethics provides a framework for reflection on the place of knowledge, will, and passions in the moral life.[35] But cultivating the weakness that constitutes character formation is a lifelong process, and moral decisions not only arise from personal virtue but also contribute to the formation of personal virtue.

True education, as Augustine noted, is to learn what to desire. As it turns out, this is a gracious cooperation between God and us.[36] Moral education in the virtues is part of the process. Moral development is influenced by habits and habits are formed by choices. Scripture witnesses to this in such exhortations as "think about these things" (Phil. 4:8), "put away" vices such as slandering (Eph. 4:31), and "make every effort to support your faith with goodness" (2 Pet. 1:5). But one does not become a virtuous person merely by pulling oneself up by the bootstraps. God gives what God requires, and the grace of the new creation in Christ accomplishes what we can never attain by human moral striving. So Peter says that God's divine power "has given us everything needed for life and godliness, through the knowledge of him who called us by his own glory and goodness [or virtue, *arete*]" (2 Pet. 1:3). What Athens requires Christ inspires. What a high calling! Is it too high? Impossible?

Is Compromise Inevitable?

Søren Kierkegaard is reported to have said that a person could no more be able to live exclusively according to the highest Christian concepts all the time than he or she would be able to live by eating at the Lord's Table. Richard Longenecker says something similar: "For most Christians the maxim seems to be this: Follow the personal ethics of the New Testament as far as circumstances allow, yet realize that we live in an immoral society and that therefore some compro-

35. Wright, *The Business of Virtue,* p. 109.
36. See Iain Benson, "Virtues," in Banks and Stevens, eds., *Everyday Christianity,* pp. 1069-72.

mises must be made in the realm of human affairs."[37] And even John Calvin admitted with regard to keeping God's law, "At least more is required of us than we are able to pay."[38]

Do we compromise prayerfully and repent afterwards?[39] Do we never compromise, take up the cross, and possibly lose our lives in this world? Or do we never compromise in personal ethics but realize that there is a different role to play in society, which tends to make us into moral amphibians? This last approach was Luther's view and is essentially what Richard Longenecker advocates.

Emilie Griffin, an advertising executive, reflects on the spirituality of ethical decision-making:

> The reflective executive . . . [is one who] understands daily experience as a call to conversion; who lives in dialog with God, making intercession for others; who takes into account, in business decisions, the intolerable sound of the word "trade-off" and at the same time the relentless necessity of compromise; who operates within the realm of the practical knowing that with God, all things are possible; who looks long, looks hard, looks prophetically and with vision at the improbable realignments that take place in society daily; who sets aside, to the extent possible, the biases, the *scotosis*, the distortions of ancient enmities and strife; and who longs for reconciliation, solidarity, sisterhood, brotherhood — perhaps for civility most of all.[40]

The spirituality of ethical decision-making is four-dimensional. First, we honor and treasure in our hearts the categorical imperatives

37. Longenecker, *New Testament Social Ethics*, p. ix.

38. John Calvin, *Institutes of the Christian Religion* (Grand Rapids: Eerdmans, 1966), 2.5.9, p. 280. "One thing only I ask to be conceded to me, that it is vain to think we have a power of fulfilling the Law, merely because we are enjoined to obey it. Since in order to our fulfilling the divine precepts, the grace of the Lawgiver is both necessary, and has been promised to us, this much at least is clear, that more is demanded of us than we are able to pay."

39. Robert Banks, "Compromise," in Banks and Stevens, eds., *Everyday Christianity*, pp. 195-99.

40. Emilie Griffin, *The Reflective Executive* (New York: Crossroad, 1993), pp. 166-67.

that God has given us, the Ten Commandments and the twin laws of love and justice. Second, we consider the end to which we are called and summoned, and how the action we are about to take may have a consequence in harmony with that end. For example, many people have discovered that dismissing an employee — always a hard thing to do as well as to be the recipient of — was the best thing for the employee in the long run. Third, we are to walk with God, breathe in the Spirit of God, and allow God's Spirit to develop within us a virtuous life while we simultaneously develop habits of moral behavior. A Toronto doctor confessed, "I have thrown away my books on moral theology. Now I just read my Bible, pray for the leading of the Spirit, and trust my intuition." And finally, we live by grace and forgiveness. We will make mistakes, make compromises, and sometimes do more harm than good. As Luther once said, "Sin boldly but believe in Jesus more boldly still."[41]

Does ethical business leadership pay off at the bottom line? Often it does. Why? Because God designed the universe in a particular way. If there is no trust, the system God made breaks down. Does ethical business *always* pay off? Not always, at least not in the short run.

For Discussion

1. Reread Dee Hock's statement at the beginning of the chapter about hiring first and foremost for integrity. How would a hiring manager assess a potential employee's integrity?
2. Consider either one of the cases at the beginning of the chapter. What are the ethical issues? What feelings might the person have in this situation? How does it help to consider whether there is a categorical imperative (deontological), a consequence (teleologi-

---

41. Luther argues that there is a "cross" in our secular vocation, a cross that puts to death the old self, a cross that is not limited to sacrificial love for the neighbor. "Our vocation is also the location of God's sanctifying work of mortifying the flesh, of putting to death the sinful self . . . ; all of this is so that on the last day only the self that is righteous in Christ will live." Marc Kolden, "Luther on Vocation," *Word and World* 3, no. 4: 388.

cal), or a character factor involved? How would you personally respond? Why? How might you pray in each situation?

3. Do an ethics audit of your own organization using the following guide:

When your organization was founded, what significant events were taking place in the industry or profession? Since that time, what major changes have taken place that have affected your organization's ethics?

What have been the critical turning points in the history of your organization? What impact have these had on your organization's values?

What is the actual — not necessarily the stated — source of the ruling principles and cherished ways of behaving in your organization?

What individuals have been exemplars of the core values of the organization? What are the characteristics and virtues that these people have exhibited?

What corporate practices, ceremonies, and rituals express what is cherished by your organization?

What, if any, values of the organization would you like to change? What symbols, cherished ways of behaving, and undergirding beliefs would need to be altered for such change to happen?

What are the actual values for each of the "stakeholders" of your organization? What ethic are you committed to practicing for staff, colleagues, clients/customers, and the larger community? What commitments do you expect from each stakeholder?

Does your organization serve any purpose that transcends making money? If so, what is it? Is the world a better place because your organization is in it? Are your employees themselves better for working in your organization?[42]

---

42. Adapted from Michael Goldberg, ed., *Against the Grain: New Approaches to Professional Ethics* (Valley Forge, Pa.: Trinity Press, 1993), pp. 193-94.

For Further Reading

Adeney, Bernard. *Strange Virtues: Ethics in a Multicultural World.* Downers Grove, Ill.: InterVarsity Press, 1995.

Donaldson, Thomas, and Patricia H. Werhane, eds. *Ethical Issues in Business: A Philosophical Approach.* Upper Saddle River, N.J.: Prentice Hall, 1996.

Gill, David W. *Doing Right: Practicing Ethical Principles.* Downers Grove, Ill.: InterVarsity Press, 2004.

Hauerwas, Stanley. *Vision and Virtue: Essays in Christian Ethical Reflection.* Notre Dame, Ind.: University of Notre Dame Press, 1974.

Hill, Alexander. *Just Business: Christian Ethics for the Marketplace.* Downers Grove, Ill.: InterVarsity Press, 1997.

Kouzes, James M., and Barry Z. Posner. *Credibility: How Leaders Gain and Lose It, Why People Demand It.* San Francisco: Jossey-Bass, 1993.

MacIntyre, Alasdair. *After Virtue.* Notre Dame, Ind.: University of Notre Dame Press, 1981/1984.

Wright, Clive. *The Business of Virtue.* London: SPCK, 2004.

9

$\blacklozenge \quad \blacklozenge \quad \blacklozenge$

Being Creative

Work should be and can be productive and rewarding, meaningful and maturing, enriching and fulfilling, healing and joyful. Work is one of our greatest
privileges. Work can even be poetic.

Max DePree

There can be no capitalist development without an
entrepreneurial class; no entrepreneurial class without a moral charter; no moral charter without religious premises.

Gianfranco Poggi

In the classic film *Wall Street* Gordon Gekko (Michael Douglas)
typifies the entrepreneur. "The lesson in business," he tells Bud
Fox (Charlie Sheen), is "don't get emotional about stock, it clouds
the judgment." Gekko is constantly in a telephone conversation, us-

ing language such as "block anybody else's merger efforts," "Christmas is over, business is business," and "I want every orifice in his body flowing red." In a famous scene, Gekko redefines greed. "Greed is good; greed is right; greed works. Greed clarifies, cuts through, and captures that essence of the evolutionary spirit." It is interesting that Gekko uses the word "spirit" in a film that exemplifies the secular humanism that has dominated the cultural environment of business in the Western world for several decades. But a change occurring in Western culture makes the question of a search for a spiritual foundation apt if not urgent. Indeed, research has shown that money is not the only thing that drives entrepreneurs. It is the desire to be masters of their own souls, to make something new, to make a difference.

So in this chapter we will explore the nature of entrepreneurship; we will revisit Max Weber's thesis in *The Protestant Ethic and the Spirit of Capitalism* and we will consider how spirituality relates to continuing creativity in enterprises, businesses, and organizations.

Entrepreneurship and the Drive to Creativity

Heather Quinn had an idea. She was a dress-maker, but an auto accident left her unable to continue in her profession. As a person with a disability, she began to see that one of the deep frustrations of other people with disabilities was the difficulty they had in finding clothing that would fit them. So she began to design clothing for people with disabilities and developed a business that does precisely that. From where did that creative idea and the will to implement it come?[1]

Bob, whom we met in an earlier case study, had a vision to make the experience of buying a used car just as satisfying as buying a new factory-delivered model. Putting flesh on the idea took him months of hard work and sacrifice. But this is part of entrepreneurship — creativity, vision, courage, and stick-to-itiveness.

---

1. This story is told by Gordon Smith in "The Soul of the Entrepreneur," *Vocatio,* forthcoming.

Rodger Woods is an architect. But he does not simply design buildings. He envisions the creation of architectural and development companies that will make the world a better place and, at the same time, provide employment for people, especially the marginalized. But he doesn't just think about it. He makes it happen, for that is what entrepreneurs do.

These three people had leading roles in starting new or reforming existing businesses. But entrepreneurship is also expressed in developing new products and services within long-standing companies or in finding new and better ways of delivering a service. People at "lower levels," as well as top echelons, in organizations can be entrepreneurial, and some businesses now reward good ideas that emerge from employees. We know that we work in a world in which terms like "de-jobbing" suggest that life-long employment is no longer a given.[2] In a rapidly changing world and a global economy we must keep reinventing ourselves. Not only people but also organizations, churches, academic institutions, and political systems need to be entrepreneurial. "Innovate or die" is simply the way it is. But where does this creativity come from?

Unquestionably, entrepreneurial activity requires faith, whether that faith is a "push" from within — a drive that arises from unmet human needs — or a "pull" from without — a calling from a significant Other. Most contemporary theories of entrepreneurship do not consider this. Factors usually identified include (1) personality — traits such as risk-taking, independence, internal locus of control, self-confidence,[3] (2) the environment or "the times," and (3) possession of skills that can be learned.[4] The most plausible theory is the systemic one, namely that multiple interdependent factors are at work to create the entrepreneurial imperative that has led to the flourishing of Western capitalism. With the exception of the much

2. See Jeremy Rifkin, *The End of Work: The Decline of the Global Work-Force and the Dawn of the Post-Market Era* (London: Penguin, 2000).

3. John E. Tropman and Gersh Morningstar, *Entrepreneurial Systems for the 1990s: Their Creation, Structure, and Management* (New York: Quorum Books, 1989), p. 7.

4. Peter F. Drucker, *Innovation and Entrepreneurship: Practice and Principles* (New York: Harper & Row, 1985).

debated 1904-1905 essay by Max Weber, there has been surprising little study and literature written on the spiritual and religious sources of entrepreneurship. It is this factor we are considering in this chapter.

Entrepreneurship involves three facets — envisioning, inventing (creativity), and implementing. If any one of these factors is missing, an activity is less than fully entrepreneurial. The term has an interesting history. *Entrepreneur* — "one who organizes, manages, and assumes the risks of a business or enterprise" (Webster) — is a French word. In the Middle Ages *entrepreneur* was used to describe any clergy who were in charge of great architectural works such as a cathedral or a castle. In one person were combined the functions of inventor, planner, architect, manager, employer, and supervisor. Only later in the eighteenth century was the term used for economic activity.[5] The trio of qualities noted above — envisioning, inventing, and implementing — seems indispensably linked with the idea of entrepreneurship: not just envisioning, not just inventing, not just implementing, but all three. Admitting the complexity of defining an entrepreneur, Robert Hebert and Albert Link suggest a similarity with Heffalump in A. A. Milne's *Winnie-the-Pooh:* "All who claim to have caught sight of him report he is enormous, but they disagree on his particularities."[6] But what makes the entrepreneur tick?

Weber's "Partial, Complex, and Momentous" Thesis

The Protestant work ethic is blamed, not without reason, for many anti-leisure attitudes — the so-called "Calvinist feeling that work

---

5. An earlier form of the word, *entreprendeur,* was used as early as the fourteenth century. The term was used in the sixteenth and seventeenth centuries for government contractors. But in the eighteenth century this French term becomes infused with "a precise economic content" in the writings of the businessperson Richard Cantillon. Robert F. Hebert and Albert N. Link, *The Entrepreneur: Mainstream Views and Radical Critiques* (New York: Praeger Publishers, 1982), pp. 12-13.

6. Hebert and Link, *The Entrepreneur,* p. 114.

alone is good."[7] A bulletin posted by a merchant for his employees in 1822 suggests just this:

1. This store must be opened at Sunrise. No mistake. Open 6 o'clock A.M. Summer and Winter. Close about 8:30 or 9:00 P.M. the year round.
2. Store must be swept, dusted; doors and windows opened; lamps filled, trimmed, and chimneys cleaned; counters, base shelves, and show cases dusted; pens made; a pail of water and also the coal must be brought in before breakfast, if there is time to do it, and attend to all the customers who call.
3. The store is not to be opened on the Sabbath day unless absolutely necessary and then only for a few minutes.
4. Should the store be opened on Sunday, the clerks must go in alone and get tobacco for customers in need.
5. The clerk who is in the habit of smoking Spanish cigars, being shaved at the barbers, going to dancing parties and other places of amusement, and being out late at night, will assuredly give his employer reason to be ever suspicious of his integrity and honesty.
6. Clerks are allowed to smoke in the store provided they do not wait on women with a "stogie" in the mouth.
7. Each clerk must pay not less than $5.00 per year to the Church and must attend Sunday School regularly.
8. Men clerks are given one evening a week off for courting and two if they go to prayer meeting.
9. After the 14 hours in the store the leisure hours should be spent mostly in reading.[8]

The popular version of the Protestant work ethic includes the following beliefs: idleness is sinful; industriousness is a religious ideal; waste is a vice; frugality is a virtue; leisure is earned by work and a

7. Max Weber, *The Protestant Ethic and the Spirit of Capitalism,* trans. Talcott Parsons (New York: Charles Scribner's Sons, 1958), p. 42.
8. Erwin O. Smigel, ed., *Work and Leisure: A Contemporary Social Problem* (New Haven, Conn.: College and University Press, 1963), Introduction.

preparation for work; complacency and failure are outlawed; ambition and success are sure signs of God's favor; and wealth is a special sign of God's favor.[9]

Some of this stems directly from the Protestant Reformation. The magisterial reformers — Luther and Calvin — not only "reformed" the way in which people came to know their acceptance with God but also their attitude to the world and work in particular. Lutheranism enjoined the worker to consider his or her economic activity as a calling *(Beruf)*, though according to Max Weber the Lutheran's commitment to a worldly calling or station does not involve strenuous effort to master, rationalize, and innovate.[10] As Weber viewed the matter, something more was needed to ratchet up the believer's intensity to a passion for entrepreneurship. Gianfranco Poggi puts it this way, "Only a religious vision that turns worldly reality into a field of experimentation, and the individual into a 'tensed-up being,' relentlessly working that field in the pursuit of a dynamic design, could plausibly be said to have offered such an inspiration."[11] According to Weber, this is what Calvinism supplied.

Michael Novak notes at least two good reasons why Max Weber has earned an immortal place in intellectual history. First, "he identified something new in economic history and glimpsed . . . its moral and religious dimensions. Second, he suggested in advance why Marxism, both as an explanatory theory and a vision of paradise, was doomed to fail: Its resolute materialism excluded the human spirit."[12]

9. Robert Banks, "Work Ethic, Protestant," in Robert Banks and R. Paul Stevens, eds., *The Complete Book of Everyday Christianity* (Downers Grove, Ill.: InterVarsity Press, 1997), pp. 1129-32.

10. Gianfranco Poggi, *Calvinism and the Capitalist Spirit: Max Weber's Protestant Ethic* (London: Macmillan, 1983), pp. 41, 60-61. Weber points to Luther's many statements against usury or interest in any form as evidence that Luther had a more traditionalist approach: A person does not by nature wish to earn more and more money (Weber, *The Protestant Ethic*, pp. 60, 82). Weber argues that the Bible, and the Old Testament in particular, actually favors this traditionalist view, which is exemplified in the words of Jesus: "Give us this day our daily bread" (p. 83).

11. Poggi, *Calvinism and the Capitalist Spirit*, p. 61.

12. Michael Novak, *The Catholic Ethic and the Spirit of Catholicism* (New York: The Free Press, 1993), p. 9.

Weber's thesis can be summarized in this way: For capitalism to flourish there must be both intensive activity and the imperative to save. The rise of both spirits can be traced to Calvinism. As to the first, with the closing of the monastery door as a way to prove one's merit before God, the fervent believer was enjoined to prove him- or herself by intensive work in the world in a calling. For the second, the drive to save, Calvinism taught self-denial and self-sacrifice, the very delayed gratification that is essential for accumulating capital. The theological underpinning for this, according to Weber, was supplied by what he viewed as Calvinism's twin doctrines of the transcendence of God and predestination. These allowed believers to operate in the world as God's instruments and in the process to gain some assurance of their own status as the elect. The first doctrine "cranks up the tension" and the second "opens the believer to the world."[13]

> The exhortation of the apostles to make fast one's own call is here interpreted as a duty to attain certainty of one's own election and justification . . . in the daily struggle of life. . . . In order to attain that self-confidence intense worldly activity is recommended as the most suitable means. It and it alone dispenses religious doubt and gives the certainty of grace.[14]

"Thus," argues Poggi, "all the Calvinist faithful's ethical eggs were placed in the basket of his calling."[15] Weber put it this way:

> The attainment of [wealth] as a fruit of labour in a calling was a sign of God's blessing. And even more important: the religious valuation of restless, continuous, systematic work in a worldly calling, as the highest medium of asceticism, and at the same time the surest and most evident proof of rebirth and genuine faith, must have been the most powerful conceivable lever for the expansion of that attitude toward life which we have here called the spirit of capitalism.[16]

13. Poggi, *Calvinism and the Capitalist Spirit*, pp. 65, 70.
14. Weber, *The Protestant Ethic*, p. 12.
15. Poggi, *Calvinism and the Capitalist Spirit*, p. 66.
16. Weber, *The Protestant Ethic*, p. 172.

Implicit in the Calvinism that Weber studied is a potentially useful concept of the stewardship of money and of time, which involves a methodological approach to time that monitors the environment and makes adjustments in order to maximize the use of time. In contrast, Catholicism proposed extensive interpenetration of the sacred and profane thus discouraging "the faithful from treating the latter as a religiously neutral field, deprived of ritual significance, and open to his 'tinkering' and rearranging." Calvinism, on the other hand, led believers to adopt an ethical posture — an inner-worldly asceticism in the context of intensive 'tinkering' in the world.[17] When you combine the attainment of wealth (acquisitive activity) as the fruit of labor in a calling as a sign of God's blessing with the limitation of consumption (saving), the inevitable result is the accumulation of capital.[18] This attitude is typified by the famous words of the evangelical John Wesley, founder of the Methodist movement, in his sermon on the use of money: "Gain all you can [a push for entrepreneurship], save all you can [a push for capitalism], give all you can."[19] Gianfranco Poggi's conclusion is apt: Weber's argument is "partial" (addressing a distinctive part of a large historical phenomenon), "complex" ("it comprises a number of discrete points, connected by a correspondingly high number of steps or transitions") *"and momentous."*[20]

Weber's thesis is hard to verify empirically but, as the British economist Brian Griffiths notes, "the Protestant ethic turns out to be a specific example of a far more general thesis: namely, that the economic process is related in an important way to cultural and religious values."[21]

---

17. Poggi, *Calvinism and the Capitalist Spirit,* pp. 56-57.

18. Weber, *The Protestant Ethic,* p. 172.

19. John Wesley, "The Use of Money," in Max L. Stackhouse, Dennis McCann, and Shirley Roels, eds., *On Moral Business: Classical and Contemporary Resources for Ethics in Economic Life* (Grand Rapids: Eerdmans, 1995), p. 197.

20. Poggi, *Calvinism and the Capitalist Spirit,* p. 79, emphasis mine.

21. Brian Griffiths, *The Creation of Wealth* (London: Hodder and Stoughton, 1984), p. 31.

Recovering the Reformational Calling

The popular version of Weber's Protestant work ethic could be more accurately described as the "post-Protestant work ethic." Weber rarely quotes Calvin. He relies heavily on his observations that capitalism seems to have flourished better in Protestant countries than in Catholic ones, a fact explained differently by David Landes.[22] Weber also relied heavily on later Puritans such as Richard Baxter, Pietists in England and Holland, Methodists, and deists like Benjamin Franklin.[23]

Among the nominally religious and early post-Protestants, people moved away from dependence on the sufficiency of Christ's work for salvation and, during the Industrial Revolution, invested work with more religious significance as a means of proving one's acceptance with God. The vocation of rest — given proper emphasis by Calvin and the early Puritans — was lost.[24] Weber correctly observed that what got worked out in the Reformed churches and sects was a "reversion to the doctrine of salvation by works" rather than justifica-

22. David Landes, "Religion and Enterprise: The Case of the French Textile Industry," in Edward C. Carter II, Robert Forster, and Joseph Moody, eds., *Enterprise and Entrepreneurs in Nineteenth-Century France* (Baltimore: Johns Hopkins University Press, 1976). Landes explains that the phenomenon of relatively slower development of industry in France, in comparison with England, was due not so much to Catholicism as to the fact of family firms whose primary concerns were safety, continuity, and privacy. It can be argued, however, that even these were an expression of Catholic culture.

23. Weber, *The Protestant Ethic*, pp. 50, 53, 180. In support of the alleged Protestant "duty of the individual toward the increase of his capital which is assumed as an end in itself" Weber quotes Franklin: "He that loses five shillings, not only loses that sum, but all the advantage that might be made by turning it in dealing, which by the time that a young man becomes old, will amount to a considerable sum of money" (Weber, *The Protestant Ethic*, pp. 50-51). Later Weber argues that in answer to why money should be made Franklin quotes Prov. 22:29, "Seest thou a man diligent in his business? [NIV "skilled in his work"] He shall stand before kings," a matter Weber maintains was drummed into Franklin by his Calvinist father (Weber, *The Protestant Ethic*, p. 53).

24. Robert Banks, "Work Ethic, Protestant," in Banks and Stevens, eds., *Everyday Christianity*, p. 1129.

tion by grace through faith: God helps those who help themselves.[25] But Weber was incorrect in concluding that Lutheranism, "on account of its doctrine of grace, lacked a psychological sanction of systematic conduct to compel the methodical rationalization of life."[26]

Both Luther and Calvin recalled people to the foundational document of the Christian faith (the Bible) and to the essential gospel experience. Thus they argued that the primary spiritual posture — and therefore the psychological force for life in this world — was neither existential anxiety (fear that one might not be approved by God) nor self-justification. Rather, true spirituality is a combination of *gratitude* to God and *love* of neighbor. This is what should make people "tick." While these truly spiritual motives do not create "tensed up" people, they do provide an empowering motivation for passionate and creative work, a motivation that can be sustained indefinitely, as I will attempt to show much later. Luther expressed this beautifully using the analogy of marriage (an analogy Calvin also used):[27]

> When a husband and wife really love each other, have pleasure in each other, and thoroughly believe in their love, who teaches them how they are to behave one to another, what they are to do or not to do, say or not to say, what they are to think? Confidence alone teaches them all this, and even more than is necessary. For such a man there is no distinction in works. He does the great and the important as gladly as the small and the unimportant, and vice versa. Moreover, he does them all in a glad, peaceful, and confident heart, and is an absolute willing companion to the woman. But where there is any doubt, he searches within himself for the best thing to do; then a distinction of works arises by which he imagines he may win favor. And yet he goes about it with a heavy heart and great disinclination. He is like a prisoner, more than half in despair and often makes a fool of himself. Thus a Christian man who lives in

25. Weber, *The Protestant Ethic*, p. 115.
26. Weber, *The Protestant Ethic*, p. 128.
27. John Calvin, *Institutes of the Christian Religion* (Grand Rapids: Eerdmans, 1966), 2.12.7.

this confidence toward God knows all things, can do all things, ventures everything that needs to be done, and does everything gladly and willingly, not that he may gain merits and good works, but because it is a pleasure for him to please God in doing these things. He simply serves God with no thought of reward, content that his service pleases God. On the other hand, he who is not at one with God, or is in a state of doubt, worries and starts looking for ways and means to do enough and to influence God with his many good works [Weber's "tensed up" person].[28]

Since the times of the magisterial reformers Luther and Calvin and the post-Protestantism that Weber studied, the Western world has experienced several decades of secular humanism. Speaking to this, Keynes observed fairly that "modern capitalism is absolutely irreligious, without internal union, without much public spirit, often, though not always, mere congeries of possessors and pursuers."[29] The human spirit and God's Spirit have been quenched. Business is business. Greed is good. All too commonly, self-interest is the primary motivation for entrepreneurship. The unhappy divorce of church/religion and business has left business on its own, and Christians (and other people of faith) living schizophrenic lives: God on Sunday, Mammon on Monday. The corporation is simply a profit-making machine. Two hundred years ago George III's Chancellor, Baron Thurlow, said: "How can you expect a corporation to have a conscience, when it has no soul to be damned and no body to be kicked?"[30] There is, however, a cultural paradigm shift under way, due in part to postmodernism (however we define it). Speaking to the philosophical underpinnings of postmodernism, Thomas Oden says, "Postmodernity whether East or West will be searching for a way back to the eternal verities that grounded society before the devastations of

---

28. Martin Luther, "Treatise on Good Works," in *Luther's Works*, trans. W. A. Lambert, ed. James Atkinson (Philadelphia: Fortress Press, 1966), vol. 44, pp. 26-27.

29. Quoted in Charles Handy, *The Hungry Spirit: Beyond Capitalism — A Quest for Purpose in the Modern World* (London: Hutchinson, 1997), p. 31.

30. Quoted in Handy, *The Hungry Spirit*, p. 157.

late modernity."[31] The growing interest in recovering the soul of work, a subject we have already considered, gives evidence of this.

Towards a Christian Spirituality of Entrepreneurship

A spirituality of entrepreneurship must inquire about motivation, about the sources of entrepreneurship. We have already seen that being made in the image of God and participating in God's grand plan of transforming everything gives humans inventiveness, creativity, and initiative.

Being Priests of Creation

It is often alleged that the Judeo-Christian view of the "creation mandate" is license to manipulate and control. Lynn White's classic 1967 article on this subject is still being read. White blames the present crisis on "orthodox Christian arrogance toward nature" and recalls us to Francis of Assisi, who substituted the idea of the equality of all creatures for the idea of humanity's limitless rule of creation. Nevertheless, White notes that the problem is essentially spiritual. "Since the roots of our trouble are so largely religious, the remedy must also be essentially religious, whether we call it that or not."[32] God intended that creation should not simply be preserved intact but should flourish. Humankind was commissioned to be entrepreneurial in just this — to be stewards in developing creation for the common good and for God's glory. But not only to be stewards.

Adam and Eve were the first priests of creation. Alexander Schmemann develops this crucial perspective in this way: Adam and Eve were placed in the garden to bless God in eating, relating, and

---

31. Thomas Oden, *Two Worlds: Notes on the Death of Modernity in America and Russia* (Downers Grove, Ill.: InterVarsity Press, 1992), p. 45.

32. Lynn White Jr., "The Historical Roots of Our Ecological Crisis," *Science* 155, no. 3767 (10 March 1967): 1203-7.

working, offering up their lives to God, and finding communion with God in the entirety of their human experience.

> In the biblical story of creation man is presented . . . as a hungry being, and the whole world his food. . . . The "original" sin is not primarily that man has disobeyed God; the sin is that he ceased to be hungry for Him and for Him alone, ceased to see his whole life depending on the whole world as a sacrament of communion with God. The sin was not that he neglected his religious duties. The sin was that he thought of God in terms of religion, i.e. opposing Him to life. The only real fall of man is his noneucharistic [non-thanksgiving] life in a noneucharistic world.[33]

Work and creativity are therefore part of our love for God; they are ways of blessing God and creation. Entrepreneurs are priests of God. As Novak says, we "bring the Creator's work to its intended fulfillment by being co-creators in a very grand project."[34] We are creating creatures. Underscoring this creativity is the truth that matter matters. The "stuff" of creation is neither evil nor meaningless. Rightly, Christianity and Judaism have been called the most materialistic of all religions. But there is a further issue that relates to our motivation.

Cultivating a Proper Selfishness

The expectation of gain or profit is certainly one of the most complicated issues. Both Adam Smith and many contemporary authors argue that while the entrepreneur's efforts may result unintentionally in the well-being of society, their primary aim is to make a profit. This, however, is not simply the case, even though there is nothing ethically

---

33. See Alexander Schmemann, *For the Life of the World* (Crestwood, N.Y.: St. Vladimir's Seminary Press, 1988), pp. 11, 18.

34. Michael Novak, *Business as a Calling: Work and the Examined Life* (New York: The Free Press, 1996), p. 37.

wrong with desiring a profit.[35] Don Flow, a businessperson, uses the analogy of blood in the human body. We need blood to live but we do not live for our blood. We need profit for a business to survive but businesses do not exist for their own survival; they exist to produce goods and services that sustain and enhance human experience.[36]

While scripture condemns self-love — preoccupation with oneself as a form of idolatry, and selfish ambition as a work of the flesh (Gal. 5) — through which a person is defined by accomplishments, scripture has a place for self-affirmation — appreciating one's value, dignity, talents, and capacities. Scripture also has a concern for profitability — seeing that one's life and one's investment lead to a worthwhile end (Matt. 16:26). Charles Handy calls this a "proper selfishness."[37] We are inspired by the worth and dignity attributed to humankind by God. We are also inspired by the Spirit of God.

Being Empowered by the Spirit of God

Christians commonly believe that God gives his Spirit and spiritual gifts to people solely for work and ministry in the church. But spiritual gifts are not just for the edification of believers. They are for the world, for entering into God's beautiful work of transforming creation, culture, community, and people. The Holy Spirit empowers us to do good and beautiful things. And to explore this we turn to the only person in the Old Testament of whom it is said "he was filled with the Holy Spirit." His name is Bezalel and he is my patron saint — a carpenter, an artisan, an artist, and a teacher (Exod. 31:1-11; 35:10-19; 35:30–36:5). In this cryptic but wonderfully evocative Old Testament

---

35. Ed Silvoso notes how in the Old Testament David, facing the challenge of defeating Goliath, asked, "What shall be done for the man who kills the Philistine, and takes away the reproach from Israel?" (1 Sam. 17:26). See Ed Silvoso, *Anointed for Business: How Christians Can Use Their Influence in the Marketplace to Change the World* (Ventura, Calif.: Regal, 2002), p. 62.

36. Don Flow, "Profit," in Banks and Stevens, eds., *Everyday Christianity*, pp. 809-13.

37. Handy, *The Hungry Spirit*, p. 86.

story, a cameo, we have a prophetic picture of what all believers are meant to be and do in the world now that the Spirit has been poured out on all.

In Exodus 31 and 35 we learn that God filled Bezalel with his Spirit and with wisdom, discernment, and skill to devise artistic designs, to work in gold, silver, bronze, precious stones, and wood — all to make a sacred place to meet with God — the tent or tabernacle, which was the people's means of knowing that God was really present in every-day life.[38] Wisdom is practical intelligence and vision — seeing, designing, and figuring out how to do something. Discernment is clarity in problem-solving. Skill is the practical ability to make it happen, hands and heart joined in doing so. This is the gift of the Spirit that God gives to his people in the workplace, uniquely of course under the older covenant, when only a few had direct interaction with the Spirit of God, and then often temporarily, but under the new covenant in Jesus, personally, universally, and permanently.

In Exodus 36:2 we learn yet one more thing. God called and empowered not only Bezalel and his helper, Oholiab, but also other skilled people "to whom the LORD had given skill [and] whose heart was stirred to come to do the work." The Hebrew literally means that their hearts were lifted up to become involved in this work. The Spirit moves us inwardly to want to do what God has called us to. Frederick Buechner says,

> There are all different kinds of voices calling you to all different kinds of work, and the problem is to find out which is the voice of God rather than of Society, say, or the Super-ego, or Self-Interest. By and large a good rule for finding out is this. The kind of work God usually calls you to is the kind of work (a) that you most need to do and (b) that the world most needs to have done. . . . Neither the hair shirt nor the soft berth will

38. Alan Cole says, "If the law was a verbal expression of God's holiness, the Tent was a visible parable of it, and the nation of Israel was intended to be a walking illustration of it." And "the entire aim of the construction of the Tent is so that God's presence may be experienced in the very midst of Israel." Alan Cole, *Exodus: A Commentary* (Downers Grove, Ill.: InterVarsity Press, 1973), pp. 23, 39.

do. The place God calls you to is the place where your deep gladness and the world's deep hunger meet.[39]

We ask to know the will of God when he has written it into the story of our lives. Listen to your life (which is the subject of the next chapter). Each of us is empowered to make something beautiful. I remember, when I was a carpenter, sneaking in on my partner Graeme Smith as he was fitting a very complicated piece of corner bead around a curved arch. He put it on, then took it off, readjusted it once again, and then, standing back, without knowing anyone was within earshot, said, "Beautiful." Beauty is not just in music and graphic art, but in a meal or a deal, a voice or an invoice, an operation or a cooperation, a community formed or an immunity created, a test or a quest, a swept floor or forgiven heart, a canvas painting or a computer program, a plaything or a work thing, a toy or a tool. In my "Everyday Life Spirituality" course when students introduced themselves on the first evening, one woman said, "I am just a hairdresser." At the end of the course she said, "I make people beautiful, and I do a lot of counseling."

Following Jesus the Entrepreneur

Onto the stage of human history strides Jesus. We can consider Jesus to be a model entrepreneur not only because his three-year public ministry for the kingdom of God involved envisioning, inventing, and implementing, but also because his occupation as a *tekton* (Greek), usually translated "carpenter," likely involved making a project happen as much as designing and building a boat or a house. Bruce Barton in 1924 wrote a book entitled, *The Man Nobody Knows,* a book often scorned but that contains some truth. The gospels, Barton argues, picture Jesus running a small entrepreneurial business, engaging the powers, enjoying a feast, befriending the marginalized, and changing the course of history. As Barton says,

39. Frederick Buechner, *Listening to Your Life: Daily Meditations with Frederick Buechner* (San Francisco: HarperSanFrancisco, 1992), pp. 185-86.

Jesus had no funds and no machinery. His organization was a tiny group of uneducated men, one of whom had already abandoned the cause as hopeless, deserting to the enemy. He had come proclaiming a Kingdom and was to end upon a cross; yet he dared to talk of conquering all creation.[40]

What was the secret of his "entrepreneurial success"? From the gospels Barton extracts several principles by which he argues that Jesus was the founder of modern business: Whoever will be great must render great service; whoever will find himself at the top must be willing to lose himself at the bottom; the big rewards come to those who travel the second, undemanded mile.[41] A contemporary development of the same theme, *Jesus CEO,* invites yet another book with the title *Jesus Entrepreneur!*[42]

Undoubtedly, the world has changed since the days of Puritanism that Weber analyzed. We have moved from a culture informed by belief in a supreme being in which people lived out their lives in a calling, answerable in the end to God, to an anti-rational, humanistic, and often nihilistic culture. Perhaps secular humanism has run its course. In recent years there has, in the West, been a recovery of spirit or soul. It is a mixed and ambiguous movement. One could cynically suggest it is just one more manipulative device to be used by managers to crank up motivation in flagging workers — of instrumental rather than intrinsic value. The nature of true spirituality is that it is essentially gratuitous. But the New Business Spirituality invites a recovery of the great truths and spiritual themes that fired the entrepreneurship of Jews, early Christians, Catholics, Protestants, and all peoples of faith: priests of creation, a proper selfishness, the inspiration and gifting of the Holy Spirit, and the example of Jesus. What can be certainly maintained is that, except in the Third World, where tra-

---

40. Bruce Barton, *The Man Nobody Knows: A Discovery of the Real Jesus* (New York: Triangle Books, 1924), p. 89.

41. Barton, *The Man Nobody Knows,* p. 177. In contrast, see Edmund F. Byrne, *Work, Inc.: A Philosophical Inquiry* (Philadelphia: Temple University Press, 1990), p. 66. Byrne claims Jesus was not a good role model for work.

42. Silvoso develops this in *Anointed for Business,* p. 40.

ditional Christian faith is flourishing, we are witnessing a recovery of entrepreneurship through spirituality *without religion* and therefore without a transcendent and universal basis for entrepreneurial initiative. Will the religious/spiritual form of the new humanism prove enough without a transcendent center? Is something more needed? Gianfranco Poggi concludes: There can be "no capitalist development without an entrepreneurial class; no entrepreneurial class without a moral charter; no moral charter without religious premises."[43]

For Discussion

• **AN ENTREPRENEUR'S DILEMMA** •

Jim Laxton watched the second hand of the clock make another revolution — 2:17 A.M. Another in a string of sleepless nights. While his body craved rest, Jim's mind continued to be agitated. There must be some solution. What was God saying? Time to decide was running out. For the thousandth time, this forty-two-year-old entrepreneur considered the path that had led him into the current situation. He weighed the options before him.

It was in a Christian graduate school that Jim had met and befriended George, a part-time student with dreams to form a venture capital company composed of Christian investors and a Christian management team. Upon graduation, Jim had sensed a calling back to the marketplace where he had worked for fifteen years as a manager for a large insurance company. Jim decided to join George's new enterprise, Innovative Venture Capital Corporation, and soon was assigned as project manager to the venture capital company's first investment in a new business. Urban Interiors manufactured and distributed unique, patented wall assembly systems. The challenge facing Jim was to find ways to develop the market for the new wall assembly system and to help set up a consistent and efficient manufacturing process. All this was to be done with relatively limited

43. Poggi, *Calvinism and the Capitalist Spirit*, p. 83.

funds that were being raised through George's venture capital company.

Two years had passed since then. Urban Interiors' business was growing, but slowly. The accounts payable had also been steadily building, and investment in the business had not kept pace. As a result, there was serious undercapitalization. An emergency meeting of the board of directors of Innovative Venture Capital Corporation was convened. Jim put his case before the board, asking that additional funds be invested in Urban Interiors. He was fairly sure that with additional funding the business would soon turn the corner and have a positive cash flow. After considerable discussion and deliberation, the board decided that Innovative should not increase its investment in Urban Interiors. They realized that without further funds, Urban Interiors could not survive and thus they would lose their entire investment. They had offered to sell Urban Interiors to Jim for $1 and a percentage of profits in the future if the business survived.

For the past five months, Jim had not received a salary. He had lived on savings. If he bought Urban Interiors, there was little likelihood of a salary for at least another year. While he had sufficient savings to do this, Jim was very concerned about the risks this would create for his family. Jim's wife Lorraine would support Jim whichever way he decided to go. Sometimes that felt like a mixed blessing. One major consideration was the eleven people who worked for Urban Interiors. They had jelled into a solid team, and Jim had significant relationships with most of them. They looked to him for leadership and strength. Jim was still very excited about the products Urban Interiors produced. They were of excellent quality, and customers were very satisfied. It was just difficult and expensive to get the marketing message out. Jim sought the advice of his friend Paul, a lawyer, who laid out several options. Jim could accept the offer and try to make a go of the business. This would involve significant personal sacrifice and risk. He could walk away and find other work. Or he could allow the business to file for bankruptcy and hope that he might be able to buy assets from the trustee. This would be very risky as there was no guarantee that the trustee would sell to him, and in any event, he would have to dig into his savings to pay for the assets. Additionally, he would have to find new sources of supply. He might also lose some key employees in the process. Suppliers and employees would be hurt if this happened.

The board of Innovative had asked for Jim's answer by Friday, the day after tomorrow. Jim was still unsettled as to how to proceed. He loved the challenge and freedom that came with leading a business. But he had never realized that the cost would be so high. 2:23 A.M. Not much time left to decide!

•   •

1. Think of entrepreneurs you know. What are their positive characteristics? What are their weaknesses?
2. What issues are faced by each of the people in this case: George (a director of the venture capital company, Innovative Venture Capital Corporation); Jim (project manager of Urban Interiors); and Paul (a lawyer)? What feelings might George and Jim have? What are the real options for the venture capital company? What are the real options for Jim? For what reasons would further risk be warranted? What gains, other than monetary, might be made by continuing the business? When would be the right time to pull the plug on the business? What insight does Christian theology bring to this case?

For Further Reading

Drucker, Peter F. *Innovation and Entrepreneurship: Practice and Principles.* New York: Harper & Row, 1985.

Handy, Charles. *The Hungry Spirit: Beyond Capitalism — A Quest for Purpose in the Modern World.* London: Hutchinson, 1997.

Schmemann, Alexander. *For the Life of the World.* Crestwood, N.Y.: St. Vladimir's Seminary Press, 1988.

Silvoso, Ed. *Anointed for Business: How Christians Can Use Their Influence in the Marketplace to Change the World.* Ventura, Calif.: Regal, 2002.

10

$\blacklozenge \quad \blacklozenge \quad \blacklozenge$

Letting Life Speak

But the door into life generally opens behind us, and a hand is put forth which draws us in backwards. The sole wisdom for a man or boy who is haunted with the hovering of unseen wings, with the scent of unseen roses, and the subtle enticements of "melodies unheard" is work. If he follows any of those, they will vanish. But if he works, they will come unsought.

George MacDonald

Marketplace spirituality is not only about the disciplines we can thread into our daily life, such as prayer, Bible reading, seasons and patterns of reflection, and meditation; it is also about the reality that life and work are themselves spiritual disciplines, pointing us Godward and teaching us about ourselves. To explore this we will open an obscure Old Testament book, Ecclesiastes, which was written, or so it seems, by a "successful" businessperson. If the writer was not a businessperson, then that person was some other leader in the community, for the Hebrew title Qoheleth (the Greek name is Ecclesiastes) denotes someone who is prominent in the assembly, a professor or teacher who has an impressive résumé.

Ecclesiastes is an enigmatic book that raises more questions than it answers. But unlike Job, who addresses his questions directly to God, at first it seems that the Professor is simply asking them for himself. We get to overhear these questions, like overhearing someone talking while asleep or two people chatting in the next restaurant booth. But the writer of Ecclesiastes means us to hear these questions, because it is just possible that this is written from the perspective of a secularist, someone who believes only in humankind, who sees everything "under the sun," the code words used thirty times in the book. "Under the sun" means having no reference to a supreme being, no relationship beyond what can be grasped with the human mind or human instrumentality — without God. So either this book is the Professor's own questioning — as I suppose — or it is an apologetic designed to start where the secularist must start — with life under the sun.

And what he sees is this: "The words of the Teacher, son of David, king in Jerusalem. 'Meaningless! Meaningless!' says the Teacher. 'Utterly meaningless! Everything is meaningless'" (1:2 [NIV]). Whether written by Solomon or one who takes on the role of Solomon, building, acquiring, inquiring, enjoying, he has a hard question to ask — What is the meaning of life? "What do people gain from all the toil at which they toil under the sun?" (1:3). So you design a new computer program. So you spend your life making electronic widgets. You create a new business. What do you really gain?

God makes himself known in our everyday life not, like the prophets, with the force of a cannon or a guided missile with nuclear warhead — "thus says the Lord," but more with the force of a hint — thus hints the Lord! There is a hint in our hearts that there may be more than the endless flow of activities and experiences, a "more" that points to a supreme and personal God who, at the conclusion of this study, will be one we are invited to fear, to fear in the sense of showing loving, ethical awe. A cartoon pictures two fish in a bowl. One says to the other, "I just figured out the meaning of life! Water!"

This cartoon points in the same direction as Ecclesiastes does — to the discovery that the greatest gift of God in life is life itself. And we find God, not outside of life, not by jumping out of the fishbowl, but *in* life. But you really can't come to that conclusion without traveling the whole journey — asking what is it all for, what do I really gain, what will be after me, and, is there any good?

So where do we get meaning? The quick answer is not "under the sun," but in God. But often this sounds like the answer given by the Sunday School student who was asked, "What is brown, furry, lives in trees, and eats nuts?" The nine-year-old answered, "I know the correct answer is supposed to be Jesus, but it seems to me a lot like a squirrel." The Professor won't let us rush to the answer to his question because the process is revelatory. In this book God is creator and reality. The surrounding water is a stubborn reality that cannot be entirely shaped by us. It is not only stubborn but also mysterious, especially when we consider, as the Professor does in 11:5, "Just as you do not know how the breath comes to the bones in the mother's womb, so you do not know the work of God, who makes everything."

But God is also sovereign. God has made life frustrating. Ecclesiastes is the Old Testament exposition of Paul's statement in Romans 8 that the creation was subjected by God to futility by the very one who subjected it in hope. The creation is groaning (8:20-22). Since the emphasis of Ecclesiastes is "let life speak," we will let life speak on three themes: time, money, and success.

The Time of Our (Business) Lives

My mother used to say to me repeatedly in my young adult years, "What's the hurry?"

Perhaps I thought, I don't have enough time. Or no time at all. Or time is running out! Augustine of Hippo is reported to have said, "Time never takes time off."[1]

---

1. Quoted in William T. McConnell, *The Gift of Time* (Downers Grove, Ill.: InterVarsity Press, 1983), p. 61.

In a wonderful contrast, Ecclesiastes says, "For everything there is . . . a time" (3:1-11), though this is not quite the same thing as saying "there is time *for* everything." We need to ponder this because we in the North, West, and much of Asia are acculturated to see time as a resource to be managed, to squeeze out of it everything we can, like the last drippings of a lemon squeezed on a fish. In the East and South, culture is more event-oriented than future-oriented, with occasions like weddings and funerals happening at approximate times and lasting until the meaning of the event is fully experienced.

It is tempting to approach the subject of time deductively — taking the major themes of theological reflection and extrapolating on this: God created time; it is part of the creation order. He created time good. Indeed the first mention of holiness in the Bible is for holy time. "So God blessed the seventh day and hallowed it" (Gen. 2:3). Time, along with the rest of creation, has been trusted to humankind as God's vice-regents, to be stewards of time but not owners. Time, along with everything else, has been twisted by the Fall, by sin — so it has been touched by the curse, and while we can experience substantial redemption in this life through the work of Christ, until this world is transfigured into the new heaven and new earth our experience of time will be ambiguous.

If we are exegetes of the New Testament we might want to explore the difference between the two words for "time" in Greek — *chronos* or clock time, which can be managed, dissected, digitalized, and processed, but not expanded, and *kairos,* a word that sometimes means clock time but in most contexts means the time of opportunity, time fraught with eternal dimensions, or time that is a call to judgment or salvation. It is "timely" time, as when Paul in Ephesians 5:16 and Colossians 4:5 speaks of "Making the most of every opportunity."[2] These last verses sadly have been twisted by Christian time management consultants to mean, Squeeze all you can out of the limited resource you have, rather than to seize the kingdom irruption when the moment provides.

All of this — the deductive approach — might be of some value,

2. McConnell, *The Gift of Time,* p. 96.

but it is not the route taken by the Professor. He is expounding experience, not theology, and finds in the experience of time a pregnant hint that points Godward. In other words, he is an inductive theologian, much like Luther, who said it is by living and dying, by being damned and being saved that one becomes a theologian, not by reasoning and speculating.

Experiencing Time

First the Professor says that we experience time in seasons, and here he lists a series of contrasts: a season for birthing, planting, healing, building, laughing, dancing, gathering stones, embracing, searching, keeping, mending, speaking, loving, and making peace. Yes, this we understand — life has its seasons. But what about dying, uprooting, killing, tearing down, weeping, mourning, scattering stones, refraining from embracing, giving up, throwing away, tearing, being silent, hating, making war (3:1-8)? But this is how we experience life — seasonally. Even a peace-loving nation will find itself at war, and the passionate lover will in time refrain; a business will be shut down, and the humorist will weep; and we shall in time die.

But second, *this is not an endless round, or an ebb and flow that have no inner coherence or sense,* as though we were flotsam and jetsam on the tides of time. Time is not part of the "burden" God has laid on humans, like the stretching of the violin string that will nevertheless produce a beautiful sound. The Professor says in 3:11, "God has made everything beautiful in its time" (NIV). Here, surely, is where the Professor comes closest to the New Testament references about *kairos* — or meaningful time, but not just in the sense that we have a strategic moment in which we can do something. He is saying that there is something beautiful going on: There is beautiful time, just as there is a beautiful art, physical beauty, the beauty of a mathematical theorem or a computer program. There is something exquisite and aesthetic, something that calls forth "Aha" in us, or "Oohs and ahs," something "holy" in being present with the present.

But this hint about the beautiful moment points rather sadly to its opposite: not being present, letting the present slip by without seeing its beauty, or being so future-oriented, so much on to the next thing you are going to do — in business or in personal planning — that you are not really present at all — something I have personally wrestled with.

But third, the Professor is really saying that time is an evangelist to take us beyond the present to recognize we are being sought by God himself. Verse 11 again says, "He has set eternity in the hearts of men and women; yet they cannot fathom what God has done from beginning to end" (NIV). "Eternity" is a rough translation of a word that in this context suggests something close to "heaven," the "age that will outlive this age," or "the kingdom of God."

There is a pointer in our experience of time, a pointer to God, but it is subtle. Jacques Ellul puts it this way:

> We are never satisfied with what we have accomplished. We start over and over; since planting does not satisfy, we must uproot; since tearing fails to satisfy, we must sew, etc. Our insatiable activism comes from our desire for something else — something that will finally prove stable. . . . Everything slips through our fingers. . . . We continually require that love last eternally. We want our life to have meaning.[3]

But we can't fathom what God has done from beginning to end. As Derek Kidner observes, "We are like the desperately near-sighted, inching their way along some great tapestry or fresco in the attempt to take it in. We see enough to recognize something of its quality, but the grand design escapes us, for we can never stand back far enough to view it as the Creator does, whole and entire, from the beginning to the end."[4] Kidner points out how dismaying this is for the thoughtful secularist under the sun, but how encouraging for the believer who has faith.

So what does this mean?

---

3. Jacques Ellul, *Reason for Being: A Meditation on Ecclesiastes,* trans. Joyce Main Hanks (Grand Rapids: Eerdmans, 1972), pp. 242-43.

4. Derek Kidner, *The Message of Ecclesiastes: A Time to Mourn and a Time to Dance* (Downers Grove, Ill.: InterVarsity Press, 1976), p. 39.

A Spirituality of Treasuring Time

First, time is a gift of God. It is not simply a resource to be managed and manipulated — a thing that is our enemy, our antagonist, always frustrating us, always denying us all we need. If it is a gift of God, then we should respect the wishes of the giver in how we use it.

Second, we are stewards, trusted with time but not owning it, and we are accountable to God for our stewardship. Are we able to discern the opportunities presented to us, the "beautiful" in the moment, the season, or the work we are presently doing, or the doing of nothing — which is really doing something and not just experiencing a void? There is, of course, a place for time planning, for discerning the important from the urgent. Stephen Covey has helpfully shown how most people dwell in the urgent and not the important, and those he calls "effective people" move away from the urgent (but not important) to spend time on the important.

Jacques Ellul observes that if we are going to see how beautiful something is, a moment, a season, a work, or an experience, "we are called to discernment rather than doing things any time we choose, however we choose."[5] John Wesley once said, "Though I am always in haste, I am never in a hurry, because I never undertake more work than I can go through with calmness of spirit."[6]

Third, we have enough time, enough to do everything God wants us to do without squeezing every last drop out of the lemon, without living hurriedly, without being controlled by the clock. Robert Schuller turned busyness into a philosophy of life: "I began my lifework on the assumption that I might not live long enough to accomplish everything I'd like to. If I wanted to do anything worthwhile in my life I'd have to hurry up. I have been in a hurry ever since."[7]

Michel Quoist put this poignantly in a prayer:

> Lord, I have time,
> I have plenty of time.

5. Ellul, *Reason for Being,* pp. 237-38.
6. McConnell, *The Gift of Time,* p. 105.
7. Quoted in McConnell, *The Gift of Time,* p. 16.

All the time that you give me,
The years of my life,
The days of my years,
The hours of my days,
They are all mine.
Mine to fill, quietly, calmly,
But to fill completely, up to the brim,
To offer them to you, that of their insipid water
You may make a rich wine as you
Made once in Cana of Galilee.[8]

So time points us inward and Godward. When we turn to the next subject we are haunted by the common and deceptive phrase that "time is money."

Money — The Bottom Line

Jacques Ellul has said that the whole message of Ecclesiastes message can be summed up in the words of Georges Bernanos: "In order to be prepared to hope in what does not deceive, we must first lose hope in everything that deceives."[9] Nothing deceives us perhaps as much as the seeming security and power of money — a theme Ecclesiastes explores in chapters five and six with sprinklings of comments throughout the book.

What comes to our minds with the mention of money? Never enough. Slips through my fingers. Where does it go? Would that I had just a little more. They are just in it for the money. The bottom line.

On one hand, the Professor says that "money meets every need" (10:19). On the other hand he says, "Whoever loves money never has money enough" (5:10 [NIV]).

Let me linger a little on the first statement that "money meets every need." In his fascinating book on finding a middle ground between matters of the wallet and matters of the spirit, *Money and the*

8. Quoted in McConnell, *The Gift of Time,* p. 91.
9. Quoted in Ellul, *Reason for Being,* p. 46.

Meaning of Life, Jacob Needleman suggests that there are very few, "even shockingly few" problems of life that cannot be solved by the infusion of a finite amount of money. The reason, he suggests, is that money can buy almost anything we want. The problem is, as Needleman points out, "that we tend to want only the things that money can buy."[10]

This leads to the Professor's second wonderful conclusion, namely that "Whoever loves money never has money enough." Kemper Fullerton observes, "After all, however blind economists may be to the fact, metaphysical convictions are the only ones which have absolute power to dominate men's lives. Economic reasons cannot account for the extraordinary power in the Western civilization today which the money-making motive exerts."[11] Has the love of money taken the place of the love of God?

The Professor is not simply down on money, suggesting that we should do without it if we could. In fact, he is merely endorsing common sense that money is the answer for a lot of problems. But he will not treat money as many theologians do today, as something neutral — merely a medium of exchange that can be used for good or ill. Money is an illusionary power; it is pretentious; it lays hold of our hearts. This is why Jesus said, "Where your treasure is, there your heart will be also" (Matt. 6:21).

Indeed, in an amazing prophecy of modern consumerist society, the Professor says in 5:11, "When goods increase, those who eat them increase" — we keep earning more and more to keep buying, and our desire for money is never satisfied. Tomorrow's wants surpass today's needs. This is so true that the more one has, the more complexity and problems one has. "Sweet is the sleep of laborers, whether they eat little or much; but the surfeit of the rich will not let them sleep" (v. 12) — either through worry or overeating. If it is the former we rely on sleeping pills, and if it is the latter we spend money on exercise machines.

10. Jacob Needleman, *Money and the Meaning of Life* (New York: Doubleday, 1991), p. 112.

11. Quoted in Needleman, *Money and the Meaning of Life,* p. xvii.

The Professor anticipates the great work of Christ on the cross, which "disarmed the rulers and authorities and made a public example of them" (Col. 2:15) — thus showing their illusionary power and defeating them by his death and resurrection. The Professor disarms the power of money by saying it is empty, a vanity, and a puff of smoke. It can buy anything, even human souls (Rev. 18:13). It can even purchase the secret location of Jesus in the garden and so secure his arrest. Yet it is nothing. Why?

Three truths will help us put money in its place.

First, when sought for itself it never satisfies. You never have enough — first it is a luxury car, then a second country home, and one thing leads to another. While consumption gallops ahead, possessions serve no use except for the owner to feast his or her eyes on them (5:11). Kidner puts it this way: "If anything is worse than the addiction money brings, it is the emptiness it leaves. Man, with eternity in his heart, needs better nourishment than this."[12]

Needleman expresses this beautifully: "Do not take for God that which is not really God: this means, among many other ways of expressing it — not to look for power, safety, joy, service, love, or meaning from any other source than that which actually brings it about in the whole of reality."[13] Needleman thinks that the entire problem of life in contemporary culture can be summed up in the words of Jesus: "Render unto Caesar that which is Caesar's, and unto God that which is God's."[14]

Second, when money is trusted as a basis of security it will prove to be empty. The Aramaic word *Mammon* has the same root as *Amen* — that which is definite and seems to give security. When you trust money as a basis of security you will find it is gone like a puff of smoke. "You cannot serve God and Money," Jesus said (Luke 16:13 [NIV]). The Professor puts it this way: "There is a grievous ill that I have seen under the sun: riches were kept by their owners to their hurt, and those riches were lost in a bad venture; though they are par-

12. Kidner, *Message of Ecclesiastes*, p. 56.
13. Needleman, *Money and the Meaning of Life*, p. 61.
14. Needleman, *Money and the Meaning of Life*, p. 51.

ents of children, they have nothing in their hands" (5:13-14). Elsewhere Ellul will say we de-sacralize money by giving it away, something that the rich man in Jesus' parable in Luke 16 did not do with the poor man Lazarus at his gate.[15]

Third, you can't take it with you. An armored vehicle has never followed a hearse to the graveyard. "As they came from their mother's womb, so they shall go again, naked as they came" (5:15). One of the worst perversions in the world today is the health-and-wealth gospel. But it is a very old idea, as many ancient sages have said that wealth is a sign of God's pleasure. And many religious hucksters today promote the idea that if you love and serve God you will be blessed with material wealth. And even the Professor says that "God gives wealth, possessions, and honor" (6:2). So whatever we have comes from God. But there is no direct cause-effect relationship between faith and wealth. Scandalously, God gives wealth to some righteous and to some unrighteous. But neither will find security in it.

On this point William Diehl offers a helpful chapter on a "theology of enough" in his excellent book *Thank God It's Monday.* He notes the temptation to keep acquiring ever more luxurious cars and houses, especially as one climbs the corporate ladder. In contrast he proposes living with "enough" — rather than choosing to live at the "top end." "If we follow a theology of enough," Diehl says, "it will mean that in whatever capacity we serve, our life style will be a modest one. We will accept and use only enough wealth and power to carry out our mission effectively. Wealth and power will be employed only to the degree they are needed to fulfill our priestly role — never for our own sake."[16]

So once again we find no hope in the deceit of money. The Professor wants us to discover this simply to find that under the sun there is nothing — not work, not a career, not marriage, not projects, not possessions — that, if sought for itself, will fill the God-shaped vacuum in

---

15. Jacques Ellul, *Money and Power,* trans. LaVonne Neff (Downers Grove, Ill.: InterVarsity Press, 1984).

16. William E. Diehl, *Thank God It's Monday* (Philadelphia: Fortress Press, 1982), p. 132.

the heart. Nothing under the sun will satisfy, except God. This makes us ask what constitutes success.

The Paradox of Success

Almost every business is evaluated by the question, Is it a success? Certainly shareholders in publicly traded companies do not want to invest in a failure, unless there are tax advantages in doing so. But what about businesspeople? Must they be successful? And what does their success look like?

Success is a paradox, and here is why:

- Because truly successful people may be failures. King Midas in the myth turned everything he touched into gold. But in the end he turned his daughter and even his food into metal and starved to death.
- Because failure may be success. Charles Colson was a success in his political profession but lost his soul to the Nixon White House. In failure, after going to prison for his crimes, he succeeded in establishing a prison ministry.
- Because faithful success is mysterious. It cannot be controlled, invented, or planned.
- Because where success is possessed it is lost. The advice to move from the youthful pursuit of success to seeking significance in the second half of life may not be helpful. It is tantamount to saying, "God has a wonderful plan for the second half of my life!" Jesus' response to the rich young ruler was not "go and do something significant with your life" but "follow me."
- Because the pursuit of success is an especially direct road to true failure. On the road to success, beware of arriving. The symptom of the person who has arrived is the loss of the ability to ask questions — dead on arrival.[17]

17. I acknowledge indebtedness for some of these thoughts to Skip Li, a Seattle lawyer speaking in the "Doing God's Business" course at Regent College, 1999.

Researching the divergent themes in success literature, Stephen Covey notes how some emphasize the personality ethic: public image and techniques. He judges this to be the dominant view. The best approach, he proposes, is one that addresses character. "There are basic principles of effective living, and . . . people can only experience true success and enduring happiness as they learn and integrate these principles into their basic character" — integrity, humility, courage, justice, patience, industry, simplicity, modesty, and the Golden Rule — as basic principles of effective living.[18]

Defining Success

Jacques Ellul provides a thoughtful Christian reflection on success in his probing "Essay on Inutility." He insists that in the light of Christ's accomplishments we can hardly boast about our own.

> At a stroke we learn that in Jesus Christ salvation is given to us, that God loved us before we did anything, that all is grace; grace — gracious gift, free gift. Life and salvation, resurrection and faith itself, glory and virtue, all is grace, all is attained already, all is done already and even our good works which we strive with great difficulty to perform have been prepared in advance that we should do them. It is all finished. . . . Of what use are these works? . . . And yet works are demanded of us; they are God's command and yet a useless service. . . . If we are ready to be unworthy or unprofitable servants (although busy and active at the same time), then our works can truly redound to the glory of him who loved us first. God loved us because he is love and not to get results.[19]

18. Stephen Covey, *The Seven Habits of Highly Successful People* (New York: Simon & Schuster, 1989), p. 18.

19. Jacques Ellul, "Meditation on Inutility," in *The Politics of God and the Politics of Man,* trans. Geoffrey W. Bromiley (Grand Rapids: Eerdmans, 1972), pp. 190-99.

The Professor's Reflections on Success

Undoubtedly the Professor was an entrepreneurial leader.

> I made great works . . . houses, vineyards, gardens and parks, pools, . . . I bought slaves . . . herds and flocks . . . I also gathered . . . silver and gold . . . got singers . . . and many concubines. . . . Then I considered all that my hands had done and the toil I had spent in doing it, and again, all was vanity and a chasing after wind; and there was nothing to be gained under the sun (2:4-11).

So the Professor came to some stunning conclusions:

First, we are to work not to be useful or to prove our identity but because it is a gift of God. "There is nothing better for mortals than to eat and drink, and find enjoyment in their toil. This also, I saw, is from the hand of God; for apart from him who can eat or who can have enjoyment? For to the one who pleases him God gives wisdom and knowledge and joy . . ." (2:24-26). "It is God's gift that all should eat and drink and take pleasure in all their toil" (3:13).

Second, there is more to life than material success, which will always let us down. "The lover of money will not be satisfied with money; nor the lover of wealth, with gain. This also is vanity" (5:10).

Third, we are to "get into life" even though all our projects and even our bodies are doomed to the grave. "Whatever your hand finds to do, do with your might; for there is no work or thought or knowledge or wisdom in [the grave], to which you are going" (9:10).

Fourth, we are to take the risk of investing and not to wait around for the perfect situation. Nevertheless, we should not put "all our eggs in one basket" but rather spread the risk. "Send out your bread upon the waters, for after many days you will get it back" (11:1). This is probably a reference to the grain trade in the ancient world. You'll never make money on the grain market, the Professor says, if you keep everything in the granary in Alexandria. Be generous; give; don't live a pinched life, and you will get it back — maybe pushed down and running over. "Divide your means seven ways, or even eight, for you do not know what disaster may happen upon earth. . . . Whoever observes the wind [waiting for the perfect weather] will not sow; whoever regards the clouds will not reap" (11:2-4). The Professor seems to be on the same topic in verse 6: "In the morning sow your seed, and at evening do not let your hands be idle; for you do not know which will prosper, this or that, or whether both alike will be good."

Fifth, work is an evangelist to take us to God — who alone can fill the God-shaped vacuum in our souls. Our work is temporary, unappreciated; it will be taken over by a fool; we will experience injustice; it is just plain hard (2:18, 19, 21, 22). But it is God's will that our work is "useless." If the Professor is right, then we will not find satisfaction in our work through faith in God (the current "Christian" work heresy); instead we will find our satisfaction in God through our experience of work. It is a subtle and telling distinction.

Sixth, we are investing in eternity in the midst of our life here and now, laying up for ourselves treasures in heaven. "He has made everything suitable for its time; moreover he has put a sense of past and future into their minds. . . . I know that whatever God does endures forever; nothing can be added to it, nor anything taken from it; God has done this, so that all should stand in awe before him" (3:11, 14).

Beyond the Professor

Those are the conclusions of our Old Testament seeker. Does the New Testament offer something more? There is no word for "success" in the New Testament except for the names of two women, "Success" [Euodia] and "Lucky" [Syntyche] (Phil. 4:2). Another word in the Old and New Testaments that comes close to the meaning is the word "blessed" (Deut. 11:26-28; Matt. 5:3-12), a word that means "the inner riches of personal character conformed to God's character."[20] The ultimate goal for humankind in the Bible is righteousness — right rela-

---

20. Robert Girard, "Failure," in Robert Banks and R. Paul Stevens, eds., *The Complete Book of Everyday Christianity* (Downers Grove, Ill.: InterVarsity Press, 1997), p. 363.

tions with God, neighbor, and creation. "Strive first for the kingdom of God and his righteousness," said Jesus (Matt. 6:33).

God's evaluation of success is a scandalous inversion of human values: the widow and her penny (Mark 12:42) and the tax collector at prayer (Luke 18:14). Since Jesus calls humility the mark of true spirituality — a God preoccupation and self-forgetfulness — we might not know we were successful if we were! We have a humble God who takes the way of downward mobility (Phil. 2:6-11). Jesus counsels us to "store up for yourselves treasures in heaven" (Matt. 6:20). The only treasures we can take from this life to the next are the relationships we have made through Christ (Luke 16:9). Shockingly, Jesus suggests that the successful person in terms of human achievement is a stunning failure and a fool (Luke 12:20). And Robert Girard concludes, "The world's success story [Babylon] concludes with God's disclosure of the ultimate failure of worldly success" (Rev. 18).[21]

Most wise people when asked how they got wisdom, answer that it was through making mistakes. Failure can in fact produce sterling character. And through failure we can move from bragging to brokenness (Luke 22:54-62).[22] The greatest failure that might be experienced by an otherwise successful person would be to go unrecognized by Jesus at the last day when we all meet God face to face: "I never knew you" (Matt. 7:23; 25:12). And the ultimate success is to "enter into the joy of the master" (Matt. 25:21) and to hear "Well done, good and faithful servant!" (Matt. 25:23 [NIV]).

Behind our handling of time, money, and success is the need to control. And the Professor says in chapter 11 that we are not in complete control: You do not know what disaster may come upon the land (v. 2); when a tree falls to the south or the north, there it will lie (v. 3); you are not in control of the wind, or the formation of a baby in the mother's womb (v. 4); and you don't know which venture you undertake will succeed (v. 6). Paul Tournier, a Christian psychiatrist, shows in his book *The Adventure of Living* how the fears of failure and of success rule people. But behind these fears is the need to be in con-

21. Girard, "Failure," p. 365.
22. Girard, "Failure," pp. 365-66.

trol. And the need to control is essentially the need to play God. The push for autonomy and absolute control goes right back to the original sin in the Garden of Eden. It is life "under the sun."

The Professor concludes, though he does so sparsely, more like a hint, that the fear of the Lord is the beginning of wisdom — not a fright fear, but loving awe of God, affectionate respect, and humble dependence. God can be trusted with the outcome of our lives. God can be trusted with the investment of our talents in an enterprise. God can be trusted with what we give away.

The alternative is deadly boredom, a pinched existence, being the walking dead. Paul Tournier says, "Life is a constant game of 'double or nothing.' We are always tempted to save what we have by refusing to put it at risk again. But this means the end of the adventure."[23]

Steve Brinn, formerly vice president of the Trillium Corporation, advises this:

> Stand on your heads every morning to understand that we have everything upside down in the business world. The big deals are not the big deals in the kingdom. Read fairy tales: constantly blow the lid off the limits to see that everything is possible. Don't flee the scenes of your failures; grieve, reflect, learn. Give yourself time. It takes a long time to find out who you are in business. Break out of lifestyle enclaves. Join a revolutionary movement of some kind in your life. Never give up on things that matter.[24]

For Discussion

1. The failure that God has redeemed in my life is . . .
2. The success that is a temptation for me is . . .

23. Paul Tournier, *The Adventure of Living*, trans. Edwin Hudson (New York: Harper and Row, 1965), p. 117.
24. Steve Brinn, "Tough Business: In Deep, Swift Waters," *Vocatio* 2, no. 2 (July 1999): 3-6.

3. What God has been addressing in my life through this process is . . .
4. My own attitude to time, money, and success is . . .

For Further Reading

Buechner, Frederick. *Listening to Your Life: Daily Meditations with Frederick Buechner.* San Francisco: HarperSanFrancisco, 1992.

Ellul, Jacques. *Money and Power,* trans. LaVonne Neff. Downers Grove, Ill.: InterVarsity Press, 1984.

Foster, Richard. *Money, Sex, and Power: The Challenge of the Disciplined Life.* San Francisco: HarperSanFrancisco, 1985.

Needleman, Jacob. *Money and the Meaning of Life.* New York: Doubleday, 1991.

Stevens, R. Paul, and Robert Banks, eds. *The Marketplace Ministry Manual.* Vancouver: Regent Publishing, 2004.

11

◆　◆　◆

Pursuing Holiness

The biggest gap between our confessed theology of
Sunday (that we are saved by grace through faith, and
not by works) and our experience of Monday, is
works righteousness. . . . Our actions betray a belief
that our identity and worth are based entirely on
what we do and how well we do it.

William Diehl

The pious tradesman . . . will redeem some time for
the noble and necessary employments of religion. . . .
His devotion disposes him for business, and his business makes devotion welcome.

Richard Steele (1629-92)

F or people in business, law, or politics, "vocational holiness" may
seem to be an oxymoron. Can you be holy and enjoy making

money, inventing new products, or designing advertisements that grab people by the throat? Can you be holy and enjoy driving a Lexus and playing golf with business colleagues? Can you be holy and make electronic devices or mechanical toys, like those in the children's story, *The Velveteen Rabbit,* that eventually break their mainsprings (or burn out their batteries) and lose their stick-out handles?

The word "holy" suggests smells and bells, clerical collars, sacred buildings, monastic austerity, long church services, and people separated from the rough and tumble of enterprise. But the idea of holiness is very simple. To be holy is to be dedicated to God, oriented toward the person and purpose of God. It does not mean being evacuated from this world, and becoming religious, and cluttering the air with pious talk like Job's friends.

In this chapter we consider what makes a businessperson truly Christian. Just as a business enterprise does not become Christian because the workers meet for prayer at the beginning of each work day, so vocational holiness for a man or woman in business is not accomplished by putting a copy of *The Message* on your desk or sprinkling your conversation with God-talk. It is deeper than that, and much more beautiful. Essentially, vocational holiness has three dimensions, the first dealing with the work, the second and third with the worker. Each dimension involves dedication to God and a beautiful fruitfulness.

God-Sent-ness

"I have come to have peace with my calling," said an advertising executive at the conclusion of one of Regent College's marketplace cohorts. Why? Because he realized that he was doing "the Lord's work" and was on the Lord's mission. With Joseph in Egypt he could say to his sisters, parents, educators, supervisors, and all the people who influenced his occupational trajectory, "It was not you who sent me here, but God" (Gen. 45:8). All kinds of influences and events, many of them as unsavory as dead fish on a hot day, had led Joseph to a position of influence in Egypt during the seven-year famine. But ultimately, as he reflected, he was exactly where God wanted him to be, doing "mission" work. Since the Latin word for "send" is *mission,* Joseph might have just as well said, "It was not you who [missioned] me here but God." We live our lives forward, but, as Kierkegaard once said, we understand our lives backwards.

In the chapter on mission we saw that business originates within the ecstatic (outgoing) life of God as Sender, Sent, and Sending. God enlisted the first human creatures in that mission by calling them to build community, to unlock the potential of creation, and to fill the earth. Since resources are not evenly spread throughout the globe and human beings are created for interdependence, fulfilling that first call would necessarily involve trade. God's three-fold promise to Abraham and his descendents was a mission blessing: first to build a family — wonderfully fulfilled in the people of God in Christ composed of Jews and Gentiles; second to possess the land, which, as we have already seen, involved economic, social, and creational stewardship — largely fulfilled in Christ's work in the world and ultimately completed in the new heaven and new earth. And third, the promise was to bless the nations, a mission that is being fulfilled in evangelistic, global, interracial, creational, and cosmic ways. Our work in this world, if it is good work (although mixed with sin and deconstruction), is part of God's intended mission of humanizing the earth, developing the potential of creation, enhancing life, and blessing the nations. We can know that we are called to this mission, though it is not always obvious to us when we take our first job.

Vocational discernment is a life-long process. Many factors contribute to a life direction — personal passion, motivation, gifts and talents, circumstances, compulsions and dysfunctions, and sometimes, a direct word from God. Significantly, the Bible never uses the word "guidance." Guidance is essentially a pagan idea. The Bible reveals a guide, not a system for determining the will of the gods, which is called "divination" and involves reading "signs" or using mechanical means such as casting lots and reading the entrails of birds.

Vocational discernment can be depicted as a triangle, in which the largest part represents the way we are fashioned by God in our motivation, what some have called our "central motivational thrust."

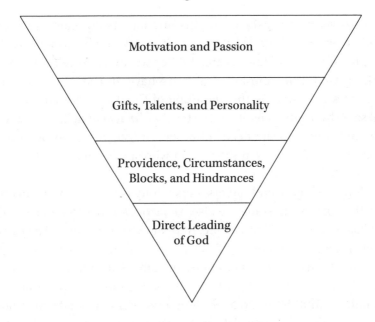

Vocational Discernment

We start with motivation and passion because it is through the heart that God mainly guides. It is a sad perversion of the Christian faith that says, "If I want to do something, it certainly can't be the will of the Lord." Just the reverse is true. If we have the mind of Christ, if God's Spirit is in us and we are immersed in the realm of the Spirit, usually what we want to do is the will of God. To discover our motivation and passion, it is good to ask, In what activity do we lose all sense of time? What do we daydream about? What kind of things, from childhood onward, have we enjoyed doing and felt we did successfully?

When I was eleven, my father gave me an electric motor. And I designed and built my first lathe for turning wood. Then at fourteen I designed and built my first boat. At twenty-four I designed and built an inner city mission. At thirty-five I designed and built a cabin. At fifty I designed and built an educational program in Kenya. Can you guess what I am stirred up in my heart to do? I am a design-and-build person. I am not very motivated to maintain or to fix things.

Next we must consider our gifts and talents. In reality gifts and talents overlap — gifts usually are temporary empowerment by the Spirit for service and talents are abilities we are endowed with. Both are from God. But from Romans 12 we have an evocative hint that Spirit gifts may well be the anointing of Creator-endowed abilities. Paul says these gifts operate in the teacher *"in teaching,"* in the person who contributes to the needs of others in *"generosity,"* in the leader through *"diligence,"* and in the person who shows mercy *"with cheerfulness"* (Rom. 12:7-8).[1]

Along with gifts and talents, personality is a factor. Many people wish that they were someone else, as Jacob wanted to be Esau. But God has made each of us unique. And knowing ourselves is a critical factor in discerning how we fit into the total economy of work and mission on earth. Providential circumstances also affect our vocational trajectory: birth, health, family background, educational opportunities. And there can be dysfunctions within us that profoundly block or hinder our sense of direction. For example, if we are addicted to the praise of others, being a people-pleaser, we will be destroyed in certain leadership roles, though those roles might well be the instrument God uses for our sanctification. Finally, sometimes God gives us a direct, even audible word of direction or brings us someone who has a prophetic message. We need to consider these supernatural words, however, in the light of who we know ourselves to be, as Moses did when he was called (Exod. 3:11; 4:10).

Gaining vocational discernment involves several activities. Pray continuously to be in constant communion with the Guide. Gather information about yourself, your passions, your interests, your central motivations, and possible occupations through reading, inventories, interviews, personal meditation, and journal-keeping. Engage selected believers who know you well in a process of discernment. Clarify your own general and particular calling, its comprehensiveness, and the sense of "ought-ness" or "I was made for this." Consider

1. See Gordon Fee and R. Paul Stevens, "Spiritual Gifts," in Robert Banks and R. Paul Stevens, eds., *The Complete Book of Everyday Christianity* (Downers Grove, Ill.: InterVarsity Press, 1997), pp. 943-49.

the negatives and positives, those who would be advantaged or disadvantaged by your vocational decision, as well as constraints (finances, health, and family responsibilities). Take time. If you must make the decision immediately, it may be only a temporary stop-gap. If you are married, you and your partner should seek God's leading and discuss and pray until you have unity, as both are affected by your decision. God's goal is not to "get the job done as quickly as possible" but to create unity. In *Marriage Spirituality* I affirm, "If it is not God's will for both of us, it is probably not God's will, no matter how much one spouse believes he or she has God's guidance."[2]

But we need another dimension of vocational discernment, a longitudinal one, as we constantly make adjustments through life, especially in the so-called mid-life transition. Many people spend the first half of their lives seeking success. In our twenties we ask, How will I make my living? In our thirties we are clarifying and defining our lifestyle choices and career. In our forties we ask, Who do I want to become? In our fifties the question is, What difference am I making in our world? And in our sixties we ask, What will be my legacy? Often it is in the forties or fifties that people ask profound questions about the meaning of their lives and the contribution they are making.

Psychiatrist Carl Jung believed that "every midlife crisis is a spiritual crisis, that we are called to die to the old self (ego), the fruit of the first half of life, and liberate the new man or woman within us."[3] In the first half of life, we relate and orient ourselves to the outer world; in the second half we adapt to the inner world. The midlife transition is a difficult birth. Jung put it this way:

> Wholly unprepared, they embark upon the second half of life. Or are there perhaps colleges for forty-year-olds which prepare them for their coming life and its demands as the ordinary colleges introduce young people to knowledge of the world and of life? No, there are none. Thoroughly unprepared we take the

2. Paul Stevens, *Marriage Spirituality: Ten Disciplines for People Who Love God* (Downers Grove, Ill.: InterVarsity Press, 1989), p. 120.

3. Carl Jung, quoted in Sue Monk Kidd, *When the Heart Waits: Spiritual Direction for Life's Sacred Questions* (San Francisco: HarperSanFrancisco, 1990), p. 9.

step into the afternoon of life; worse still, we take this step with the false presupposition that our truths and ideas will serve as hitherto. But we cannot live the afternoon of life according to the program of life's morning — for what was great in the morning will be little at evening, and what in the morning was true at evening will become a lie.[4]

At every stage of life, but particularly at crucial transitions, we are challenged to rediscover vocation and to go deeper.

One false notion that can affect our sense of vocational discernment is the belief that God has a wonderful plan for our lives — or two plans, one for the first half of our lives and one for the second. We must discover that plan, so we think, and work it. The only thing I can remember the speaker saying on the youth weekend in which I was embraced by the love of Jesus and became his follower was a lie. The speaker said that God had called him to be a missionary at sixteen years of age. He had refused to go. So God fixed it so he could never go. God, he said, made him have a motorcycle accident in which his left leg was mangled. Now no mission board would take him and he was, as he said, "doomed" to do "God's second best," which was being a pastor! I am thankful I was not converted to that man's God. God has something better than a wonderful *plan* for both halves of our lives. God has a wonderful *purpose* into which we are called, God's grand purpose of leading people into becoming fully human and changing the world until it is a totally transformed earth and heaven. Admittedly, many people do not consider what their life is really about until the so-called mid-life transition. But why wait?

The difference between a plan and a purpose is subtle but sublime. A plan, like a blueprint of a house, must be followed carefully and when you make a mistake you have to start over again, or settle for a plan B that is "second best." Usually we cannot go back to "go" and start again. But experiencing the will of God as purpose is like canoeing down a moving stream (something I love to do) and using the motion and the angle of the canoe to paddle towards one bank or the

---

4. Jung, quoted in Kidd, *When the Heart Waits*, p. 9.

other. It is called back-ferrying or front-ferrying. We are being carried along. We have mobility. God can redeem our own mistakes and even the mistakes of others, as Joseph discovered. There is no second best purpose, just as there is no second half to our life. And the solution to discovering vocational holiness is not to give the first half of our lives to pursuing success and the second half to pursuing holiness and significance, but to continuously find God's purpose right where we are.

Vocational discernment involves both the courage to experiment and faith. Why faith? Because we are bound to make many mistakes in action and motivation along the way and will need to start again and again. We never grow up from being in kindergarten. Theologian Karl Barth says that neither Christian living nor Christian ministry can ever "be anything but the work of beginners. . . . What Christians do, becomes a self-contradiction when it takes the form of a trained and mastered routine, of a learned and practised art. They may and can be masters and even virtuosos in many things, but never in what makes them Christians, God's children."[5]

God-Ward-ness

What makes a type of work holy is not the religious character of the work but first, the character of the work itself (God-sent-ness) and second, the character of the worker. In chapter 8 we considered the role of virtues in ethical decision-making. We saw that our morality is rooted in a personal relationship with the living God and our increasing conformity to the character of God. Therefore we can speak of virtuous work because time and again the New Testament apostles spoke of working with faith, hope, and love. Paul, in writing to the Thessalonians, mentioned all three of what are called the "theological virtues." "We always . . . [remember] before our God and Father your work of faith and labor of love and steadfastness of hope in our Lord Jesus Christ" (1 Thess. 1:2-3). The same trilogy appears in the fa-

5. Karl Barth, *The Christian Life, Dogmatics IV, 4: Lecture Fragments* (Edinburgh: T. & T. Clark, 1974), p. 79.

mous love song of 1 Corinthians 13: "And now faith, hope, and love abide, these three; and the greatest of these is love" (13:14). Can you make a business deal with love? Or design a new hotel with faith? Or market automobiles with hope? The answer to each question is yes. Indeed it is part of what makes our work holy, God-oriented, and God-directed.

Matthew 25 contains three parables of Jesus that in a remarkable way express and illustrate just what is involved in working with faith, hope, and love.

Faith — The Parable of the Talents (Matt. 25:14-30)

In this parable a businessman left on an extended journey and entrusted his assets (talents) to several of his employees, "each according to his ability" (25:15). To one, five talents (let's say that is $5,000), to another, two talents ($2,000), and to the third, one talent ($1,000). In the parallel story in Luke, the businessman said, "Do business with these until I come back" (Luke 19:13), which was surely the intent of the owner, not preservation but investment. When the owner finally returned he discovered that the five-talent person had made five more, as had the two-talent person, two more. The response of the businessman is significant. Their investments yielded two results. First, they received more responsibility: "You have been trustworthy in a few things; I will put you in charge of many things" (25:21, 23). Second, the owner invited the workers to share his happiness: "Enter into the joy of your master" (25:21, 23). As we have seen, this surely is one of the deepest expressions of a spirituality of work — to enter the joy of God, God's delight in seeing his creation developed, in seeing the earth humanized, and in seeing neighbors served. This is reminiscent of the famous line in the film *Chariots of Fire* when Eric Liddell, the Olympic runner, says that he feels the pleasure of God when he runs. So much for the successful workers. But what was the state of the one-talent person?

The harshest words were reserved for him: wicked and lazy. Why? Because the one-talent man kept the talent and returned it to the owner intact. The result was devastating. The one-talent person lost the one talent and, worse still, was thrust into darkness "where there will be weeping and gnashing of teeth" (25:30). The punishment seems harsh because, after all, the one-talent man did not squander the talent; he did not throw it away; he treasured it. He simply hid it in the ground, safe and secure for the owner's return, only to hear a withering rebuke.

What was so wrong about the action of the one-talent person? First he had the wrong conception of God: "I knew that you were a harsh man, reaping where you did not sow, and gathering where you did not scatter seed; so I was afraid, and I went and hid your talent in the ground" (25:24-25). Notice that this is close to the conception of God attributed by Weber to Calvin! A harsh exacting God who is to be feared inhibits risk-taking, whereas a God who is creative, loving, forgiving, and good inspires risk-taking. With such a God, failure might even become a kind of success. We are inspired by the graciousness of God in dealing with potential failures and mistakes.

Further, the one-talent person had the wrong conception of stewardship. He thought his job was to keep creation intact, rather than develop it, invest it, and bring added value to it. And finally, he had the wrong conception of the kingdom of God, that God's mighty rule is to be waited for resolutely, perhaps with the second petition of the Lord's Prayer interpreted as something in the distant future — "Thy kingdom come." There is nothing to do except to fold one's hands and wait, rather than to join the in-breaking kingdom now in intensive and fruitful activity. The issue boils down to faith.

With faith in God we can take risks and even make mistakes because we have a great and beautiful God who not only forgives but also redeems mistakes. I love the way Persian carpets are made. Workers on each side of the loom weave colored wool in the warp and woof at the direction of the master weaver, who is the only one who sees the overall design, viewing it as he does from the front. When a weaver puts in the wrong color, the master weaver does not demand that it be withdrawn, but incorporates the "mistake" into a slightly revised overall design. Such is our God.

To work with faith means to heartily trust God, to invest what we are entrusted with and, as an outcome, to enter the joy of God.

Luther spoke about this eloquently.

Now you tell me, when a father goes ahead and washes diapers or performs some other mean task for his child, and someone ridicules him as an effeminate fool — though that father is acting . . . in Christian faith — my dear fellow you tell me, which of the two is most keenly ridiculing the other? God, with all his angels and creatures, is smiling — not because that father is washing diapers, but because he is doing so in Christian faith.[6]

What you do in your house is worth as much as if you did it up in heaven for our Lord God. . . . We should accustom ourselves to think of our position and work as sacred and well-pleasing to God, not on account of the position and work, but on account of the word and faith from which the obedience and work flow.[7]

Hope — The Parable of the Wise and Foolish Bridesmaids (Matt. 25:1-13)

Earlier, when considering "time," we looked at how, in many cultures, and certainly in the world of Jesus, the experience of time is event-oriented rather than future-oriented. This was certainly what my wife Gail and I experienced at a wedding in Kenya a few years ago. The wedding was set for 10:00 in a distant village. We hurried to get there on time, picking up a pastor friend on the way. We were already "late" but Pastor Julius said we must stop for tea, which we did. When we finally arrived at the village, having got stuck in a corn field and being retrieved by a dozen men pushing our car through the muck, it was already 10:30. Hardly anyone was there let alone the bride and groom, who arrived at 11:30 and 12:00 respectively. But the wedding didn't get under way until 4:00 and continued until sundown. Such is the picture Jesus paints.

6. Martin Luther, "The Estate of Marriage," in *Luther's Works,* trans. W. A. Lambert, ed. James Atkinson (Philadelphia: Fortress Press, 1966), vol. 45, p. 40.

7. Quoted in W. R. Forrester, *Christian Vocation: Studies in Faith and Work* (London: Lutterworth Press, 1951), pp. 147-48.

The female attendants understood there could be a delay. Both the "wise" and the "foolish" had lamps and lamp oil. Both slept with impunity when there was a long delay and an overnight stay was necessary. But when the bridegroom finally came (the next day) the maidens who had oil for a long wait were ready to go in and enjoy the feast — the perennial vision of the kingdom of God, a party. The foolish bridesmaids who only had enough oil for a short wait were told to go off to the merchants and buy some. When they finally returned, the door was shut and the voice inside said to them the most terrifying words that can be spoken to a human being on the day of final judgment: "I do not know you" (25:12).

Note: The maidens did not say, "we know you," but the bridegroom said, "You and I do not have a relationship." These same words of judgment are said in Matthew 7:23. People who call themselves Christians often speak about "knowing God" as though we could know the absolute and infinite supreme being of the universe through and through. Paul, in contrast, when he began to speak about having "come to know God" corrected himself and said, "or rather to be known by God" (Gal. 4:9).

What is the difference between the wise and foolish bridesmaids? Simply this. The wise had hope. They had oil for a long wait, whereas the foolish could only envision being met by the Lord soon, or, to use the common end-times thinking of many North American evangelicals, being evacuated soon.

Without hope we cannot sustain a delay. There is nothing worth doing except preaching the gospel while we wait for an imminent evacuation. Living with hope we know that God will bring the whole human story to a worthwhile end, and even our work in this passing world can last. Paul said, "Therefore, my beloved, be steadfast, immovable, always excelling in the work of the Lord, because you know that in the Lord your labor is not in vain" (1 Cor. 15:58). Of course that includes gospel work, but it also includes making widgets, tables, meals, and deals.

But there is a third dimension of God-directedness — love. Ironically, it is a virtue that appears to be directed not mainly toward God but toward our neighbor.

*Love — The Parable of the Sheep
and Goats (Matt. 25:31-46)*

This well-known parable is largely misunderstood. On the final judgment day when Jesus comes back and gathers all people, separating them as a shepherd separates sheep from goats, Jesus commends the righteous for feeding him when he was hungry, clothing him when he was naked, welcoming him when he was a stranger, and visiting him when he was in prison. He tells these righteous to take their inheritance, which is the kingdom prepared for them since the creation of the world — God's wonderful reign in which everything, including creation and creatures, is under his lovely rule. Jesus sends the unrighteous who didn't do these things to eternal punishment. The simple reading of the parable has motivated generations to do good works for the poor and marginalized because they were actually serving and loving Jesus thereby. In passing, we might note the stupendous truth that Jesus himself is the recipient of our work and behavior. On that day he will say, you fixed my drains, you changed my diapers, you sold me a car, you designed my office, you negotiated my deal, you managed my company. And we will say — Really? But that is the key to the parable.

Thomas Aquinas, the great theologian of the Roman Catholic Church, described what he called the seven corporal alms deeds (having to do with our bodily life and down-to-earth caring of others) and the seven spiritual alms deeds. Note how, in a significant way, each of the alms deeds does point to an aspect of industry and business.

- To feed the hungry (the food industry)
- To give drink to the thirsty (beverage)
- To clothe the naked (clothing, design)
- To harbor the harborless (hospitality)
- To visit the sick (medicine, counseling)
- To ransom the captive (police, military)
- To bury the dead (funeral business)

And seven spiritual alms deeds indicate what ministry we can have in the world and church:

- To instruct the ignorant
- To counsel the doubtful
- To comfort the sorrowful
- To reprove the sinner
- To forgive injuries
- To bear with those who trouble and annoy us
- To pray for all[8]

Usually when we think of loving acts we imagine the poor, the dispossessed, the refugee, the single mother, and the person with a disability. What do we think about when we read "feed the hungry" and "clothe the naked"? Do we think of the food or clothing industries? Most, but not all, business activity is a way of loving our neighbor either directly or indirectly.

But the pivotal point of the parable is not listing the various good works. It is the surprise of both the righteous and the unrighteous that is the key to understanding the extraordinary dividing of the ways. The unrighteous say, "If we had known that we were actually feeding Jesus the Lord, then we would have done it." And the righteous similarly say, "Lord, when did we see you naked, a stranger, or hungry?" This shows that they were not doing it knowingly for the benefit of Jesus and for his approval. Their love was gratuitous. That difficult word means it was not "for" anything except the neighbor. It was not for the religious benefit, for seeing Jesus in the disguise of the poor and needy, behind their masks, as it were. Love simply sees the neighbor and loves. And that is what makes a vocation holy.

God-Likeness

Vocational holiness has to do with motivation — faith, hope, and love. It also has to do with a character that is increasingly being conformed to the image of Christ. The Eastern Orthodox term for this

8. Thomas Aquinas, "Treatise on Faith, Hope, and Charity," *Summa Theologica*, (Westminster, Md.: Christian Classics, 1948), Part II of second part, Q 32, art 2.

metamorphosis is "deification." The Church Fathers say that God became human, so that he might make us gods.[9] Tomáš Špidlik summarizes the tradition, usually attributed to Irenaeus, in these words: "For it was for this end that the Word of God was made man, and he who was the Son of God became the Son of Man, that man [sic], having been taken into the Word, and receiving adoption, might become the son of God."[10] While the Western church has stressed sanctification and holiness (often as a human accomplishment), the Eastern church has stressed what Peter proposes in his letter, that [we] "may become participants of the divine nature" (2 Pet. 1:4) — true godliness. God is at work in us transforming us more and more into the perfect human image of his Son Jesus (2 Cor. 3:18). It is this aspect of holiness that we now consider.

In his letter to the Galatians, Paul contrasts the works of the flesh and the fruit (singular) of the Spirit. In business, the works of the flesh are present around us and in us (Gal. 5:19-21 [NIV]). We function in a complex web of relationships among fallen people and institutional structures.

- "sexual immorality," "impurity," "debauchery" — sexual exploitation, harassment, discrimination
- "idolatry" — driven-ness, workaholism, greed, materialism
- "witchcraft" — power-brokering
- "hatred," "discord," "jealousy," "fits of rage" — relational manipulation
- "selfish ambition," "dissensions," "factions," "envy" — predatory competition, creating envy and covetousness
- "drunkenness," "orgies" — using alcohol to manipulate or anesthetize, using sex to sell or accommodate customers

Probably nothing is so universally documented and scientifically described as original sin. Theodore Dalrymple, a prison doctor in the

9. Archimandrite George, Abbot of the Holy Monastery of St. Gregorios, Mt. Athos, "Deification: The Purpose of Life" (unpublished), p. 8.

10. Tomáš Špidlik, *The Spirituality of the Christian East: A Systematic Handbook* (Kalamazoo, Mich.: Cistercian Publications, 1986), p. 355.

United Kingdom, admits that a few people in the world — and he has seen some — seem wired to do evil without any conscience. The rest, when not held back by law and civilization, actually enjoy hurting their neighbor, whether in Rwanda, Iraq, or Palestine.

> My vision of humanity has darkened, not since I read about Nazi Germany and Soviet Russia, which seemed to me exotic and distant, culturally and politically, but since I began to investigate the lives of ordinary British people in modern conditions. I have come to the conclusion that the default setting of man is to evil and that, if not all, then many and perhaps most men will commit evil if they can get away with it.[11]

In business, destroying the competition, stepping on a few faces to get ahead, lying and stealing to make a sale or a deal, are all too common. Significantly, *Harpers* magazine in 1989 commissioned several New York advertising agencies to "advertise" the seven deadly sins. They were brilliant.

The one on *lust* was entitled: "Where would we be without it?" Showing a man and woman in a passionate embrace, the ad continued, "Any sin that's enabled us to survive centuries of war, death, pestilence, and famine can't be called deadly." And the piece on *sloth* pictured Adam and Eve in paradise with the caption, "If the original sin had been sloth, we'd still be in paradise."

In contrast to the deadly sins and works of the flesh, the fruit of the Spirit includes (Gal. 5:22-23 [NIV]):

- Love
- Joy
- Peace
- Patience
- Kindness
- Goodness
- Faithfulness

11. Theodore Dalrymple, "Nick Berg's Executioners All Too Clearly Enjoyed Beheading Him," *The Daily Telegraph* (Sydney) (Thursday, 13 May 2004), p. 24.

- Gentleness
- Self-control

Paul is not saying that we have a higher and lower nature, the higher being spiritual and the lower being physical. As should be obvious, most of the "works of the flesh" are not physical. But they are expressions of human nature without Christ, turned in on itself. Whereas, with the coming of Christ and the Spirit, we are in a new age. Paul's concern is not anthropological — the makeup of the human person — but eschatological (end times) — how we live in the light of the fact that end times have come with the outpouring of the Spirit.

As we turn from life outside of Christ (the flesh) and walk in step with the Spirit, God increasingly unfolds Christ-likeness in us — love, joy, peace, patience, kindness, goodness, faithfulness, gentleness, and self-control. Fruit is not something produced by beating the apple tree, but by nurturing and fertilizing it. Fruit of the Spirit is not produced by spiritual self-flagellation or self-hatred, this latter being the cloak of pride turned inside out. But it can be nurtured by feeding on God moment by moment.

So vocational holiness comes from God-sent-ness, God-ward-ness, and God-likeness. The irony of exploring this theme is that if we were holy, or even increasingly becoming so, we would not know it! Or at least we wouldn't boast about it if we knew.

For Discussion

Consider and discuss Jacques Ellul's "Meditation on Inutility" in light of pursuing vocational holiness:

> In spite of God's respect and love for man, in spite of God's extreme humility in entering into man's projects in order that man may finally enter into his own design, in the long run one cannot but be seized by a profound sense of inutility and vanity of human action. . . . At a stroke we learn that in Jesus Christ

salvation is given to us, that God loved us first before we did anything, that all is grace; grace — gracious gift, free gift. Life and salvation, resurrection and faith itself, glory and virtue, all is grace, all is attained already, all is done already, and even our good works which we strive with great difficulty to perform have been prepared in advance that we should do them. It is all finished. We have nothing to achieve, nothing to win, nothing to provide. . . . But what about works? Not just the deadly works of the law . . . but the works of faith . . . the fruits of the Spirit — of what use are these works? . . . Here again we come up against the same inutility, the same vanity, as we contemplate God's omniprescience and stand in the perfect presence of his love. And yet works are demanded of us; they are God's command and yet a useless service. . . .

To be controlled by utility and the pursuit of efficacy is to be subject to the strictest determination of the actual world. . . . If we are ready to be unworthy or unprofitable servants (although busy and active at the same time), then our works can truly redound to the glory of him who freely loved us first. God loved us because he is love and not to get results. . . . To do a gratuitous, ineffective, and useless act is the first sign of our freedom and perhaps the last. . . . If we do not pray, if we do not the works of faith, if we do not seek after wisdom, if we do not preach the gospel, nothing in history, nor very probably in the church, would look much different. The world would go its way, and the kingdom of God would finally come by way of judgment. And yet there would be lacking something irreplaceable and incommensurable, something that is measured neither by institutions nor metaphysics nor products nor results, something that modifies everything qualitatively and nothing quantitatively, something that gives the only possible meaning to human life, and yet that cannot belong to us, that cannot be its fruit. . . . This is freedom: man's freedom within God's freedom; man's freedom as a reflection of God's freedom; man's freedom exclusively received in Christ; man's freedom which is free obedience to God and which finds unique expression in childlike acts, in prayer and witness, as we see these in the Second Book of Kings, within the tragic acts of politics and religion.[12]

For Further Reading

Diehl, William E. *The Monday Connection: On Being an Authentic Christian in a Weekday World.* San Francisco: HarperSanFrancisco, 1991.
Palmer, Parker. *The Active Life: Wisdom for Work, Creativity, and Caring.* San Francisco: HarperSanFrancisco, 1990.

12. Jacques Ellul, "Meditation on Inutility," *The Politics of God and the Politics of Man,* trans. Geoffrey W. Bromiley (Grand Rapids: Eerdmans, 1972), pp. 190-99.

———— ◆ ◆ ◆ ————

The Contemplative Leader

The first responsibility of a leader is to define reality. The last is to say thank you. In between the two, the leader must become a servant and a debtor. That sums up the progress of an artful leader.

Max DePree

It occurred to him that what had appeared perfectly impossible before, namely that he had not spent his life as he should have done, might after all be true. . . . And his professional duties and the whole arrangement of his life and of his family, and all his social and official interests, might all have been false.

"But if that is so and I am leaving this life with the consciousness that I have lost all that was given me and it is impossible to rectify it — what then?"

Tolstoy, *The Death of Ivan Ilych*

Contemplative leaders are saints dressed in ordinary business clothes. But they are not plaster saints with halos. They know the complexity of working in the real world of trade-offs, deals, and half-truths. They are acquainted with compromise but are never out of touch with God. They live by grace, God's gratuitous unselfing of himself that enables them to go the extra mile, to offer extraordinary service, to see the slimiest competitor as one made in God's image, albeit distorted and twisted. At the same time their identity is not wrapped up in making the best deal, or advancing on the corporate ladder, or owning more than others. They know themselves to be deeply approved by God. Their identity is to be children of God, priests, prophets, and rulers. It is not the work itself that makes them acceptable to God. They have what Luther called gospel confidence. So it doesn't matter whether they do little things — like pushing invoices across a desk, or drawing up spread-sheets on the screen — or big things — like concluding a multi-million-dollar deal. As William Tyndale, the English Reformer, said, "There is no work better than another to please God; to pour water, to wash dishes, to be a souter [cobbler], or an apostle, all is one, to wash dishes and to preach is all one, as touching the deed, to please God."[1]

Contemplative leaders know that God is present in the marketplace. God is at work in businesspeople's relationships with their co-workers. God is also in charismatic events, moments when they celebrate a great idea (from God), or turn to God in desperation and find God to be there. They see God continuing God's work of creating, sustaining, providing, instructing, revealing, giving justice, making covenants, building community, and redeeming. They know that they are doing the Lord's work. Contemplative leaders know that God is bringing people to himself in the mission field of the marketplace. They pray. They lift all to God — meetings, contacts with others, decisions, and intercession for the company or institution. Contemplative leaders engage in spiritual warfare. They face a multi-level resistance that is well described in the Anglican prayer book as "the world, the flesh,

---

1. William Tyndale, "A Parable of the Wicked Mammon," in *Treatises and Portions of Holy Scripture* (1527; reprint, Cambridge: Parker Society, 1848), pp. 98, 104.

and the devil." They deal with the *world* by non-conformity (Rom. 12:1-2) yet loving the world as God does. They deal with fallen structures by engagement and transformation, making a difference where they can by participation and sometimes by non-violent suffering. They deal with the *flesh* by crucifying the flesh (not the body but life lived without God and turned in on oneself) and by walking in the Spirit (Gal. 5:24-25). They deal with the *devil* by the Word and prayer.

Contemplative leaders are servants. The commonly used phrase, "servant leadership," brings together two concepts that normally cannot coexist. Servant leadership, based on the statement of Jesus in Matthew 20:25-28, gathers up the vision of Isaiah about the one who would serve the Lord in the world — the people, the remnant, the Messiah, and now the whole people. But contemplative leaders know that being servant leaders does not mean doing everything others want them to. They want not only to get the job done but also to do the right thing. They are servants of the Lord. They know that the "need" is not the "call." Being the Lord's servants does not mean practicing passivity and compliance. They are ambitious, creative, and entrepreneurial. They know that ungodly ambition is where we define ourselves by what new achievements we have accomplished; godly ambition is seeking the best for others, for creation, and for the kingdom of God. God in creation expressed a dimension of ambition when he created the opportunity for the development of his creation. In the mind of God, the City of God always stood as the final destiny of humankind, and this vision inspires contemplative leaders daily. Contemplative leaders live by metaphor and vision. They know that people are drowning in the water for lack of meaning. So they throw poems, visions, and metaphors to people floundering in the waves. They have practical heavenly-mindedness.

Contemplative leaders combine the qualities of Mary and Martha. They have a rhythm of engagement and withdrawal, a mixed life. But the rhythm of work and Sabbath is not the alternation between profane and holy. All of life is sacred for them, including family time, time with friends, rest, sleep, and worship. But contemplative leaders do not restrict worship to religious services. They find cause for celebration all day long, recognizing that God is present in the marketplace, that ultimately God receives all their work, and in the last day will say, "You did it *to* me, not just *for* me." Faith, hope, and love are in contemplative leaders' hearts and work.

Contemplative leaders are in full-time ministry. They know that they are serving God and God's purposes in the work-world just as pastors and missionaries serve God's purposes in the church. Each of them is part priest, part prophet, and part ruler. They have the touch of God, though usually they are unaware of it. They touch God in intercession on behalf of people and places. They touch people and places for God, bringing a good fragrance and even beauty. They have a sphere of influence, whether to the multiple stakeholders of the large organizations they head or in lower management through a circle of influence around their work stations. And when they sin they pray for forgiveness. They may pray this many times a day.

Contemplative leaders are never bored. They are called people on a mission. They know that God is at work for their sanctification in the nitty-gritty of the daily grind, producing character and perseverance. They also have intimations in the here and now of something that one day will be the ultimate reward: entering into the joy and happiness of the Master.

For Further Reading

Griffin, Emilie. *The Reflective Executive: A Spirituality of Business and Enterprise.* New York: Crossroad, 1993.

DePree, Max. *Leadership Is an Art.* New York: Dell, 1989.

Stevens, R. Paul. *Down-to-Earth Spirituality.* Downers Grove, Ill.: InterVarsity Press, 2003.

Wright, Walter C. *Relational Leadership: A Biblical Model for Leadership Service.* Carlisle, Cumbria: Paternoster, 2000.

Bibliography

Adeney, Bernard. *Strange Virtues: Ethics in a Multicultural World.* Downers Grove, Ill.: InterVarsity Press, 1995.

Almen, Louis T. "Vocation in a Post-Vocational Age." *Word and World* 4, no. 2 (Spring 1984): 131-40.

Alter, K. S. *Managing the Double Bottom Line.* Washington, D.C.: Pact Publications, 2000.

Anderson, Ray S. *Minding God's Business.* Grand Rapids: Eerdmans, 1986.

Aquinas, Thomas. "Treatise on Faith, Hope, and Charity." In *Summa Theologica.* Westminster, Md.: Christian Classics, 1948.

Arias, Mortimer. *Announcing the Kingdom: Evangelization and the Subversive Memory of Jesus.* Lima, Ohio: Academic Renewal Press, 1984/ 2001.

Augustine. *Confessions.* Translated by R. S. Pine-Coffin. Harmondsworth, U.K.: Penguin Books, 1961.

Baechler, Mary. "Death of a Marriage." *INC* (April 1994).

Bang, Sunki. "Tensions in Witness." *Vocatio* 1, no. 2 (July 1998).

Banks, Robert. "Work Ethic, Protestant." In *The Complete Book of Everyday Christianity,* ed. Robert Banks and R. Paul Stevens, pp. 1129-32. Downers Grove, Ill.: InterVarsity Press, 1997.

———, ed. *Faith Goes to Work.* Washington, D.C.: Alban Institute, 1993.

Banks, Robert, and Bernice Ledbetter. *Reviewing Leadership: A Christian Evaluation of Current Approaches.* Grand Rapids: Baker, 2004.

Banks, Robert, and Kimberly Powell, eds. *Faith in Leadership: How Leaders Live Out Their Faith in Their Work and Why It Matters.* San Francisco: Jossey-Bass, 2000.

Banks, Robert, and R. Paul Stevens, eds. *The Complete Book of Everyday Christianity.* Downers Grove, Ill.: InterVarsity Press, 1997.

Barth, Karl. "Vocation." In *Church Dogmatics,* vol. 3, part 4, translated by A. T. Mackay, T. H. L. Parker, H. Knight, H. A. Kennedy, and J. Marks. Edinburgh: T. & T. Clark, 1961.

Barton, Bruce. *The Man Nobody Knows: A Discovery of the Real Jesus.* New York: Triangle Books, 1924.

Beardslee, W. A. *Human Achievement and Divine Vocation in the Message of Paul.* London: SCM Press, 1961.

Berger, Peter L. *The Capitalist Spirit: Toward a Religious Ethic of Wealth Creation.* San Francisco: Institute for Contemporary Studies, 1990.

———. *The Sacred Canopy: Elements of a Sociological Theory of Religion.* Garden City, N.Y.: Doubleday, 1967.

Berkhof, H. *Christ and the Powers.* Translated by J. H. Yoder. Scottdale, Pa.: Herald, 1962.

Bochmuehl, Klaus. "Recovering Vocation Today." *Crux* 24, no. 3 (September 1988): 25-35.

Bolman, L., and T. Deal. *Leading with Soul: An Uncommon Journey of Spirit.* San Francisco: Jossey-Bass, 1995.

Bonhoeffer, Dietrich. *Ethics.* London: SCM Press, 1976.

———. *Life Together.* San Francisco: Harper & Row, 1954.

Bosch, David J. *Believing in the Future: Toward a Missiology of Western Culture.* Leominster Herefordshire, England: Gracewing, 1995.

———. *Transforming Mission: Paradigm Shifts in Theology of Mission.* Maryknoll, N.Y.: Orbis Books, 1991.

Breton, Denis, and Christopher Largent. *The Soul of Economics: Spiritual Evolution Goes to the Marketplace.* Wilmington, Del.: Idea House Publishing Co., 1991.

Brinn, Steve. "Tough Business: In Deep, Swift Waters." *Vocatio* 2, no. 2 (July 1999): 3-6.

Buechner, Frederick. *Listening to Your Life: Daily Meditations with Frederick Buechner.* San Francisco: HarperSanFrancisco, 1992.

Bussard, Allan, Marek Markus, and Daniela Olejarova. *Code of Ethics and Social Audit Manual.* Bratislava, Slovakia: The Integra Foundation, n.d.

Byrne, Edmund F. *Work, Inc.: A Philosophical Inquiry.* Philadelphia: Temple University Press, 1990.

Byron, William J., S.J. "Business: A Vocation to Justice and Love." In *The Professions in Ethical Context,* edited by Francis A. Eigo, O.S.A. Villanova, Pa.: Villanova University Press, 1986.

Calvin, John. *Commentary on a Harmony of the Evangelists, Matthew, Mark, and Luke.* Translated by William Pringle. Grand Rapids: Eerdmans, 1956.

———. *The First Epistle of Paul the Apostle to the Corinthians.* Translated by John W. Fraser. Edited by David W. Torrance and Thomas F. Torrance. Edinburgh: Oliver & Boyd, 1960.

———. *Institutes of the Christian Religion.* Translated by Ford Lewis Battles. Philadelphia: Westminster Press, 1960.

Cantillon, Richard, Robert F. Hebert, and Albert N. Link. *The Entrepreneur: Mainstream Views and Radical Critiques.* New York: Praeger Publishers, 1982.

Capon, Robert. *An Offering of Uncles: The Priesthood of Adam and the Shape of the World.* New York: Crossroad, 1982.

Carey, William. *An Enquiry into the Obligations of Christians to Use Means for the Conversion of the Heathens.* Leicester, U.K., 1792.

Carroll, Vincent, and David Shiflett. *Christianity on Trial: Arguments Against Anti-Religious Bigotry.* San Francisco: Encounter Books, 2002.

Carter, Edward C., II, Robert Forster, and Joseph Moody, eds. *Enterprise and Entrepreneurs in Nineteenth-Century France.* Baltimore: Johns Hopkins University Press, 1976.

Chewning, Richard C., ed. *Biblical Principles and Economics: The Foundations.* Christians in the Marketplace, vol. 1. Colorado Springs: NavPress, 1989.

———. *Biblical Principles and Economics: The Practice,* vol. 3. Colorado Springs: NavPress, 1990.

———, ed. *Biblical Principles and Economics: The Foundations.* Christians in the Marketplace, vol. 2. Colorado Springs: NavPress, 1989.

————. *Biblical Principles and Economics: The Practice,* vol. 4. Colorado Springs: NavPress, 1991.

Chewning, Richard C., John W. Eby, and Shirley Roels. *Business through the Eyes of Faith.* San Francisco: HarperSanFrancisco, 1990.

Ciulla, Joanne B. *The Working Life: The Promise and Betrayal of Modern Work.* New York: Three Rivers Press, 2000.

Collins, Philip, and R. Paul Stevens. *The Equipping Pastor: A Systems Approach to Empowering the People of God.* Washington, D.C.: Alban Institute, 1993.

Conger, J., et al. *Spirit at Work: Discovering the Spirituality in Leadership.* San Francisco: Jossey-Bass, 1994.

Covey, Stephen. *The Seven Habits of Highly Effective People.* New York: Simon & Schuster, 1989.

Cranfield, Jack, and Jacqueline Miller. *Heart at Work: Stories and Strategies for Building Self-Esteem and Reawakening the Soul at Work.* New York: McGraw Hill, 1996.

Davis, John Jefferson. "'Teaching Them to Observe All That I Have Commanded You': The History of the Interpretation of the 'Great Commission' and Implications for Marketplace Ministries." Paper, Gordon-Conwell Theological Seminary, 1998.

DePree, Max. *Leadership Is an Art.* New York: Dell, 1989.

Diehl, William E. *Christianity and Real Life.* Philadelphia: Fortress Press, 1976.

————. *The Monday Connection: A Spirituality of Competence, Affirmation, and Support in the Workplace.* San Francisco: HarperSanFrancisco, 1991.

————. *Thank God It's Monday.* Philadelphia: Fortress Press, 1982.

Donaldson, Thomas, and Patricia H. Werhane, eds. *Ethical Issues in Business: A Philosophical Approach.* Upper Saddle River, N.J.: Prentice Hall, 1996.

Dreyer, Elizabeth A. *Earth Crammed with Heaven: A Spirituality of Everyday Life.* New York: Paulist Press, 1994.

Droel, William L. *Business People: The Spirituality of Work.* Chicago: ACTA Publications, 1990.

Drucker, Peter F. *Innovation and Entrepreneurship: Practice and Principles.* New York: Harper & Row, 1985.

Dumbrell, William. "Creation, Covenant and Work." *Crux* 24, no. 3 (September 1988): 14-24.

Ellul, Jacques. "Meditation on Inutility." In *The Politics of God and the Politics of Man.* Translated by Geoffrey W. Bromiley. Grand Rapids: Eerdmans, 1972.

————. *Money and Power.* Translated by LaVonne Neff. Downers Grove, Ill.: InterVarsity Press, 1984.

————. *The Presence of the Kingdom.* Translated by Olive Wyon. New York: Seabury Press, 1948.

————. *Reason for Being: A Meditation on Ecclesiastes.* Translated by Joyce Main Hanks. Grand Rapids: Eerdmans, 1972.

Fairholm, Gilbert. *Capturing the Heart of Leadership: Spirituality and Community in the New American Workplace.* Westport, Conn.: Praeger, 1997.

Falk, David John. "A New Testament Theology of Calling with Reference to the 'Call to the Ministry.'" MCS thesis, Regent College, Vancouver, B.C., 1990.

Fee, Gordon D. *The First Epistle to the Corinthians.* Grand Rapids: Eerdmans, 1987.

Fee, Gordon D., and R. Paul Stevens. "Spiritual Gifts." In *The Complete Book of Everyday Christianity,* ed. Robert Banks and R. Paul Stevens, pp. 943-49. Downers Grove, Ill.: InterVarsity Press, 1997.

Flow, Don. "Profit." In *The Complete Book of Everyday Christianity,* ed. Robert Banks and R. Paul Stevens, pp. 809-13. Downers Grove, Ill.: InterVarsity Press, 1997.

Foster, Richard. *Money, Sex and Power: The Challenge of the Disciplined Life.* San Francisco: HarperSanFrancisco, 1985.

Friedman, Edwin H. *Generation to Generation: Family Process in Church and Synagogue.* New York: Gilford, 1985.

Friedman, Thomas L. *The Lexus and the Olive Tree.* New York: Farrar, Straus, and Giroux, 1999.

Garfield, Charles, and Associates, with Michael Toms. *The Soul of Business.* Carlsbad, Calif.: Hay House Inc., 1997.

Gay, Craig. *With Liberty and Justice for Whom? The Recent Evangelical Debate over Capitalism.* Grand Rapids: Eerdmans, 1991.

Archimandrite George, Abbot of the Holy Monastery of St. Gregorios, Mt. Athos. "Deification: The Purpose of Life" (unpublished).

Gibbs, Mark, and T. R. Morton. *God's Frozen People.* Philadelphia: Westminster Press, 1965.

Gibson, D. *Avoiding the Tentmaker Trap.* Hamilton, Ont.: WEF International, 1997.

Gill, David W. *Doing Right: Practicing Ethical Principles.* Downers Grove, Ill.: InterVarsity Press, 2004.

Girard, Robert. "Failure." In *The Complete Book of Everyday Christianity,* ed. Robert Banks and R. Paul Stevens, pp. 363-66. Downers Grove, Ill.: InterVarsity Press, 1997.

Goldberg, Michael, ed. *Against the Grain: New Approaches to Professional Ethics.* Valley Forge, Pa.: Trinity Press, 1993.

Goodell, E., ed. *Social Venture Network Standards of Corporate Social Responsibility.* San Francisco: Social Venture Network, 1999.

Gordon, B. *The Economic Problem in Biblical and Patristic Thought.* Leiden: E. J. Brill, 1989.

Goudzwaard, Bob. *Capitalism and Progress: A Diagnosis of Western Society.* Translated by Josina Van Nuis Zylstra. Grand Rapids: Eerdmans, 1979.

Green, Michael, and R. Paul Stevens. *Living the Story: Biblical Spirituality for Everyday Christians.* Grand Rapids: Eerdmans, 2003.

Green, Thomas H. *Darkness in the Marketplace: The Christian at Prayer in the World.* Notre Dame, Ind.: Ave Maria Press, 1981.

Greenleaf, R. *Servant Leadership.* New York: Paulist Press, 1977.

Grenz, Stanley. "Community as Theology Motif for the Western Church in an Era of Globalization." *Crux* 28, no. 3 (September 1992): 10-19.

Griffin, Emilie. *The Reflective Executive: A Spirituality of Business and Enterprise.* New York: Crossroad, 1993.

Griffiths, Brian. *The Creation of Wealth.* London: Hodder and Stoughton, 1984.

Guiness, Os. *The Call: Finding and Fulfilling the Central Purpose of Your Life.* Nashville: Word, 1998.

————. *Winning Back the Soul of American Business.* Washington, D.C.: Hourglass Publishers, 1990.

Gunther, Marc. "God and Business: The Surprising Quest for Spiritual Renewal in the American Workplace." *Fortune,* 16 July 2001, pp. 58-80.

Handy, Charles. *The Hungry Spirit: Beyond Capitalism — A Quest for Purpose in the Modern World.* London: Hutchinson, 1997.

Hardy, Lee. *The Fabric of This World: Inquiries into Calling, Career Choice, and the Design of Human Work.* Grand Rapids: Eerdmans, 1990.

Hauerwas, Stanley. *Vision and Virtue: Essays in Christian Ethical Reflection.* Notre Dame, Ind.: University of Notre Dame Press, 1974.

Haughey, John. *Converting Nine to Five: A Spirituality of Daily Work.* New York: Crossroad, 1989.

Hebert, Robert F., and Albert N. Link. *The Entrepreneur: Mainstream Views and Radical Critiques.* New York: Praeger Publishers, 1982.

Heiges, Donald R. *The Christian's Calling.* Philadelphia: United Lutheran Church in America, 1958.

Helgesen, S. *The Female Advantage: Women's Ways of Leadership.* New York: Doubleday, 1990.

Helm, Paul. *The Callings: The Gospel in the World.* Edinburgh: Banner of Truth Trust, 1987.

Higginson, Richard. *Called to Account: Adding Value in God's World — Integrating Christianity and Business Effectively.* Guildford, Surrey: Eagle, 1993.

—————. *Questions of Business Life: Exploring Workplace Issues from a Christian Perspective.* Carlisle, Cumbria: Authentic Media, 2002.

Hill, Alexander. *Just Business: Christian Ethics for the Marketplace.* Downers Grove, Ill.: InterVarsity Press, 1997.

Hilton, Walter. *Toward a Perfect Love.* Translated by David Jeffrey. Portland: Multnomah Press, 1985.

Hock, Dee. "The Trillion-Dollar Vision of Dee Hock." *Fast Company* (October/November 1996): 75-86.

Hock, R. F. *The Social Context of Paul's Ministry: Tentmaking and Apostleship.* Philadelphia: Fortress Press, 1980.

Hogben, Rowland. *Vocation.* London: Inter-Varsity Press, 1940.

Holl, Karl. "The History of the Word 'Vocation.'" *Review and Expositor* 55 (1958).

Holland, Joe. *Creative Communion: Toward a Spirituality of Work.* Mahwah, N.J.: Paulist Press, 1989.

Humphreys, Kent. *Lasting Investments: A Pastor's Guide for Equipping Workplace Leaders to Leave a Spiritual Legacy.* Colorado Springs: NavPress, 2004.

John Paul II. *Laborem Exercens: On Human Work.* Washington, D.C.: Office of Publishing and Promotion Services, United States Catholic Conference, 1981.

Johnson, C. Neal. "Toward a Marketplace Missiology." *Missiology: An International Review* 31, no. 1 (January 2003): 87-97.

Kanter, Rosabeth Moss. *The Change Masters: Innovation and Entrepreneurship in the American Corporation.* New York: Simon and Schuster, 1983.

Kantzer, Kenneth C. "God Intends His Precepts to Transform Society." In *Biblical Principles and Business: The Foundations,* ed. Richard C. Chewning, vol. 1, pp. 22-34. Colorado Springs: NavPress, 1989.

Kaplan, Robert D. "The Coming Anarchy." *Atlantic Monthly* (February 1994): 44-76.

Kee, Howard C., and Montgomery J. Shroyer. *The Bible and God's Call: A Study of the Biblical Foundation of Vocation.* New York: Cokesbury–The Methodist Church, 1962.

Kidd, Sue Monk. *When the Heart Waits: Spiritual Direction for Life's Sacred Questions.* San Francisco: HarperSanFrancisco, 1990.

Kidner, Derek. *The Message of Ecclesiastes: A Time to Mourn and a Time to Dance.* Downers Grove, Ill.: InterVarsity Press, 1976.

Kolden, Marc. "Luther on Vocation." *Word and World* 3, no. 4: 382-90.

Kouzes, James M., and Barry Z. Posner. *Credibility: How Leaders Gain and Lose It, Why People Demand It.* San Francisco: Jossey-Bass, 1993.

Kraemer, Hendrik. *A Theology of the Laity.* Philadelphia: Westminster Press, 1958.

Laing, R. D. *The Politics of Experience and the Bird of Paradise.* Harmondsworth, U.K.: Penguin Books, 1967.

Lambert, Lake, III. "Called to Business: Corporate Management as a Profession of Faith." Ph.D. dissertation, Princeton Theological Seminary, 1997, available through UMI Services.

Leech, Kenneth. *True Prayer: An Invitation to Christian Spirituality.* San Francisco: Harper & Row, 1980.

Levoy, Gregg. *Callings: Finding and Following the Authentic Life.* New York: Three Rivers Press, 1997.

Lewis, C. S. *George MacDonald: An Anthology.* London: Geoffrey Bles/The Centenary Press, 1946.

Long, Edward L. *Conscience and Compromise.* Philadelphia: Westminster Press, 1954.

Longenecker, Richard. *New Testament Social Ethics for Today.* Grand Rapids: Eerdmans, 1984.

Luther, Martin. "The Estate of Marriage." In *Luther's Works,* vol. 44. Translated by W. A. Lambert. Edited by James Atkinson. Philadelphia: Fortress Press, 1966.

————. "That a Christian Assembly or Congregation Has the Right and Power to Judge All Teaching and to Call, Appoint, and Dismiss Teachers, Established and Proven by Scripture." In *Luther's Works,* vol. 39, pp. 310-11. Translated by W. A. Lambert. Edited by James Atkinson. Philadelphia: Fortress Press, 1966.

————. "Treatise on Christian Liberty." In *Luther's Works,* vol. 2. Translated by W. A. Lambert. Edited by James Atkinson. Philadelphia: Fortress Press, 1966.

————. "Treatise on Good Works." In *Luther's Works,* vol. 44. Translated by W. A. Lambert. Edited by James Atkinson. Philadelphia: Fortress Press, 1966.

MacIntyre, Alasdair. *After Virtue.* Notre Dame, Ind.: University of Notre Dame Press, 1981/1984.

Marshall, Paul. *A Kind of Life Imposed on Man: Vocation and Social Order from Tyndale to Locke.* Toronto: University of Toronto Press, 1996.

————. *Thine Is the Kingdom.* Grand Rapids: Eerdmans, 1986.

Marshall, Paul, and Lela Gilbert. *Heaven Is Not My Home: Learning to Live in God's Creation.* Nashville: Word Publishing, 1998.

McConnell, William T. *The Gift of Time.* Downers Grove, Ill.: InterVarsity Press, 1983.

McGurn, William. "Globalization Gospel Reaches the Eternal City." *Financial Post,* 23 December 2000, p. D11.

McLoughlin, Michael C. R. "Back to the Future of Missions." *Vocatio* 4, no. 2 (December 2000).

Meilaender, Gilbert. "Professing Business: John Paul meets John Wesley." *Christian Century,* 4 December 1996, pp. 1200-1204.

————, ed. *Working: Its Meaning and Its Limits.* Notre Dame, Ind.: University of Notre Dame Press, 2000.

Mihindukulasuriya, Prabo. "Business as a Calling: Work and the Examined Life" (review). *Crux* 34, no. 2 (June 1998): 46-48.

Minear, Paul S. *To Die and to Live: Christ's Resurrection and Christian Vocation.* New York: Seabury Press, 1977.

Moltmann, Jürgen. *The Coming of God: Christian Eschatology.* Translated by Margaret Kohl. Minneapolis: Fortress Press, 1996.

———. *The Trinity and the Kingdom.* Translated by Margaret Kohl. San Francisco: Harper and Row, 1991.

Morrow, John. "The Global Economy and Global Free Market Capitalism: Towards a Christian Perspective." Unpublished paper for Marketplace Ministry Seminar, Regent College, 2000.

Myers, Bryant. *Walking with the Poor: Principles and Practices of Transformational Development.* Maryknoll, N.Y.: Orbis, 1999.

Nash, Laura. *Believers in Business: Resolving the Tensions between Christian Faith, Business Ethics and Our Definitions of Success.* Nashville: Thomas Nelson, 1995.

Nash, Laura, and Scotty McLennan. *Church on Sunday, Work on Monday.* San Francisco: Jossey-Bass, 2001.

Neuhaus, Richard John. *Doing Well and Doing Good: The Challenge of the Christian Capitalist.* New York: Doubleday, 1992.

Newbigin, Lesslie. *Foolishness to the Greeks: The Gospel and Western Culture.* Grand Rapids: Eerdmans, 1986.

———. *The Gospel in a Pluralistic Society.* Grand Rapids: Eerdmans, 1989.

———. *Honest Religion for Secular Man.* Philadelphia: Westminster Press, 1966.

———. *Unfinished Agenda: An Updated Autobiography.* Edinburgh: St. Andrew Press, 1993.

Nicholls, Bruce. *Contextualization: A Theology of Gospel and Culture.* Downers Grove, Ill.: InterVarsity Press, 1979.

Nouwen, Henri. *Reaching Out: The Three Movements of the Spiritual Life.* New York: Doubleday, 1975.

Novak, Michael. *Business as a Calling: Work and the Examined Life.* New York: The Free Press, 1996.

———. *The Catholic Ethic and the Spirit of Catholicism.* New York: The Free Press, 1993.

———. *The Fire of Invention: Civil Society and the Future of the Corporation.* Lanham, Md.: Rowman & Littlefield Publishers, 1997.

———. "Human Dignity, Personal Liberty: Themes from Abraham Kuyper and Leo XIII." *Journal of Markets & Morality* 5, no. 1 (Spring 2002): 59-126.

————. *Toward a Theology of the Corporation*. Washington, D.C.: American Enterprise Institute for Public Policy Research, 1981.

Oden, Thomas. *Two Worlds: Notes on the Death of Modernity in America and Russia*. Downers Grove, Ill.: InterVarsity Press, 1992.

Oliver, E. H. *The Social Achievements of the Christian Church*. United Church of Canada, 1930; reprinted Vancouver: Regent Publishing, 2004.

Packer, J. I. "The Christian's Purpose in Business." In *Biblical Principles and Business: The Practice*, vol. 3, ed. Richard C. Chewning. Colorado Springs: NavPress, 1990.

Padilla, C. René. "The Mission of the Church in the Light of the Kingdom of God." *Transformation* 1, no. 2 (April-June 1984): 16-20.

Parker, Palmer. *Let Your Life Speak: Listening for the Voice of Vocation*. San Francisco: Jossey-Bass, 2000.

————. "On Minding Your Call — When No One Is Calling." *Weavings* (September-October 1996): 15-22.

Pattison, Mansell E. *Pastor and People — A Systems Approach*. Philadelphia: Fortress Press, 1977.

Percy, Ian. *Going Deep*. Toronto: Macmillan, 1998.

Perkins, William. "A Treatise of the Vocations or Callings of Men." In *The Work of William Perkins*, edited and with an introduction by Ian Breward. Appleford, U.K.: Courtenay Press, 1970.

Poggi, Gianfranco. *Calvinism and the Capitalist Spirit: Max Weber's Protestant Ethic*. London: Macmillan, 1983.

Preece, Gordon. "Business as a Calling and Profession: Towards a Protestant Entrepreneurial Ethic." Unpublished manuscript delivered at the International Marketplace Theology Consultation, Sydney, June 2001.

————. *Changing Work Values: A Christian Response*. Melbourne: Acorn Press, 1995.

Rae, Scott, and Kenman Wong. *Beyond Integrity: A Judeo-Christian Approach to Business Ethics*. Grand Rapids: Zondervan, 1996.

Ramsey, Paul. *Basic Christian Ethics*. Chicago: University of Chicago Press, 1977.

Reid, D. G. "Principalities and Powers." In *Dictionary of Paul and His Letters*, ed. F. F. Hawthorne, R. Martin, and D. G. Reid. Downers Grove, Ill.: InterVarsity Press, 1993.

Renesch, John, ed. *New Traditions in Business: Spirit and Leadership in the Twenty-First Century*. San Francisco: Berrett-Koehler Publishers, 1992.

Richards, Robert. *God and Business: Christianity's Case for Capitalism*. Fairfax, Va.: Xulon Press, 2002.

Richardson, Alan. *The Biblical Doctrine of Work*. London: SCM Press, 1952.

Richardson, John E. "Whistle-Blowing." In *The Complete Book of Everyday Christianity*, ed. Robert Banks and R. Paul Stevens, pp. 1114-16. Downers Grove, Ill.: InterVarsity Press, 1997.

Rifkin, Jeremy. *The End of Work: The Decline of the Global Work-Force and the Dawn of the Post-Market Era*. London: Penguin, 2000.

Rundle, Steve, and Tom Steffan. *Great Commission Companies: The Emerging Role of Business in Missions*. Downers Grove, Ill.: InterVarsity Press, 2003.

Ryken, Leland. *Redeeming the Time: A Christian Approach to Work and Leisure*. Grand Rapids: Baker, 1995.

Samuel, Vinay. "Evangelical Response to Globalisation: An Asian Perspective." *Transformation* (January 1999).

Satir, Virginia. *Conjoint Family Therapy*. Revised edition. Palo Alto, Calif.: Science and Behavior Books, 1983.

The Sayings of the Desert Fathers: The Alphabetical Collection. Translated by Benedicta Ward, S.L.G. London: Cistercian Publications, 1974/1985.

Schein, Edgar H. *Organizational Culture and Leadership: A Dynamic View*. San Francisco: Jossey-Bass, 1991.

Schleir, H. *Principalities and Powers in the New Testament*. New York: Herder & Herder, 1964.

Schmemann, Alexander. *For the Life of the World*. Crestwood, N.Y.: St. Vladimir's Seminary Press, 1988.

Schumacher, Christian. *God in Work*. Oxford: Lion Publishing, 1998.

Schuurman, Douglas J. *Vocation: Discerning Our Callings in Life*. Grand Rapids: Eerdmans, 2004.

Seerveld, Calvin. "Christian Workers, Unite." In *In the Fields of the Lord: A Calvin Seerveld Reader*, ed. Craig Bartholomew. Toronto: Toronto Tuppence Press, 2000.

Sellers, Jeff. "New Age or Kingdom Come? Description and Critique of the 'New Business Spirituality' in Light of a Biblical Spirituality of Work." MCS Thesis, Regent College, Vancouver, April 2000.

Senge, Peter M. *The Fifth Discipline: The Art and Practice of the Learning Organization.* New York: Doubleday, 1990.

Silvoso, Ed. *Anointed for Business: How Christians Can Use Their Influence in the Marketplace to Change the World.* Ventura, Calif.: Regal, 2002.

Smedes, Lewis B. *Mere Morality: What God Expects from Ordinary People.* Grand Rapids: Eerdmans, 1983.

Smigel, Erwin O., ed. *Work and Leisure: A Contemporary Social Problem.* New Haven, Conn.: College and University Press, 1963.

Špidlík, Tomáš. *The Spirituality of the Christian East: A Systematic Handbook.* Kalamazoo: Cistercian Publications, 1986.

Stackhouse, Max L. "Is God in Globalization?" Unpublished paper, Regent College, 1999.

Stackhouse, Max L., Dennis P. McCann, Shirley J. Roels, and Preston N. Williams, eds. *On Moral Business: Classical and Contemporary Resources for Ethics in Economic Life.* Grand Rapids: Eerdmans, 1995.

Stackhouse, Max L., Tim Dearborn, and Scott Paeth, eds., *The Local Church in a Global Era: Reflections for a New Century.* Grand Rapids: Eerdmans, 2000.

Stark, Rodney. *For the Glory of God: How Monotheism Led to Reformations, Science, Witch-Hunts, and the End of Slavery.* Princeton: Princeton University Press, 2003.

Steele, Richard. *Religious Tradesman or Plain and Serious Hints of Advice for the Tradesman's Prudent and Pious Conduct; from His Entrance into Business, to His Leaving It Off.* 1747; reprint Harrisonburg, Va.: Sprinkle Publications, 1989.

Steen, Todd, and Steve VanderVeen. "Will There Be Marketing in Heaven?" *Perspectives* (November 2003): 6-11.

Stevens, R. Paul. *Down-to-Earth Spirituality.* Downers Grove, Ill.: InterVarsity Press, 2003.

———. *The Equippers' Guide to Every Member Ministry.* Vancouver: Regent College Publishing, 2000.

———. "The Marketplace: Mission Field or Mission?" *Crux* 37, no. 3 (September 2001): 7-16.

———. *Marriage Spirituality: Ten Disciplines for People Who Love God.* Downers Grove, Ill.: InterVarsity Press, 1989.

————. *The Other Six Days: Vocation, Work, and Ministry in Biblical Perspective.* Grand Rapids: Eerdmans, 2000; Vancouver: Regent Publishing, 1999.

————. *Seven Days of Faith.* Colorado Springs: NavPress, 2001.

————. "The Spiritual and Religious Sources of Entrepreneurship: From Max Weber to the New Business Spirituality." *Crux* 36, no. 2 (June 2000): 22-33; reprinted in *Stimulus: The New Zealand Journal of Christian Thought and Practice* 9, no. 1 (February 2001): 2-11.

————. "Vocational Conversion: An Imaginary Puritan–Baby Boomer Dialogue." *Crux* 37, no. 4 (December 2001): 2-8.

————. "Wealth." In *The Complete Book of Everyday Christianity,* ed. Robert Banks and R. Paul Stevens, pp. 1102-6. Downers Grove, Ill.: InterVarsity Press, 1997.

Sullivan, William M. *Work and Integrity: The Crisis and Promise of Professionalism in America.* New York: Harper, 1995.

Tournier, Paul. *The Adventure of Living.* Translated by Edwin Hudson. New York: Harper and Row, 1965.

Troeltsch, Ernst. *The Social Teachings of the Christian Churches.* Translated by Olive Wyon. Louisville: Westminster/John Knox Press, 1992.

Tropman, John E., and Gersh Morningstar. *Entrepreneurial Systems for the 1990s: Their Creation, Structure and Management.* New York: Quorum Books, 1989.

Trueblood, Elton. *Your Other Vocation.* New York: Harper & Brothers, 1952.

Tyndale, William. "A Parable of the Wicked Mammon." In *Treatises and Portions of Holy Scripture.* 1527; reprint, Cambridge: Parker Society, 1848.

Vicedom, George F. *The Mission of God: An Introduction to a Theology of Mission.* Translated by Gilbert A. Thiele and Dennis Hilgendorf. St. Louis: Concordia, 1965.

Volf, Miroslav. "Human Work, Divine Spirit, and the New Creation: Toward a Pneumatological Understanding of Work." *Pneuma: The Journal of the Society for Pentecostal Studies* (Fall 1987): 173-93.

————. *Work in the Spirit: Toward a Theology of Work.* New York: Oxford University Press, 1991.

Wauzzinski, Robert A. *Between God and Gold: Protestant Evangelicalism and the Industrial Revolution 1820-1914.* Rutherford, N.J.: Fairleigh Dickinson University Press, 1993.

Bibliography

Weber, Max. *The Protestant Ethic and the Spirit of Capitalism.* Translated by Talcott Parsons. New York: Charles Scribner's Sons, 1958.

Wesley, John. "The Use of Money." In *On Moral Business: Classical and Contemporary Resources for Ethics in Economic Life,* ed. Max L. Stackhouse, Dennis P. McCann, Shirley J. Roels, and Preston N. Williams, p. 197. Grand Rapids: Eerdmans, 1995.

White, Lynn, Jr. "The Historical Roots of Our Ecological Crisis." *Science* 155, no. 3767 (10 March 1967): 1203-7.

Wilkinson, Loren. "One Earth, One World, One Church." *Crux* 28, no. 1 (March 1992): 28-36.

Willard, Dallas. *The Divine Conspiracy: Rediscovering Our Hidden Life in God.* San Francisco: HarperSanFrancisco, 1998.

Williams, Paul S. "Hermeneutics for Economists: The Relevance of the Bible to Economics." MCS Thesis, Regent College, Vancouver, 1995.

Wink, Walter. *Naming the Powers: The Language of Power in the New Testament.* Philadelphia: Fortress Press, 1984.

Wogaman, Philip J. "Christian Faith and Personal Holiness." In *Biblical Principles and Business: The Foundations,* ed. Richard C. Chewning, vol. 1, pp. 37-50. Colorado Springs: NavPress, 1989.

Wong, Siew Li. "A Defence of the Intrinsic Value of 'Secular Work' in Tentmaking Ministry in the Light of the Theology Doctrines of Creation, Redemption and Eschatology." MCS Thesis, Regent College, Vancouver, April 2000.

Wright, Christopher J. H. *Living as the People of God: The Relevance of Old Testament Ethics.* Leicester: Inter-Varsity Press, 1998.

Wright, Clive. *The Business of Virtue.* London: SPCK, 2004.

Wright, Walter C., Jr. *Relational Leadership: A Biblical Model for Influence and Service.* Carlisle: Paternoster, 2000.

Wyszynski, Stefan Cardinal. *All You Who Labor: Work and the Sanctification of Daily Life.* Manchester, N.H.: Sophia Press, 1995.

Yamamori, Tetsunao, and Kenneth A. Eldred, eds. *On Kingdom Business: Transforming Missions Through Entrepreneurial Strategies.* Wheaton, Ill.: Crossway, 2003.

Yoder, John Howard. *The Politics of Jesus.* Grand Rapids: Eerdmans, 1972.

Zizoulas, John D. *Being in Communion.* Crestwood, N.Y.: St. Vladmir's Seminary Press, 1993.

Index

Index